25

THE VOICE OF FIGHTING RUSSIA

JOSEPH STALIN
Chairman of the Council of People's Commissars

THE VOICE
OF
FIGHTING RUSSIA

Edited by

LUCIEN ZACHAROFF

Preface by

HEWLETT JOHNSON
Dean of Canterbury

ALLIANCE BOOK CORPORATION

New York

CONTRIBUTORS TO THIS BOOK

Chairman of the Council of People's Commissars of the U.S.S.R.: Joseph Stalin.

Novelists, Poets, Critics: M. Sholokhoff, Alexei Tolstoy, Vs. Ivanoff, P. Pavlenko, V. Katayev, L. Sobolev, V. Stavsky, Vs. Vishnevsky, Anna Karavayeva, K. Simonoff, V. Ilyenkoff, Toor Brothers, L. Kassil.

War Correspondents, Other Journalists: N. Kruzhkoff, E. Vilensky, El. Kononenko, M. Suvinsky, P. Tzvetoff, O. Kurganoff, K. Taradankin, V. Poltoratzky, Gr. Mishulovin, Tatiana Tess, L. Khvat, Vl. Rudny, A. Sharoff, A. Dunayevsky, V. Znamensky, M. Gordon, A. Sadovsky, G. Kryloff, P. Grinev, Z. Lipavsky, A. Krassnoff, D. Novopliansky, M. Smirnoff, S. Kachaloff, M. Kotoff, V. Miaskovsky, L. Petrovich, V. Gleboff, V. Stolpner, A. Kordoff, A. Gutman, A. Koroboff, A. Bakovikoff, L. Botvinsky, V. Shumoff, B. Galich, I. Vensky, Y. Medvedovsky, A. Tzelikova, O. Smirnoff, N. Vasilyev.

Red Army Men and Commanders: Senior Sergeant N. Shabota, Junior Political Instructor M. Bulkin, Senior Political Instructor I. Deygen, Battalion Commissar Y. Gorodskoy, Air Navigator Sh. Kordonsky, Captain A. Sovin, Lieutenant I. Chuproff, Tankist M. Zagrebelny, Political Instructor P. Troyanovsky, Cadet P. Litovetz, Red Armyman V. Tikhomiroff.

CONTENTS

LIST OF ILLUSTRATIONS

EDITOR'S FOREWORD

JAPAN'S ATTEMPT to stab the United States in the back endows this book about the Soviet battle against similarly treacherous aggression with new significance to Americans.

Even before Tokyo decided to wind up its professions of peace at Washington with a surprise attack at Pearl Harbor, this was a powerful human document in which the embattled Soviet people told of their epic defense against the Axis.

Today this work is pregnant with a deeper meaning. The two peoples are companions-in-arms, each being the greatest obstacle in its own hemisphere to the Axis march to the enslavement of all mankind, each helping the other and the rest of the threatened or conquered countries by an all-out application on its farflung sector of the world-wide front.

This book has a collective author. It was written by correspondents in advance positions with the Red Army, Navy, and Air Force, by novelists and poets who abandoned their peaceful studies to write from the front, by the valorous men and commanders of the Soviet armed forces, the participants in the heroic battles. It was written by industrial workers and collective farmers, by women, old people and children, who by their labor in the rear are aiding the struggle, often as hard-hitting guerrillas behind the enemy lines.

Here is a balanced firsthand account of every phase of the

opening weeks of the war between the Soviet Union and Nazi Germany. The editor deemed it advisable to include three speeches by Premier Stalin whose statesmanship and military leadership inspired many of the exploits described in this book; these particular speeches constitute the program of action, the grand strategy of some 200,000,000 Soviet citizens who, in the German invasion, have shown unprecedented national unity. Also included is the exchange of letters between the Soviet Premier and the President of the United States.

To us in America this book is further important as a reflection of the unbending will of the Soviet people who, at the front and behind the lines, are waging a grim, decisive, merciless struggle for their native land, for their honor and freedom, thus making certain the final victory over the common enemy of all civilization—Fascism.

In an effort to preserve the spirit of the manuscript, whose pages are permeated with gunpowder smoke, the editor considered it his prime function to avoid all unnecessary editing. His was not a job of streamlining and polishing, since the unaffected and straightforward reports of eyewitnesses and participants of "the greatest battle in history" are entitled to our attention in whatever form their authors may choose to present them. This is, frankly, the voice of the Soviet people expressing their innermost reactions and attitudes, since originally all these reports were made for the purpose of sharing their experiences of the battlefield among themselves. Matter-of-fact reports to themselves, to us they are sagas and an indestructible guarantee that those 200,000,000 men, women, and children are in *our* struggle until the day of our common victory.

LUCIEN ZACHAROFF

New York City
February 2, 1942

PREFACE

By HEWLETT JOHNSON
Dean of Canterbury

ON THE ICE-STREWN, snow-swept plains of Russia we see the culminating battles of a struggle which has its roots in the day when morality and science began their long warfare against immoral and unscientific elements in our social, industrial and commercial order.

It is no accident or strange turn of the wheel which now flings Germany against Russia. Germany and Russia represent principles and tendencies which stand fundamentally opposed and which were bound sooner or later to come to grips. Germany stands for three principles which are undemocratic, immoral and unscientific; Russia stands for the three opposed principles. Russia may have had and still has many vices and dark spots, hangovers from an evil past; Germany, on the other hand, may have had and has many excellent virtues inherited also from an industrious and cultured past, but over and above these good and bad hangovers stand the three principles of which I speak. They confront one another now in their most extreme forms and contend in the present titanic struggle for world mastery:

1. Fascist Germany under her present rulers maintains that there is and always must be a dominant class and a servile class. Germany perpetuates and exaggerates class differences. Russia believes in a classless society, avoiding great extremes of wealth and poverty, providing education, security of life and full op-

portunity for developing the latent powers of each individual in her realm.

2. Fascist Germany believes in the dominant race and the servile race. It believes that a mystical difference in blood makes some peoples master peoples and others servile peoples. It is her deliberate aim, should she succeed in the world war, to make France purely agricultural, keeping to herself, as the chosen and dominant race, the industrial side of life with its power and weapons and amenities. Russia believes in a brotherhood of nations and makes that brotherhood a reality in the 170 different national groups which comprise her Union.

3. Fascist Germany believes in war as desirable and necessary; Russia believes in and works for a warless world. She fights, but only in self-defense and under bitter provocation, not on principle and as something of necessity and desirable.

It is on account of these principles that we in the democratic countries find ourselves logically and inevitably on the side of Russia and not of Germany in this world struggle. When a nation fights thus for great moral and, I would add, Christian principles, her strength is as the strength of ten. Such is the strength of Russia today.

Hitler signed his death warrant when on June 22, 1941, he assaulted the Soviet Union whose courage is matched by her brains and her skill. Russia is strong with a growing strength, strong in the arts of war because strong in the arts of peace, strong to protect life because strong to promote life.

But the struggle is terrific and the cost appalling. It was a stronger Germany that attacked the East than that which attacked the West, stronger in all the war weapons and war potential gathered from the defeated countries, and stronger because Finns, Rumanians and Hungarians augment her armies.

Against that mighty massed attack our heroic and gallant ally stands firm. Russia breaks the blitz on the land as England broke it in the air, and now she is beginning to hurl back the mighty Germany and her satellites.

It is magnificent, but the struggle is intense, and when she calls for our help we must run to give it. Moral, economic and military help must be given to the utmost of their capacity by all nations and by every individual who would denounce the Fascist theory of dominant class, dominant race and war as a necessity and glory, by all who love freedom, a fair chance to each, a brotherhood of peoples and a world at peace.

May the stirring stories told in this grand book drive the spurs deep into our sides till we leap into action on Russia's behalf.

BOOK I

INTRODUCTION

EXCHANGE OF COMMUNICATIONS BETWEEN THE PRESIDENT OF
THE UNITED STATES AND JOSEPH STALIN, CHAIRMAN OF THE
COUNCIL OF PEOPLE'S COMMISSARS

*(The following is a paraphrase of the text of a letter addressed by the
President under date of October 30, 1941, to Mr. Joseph Stalin, as released
by the Department of State of the United States)*

I HAVE EXAMINED the record of the Moscow Conference and
the members of the mission have discussed the details with me.
All of the military equipment and munitions items have been
approved and I have ordered that as far as possible the delivery
of raw materials be expedited. Deliveries have been directed to
commence immediately and to be fulfilled in the largest possible amounts.

In an effort to obviate any financial difficulties, immediate
arrangements are to be made so that supplies up to one billion
dollars in value may be effected under the Lend-Lease Act. If
approved by the government of the U.S.S.R., I propose that the
indebtedness thus incurred be subject to no interest and that the
payments by the government of the U.S.S.R. do not commence
until five years after the war's conclusion and be completed over
a ten-year period thereafter.

I hope that special efforts will be arranged by your government to sell us the available raw materials and commodities which the United States may need urgently under the arrangement that the proceeds thereof be credited to the Soviet government's account.

At this opportunity I want to tell you of the appreciation of the United States government for the expeditious handling by you and your associates of the Moscow supply conference, and to send you assurances that we will carry out to the limit all the implications thereof. I hope that you will communicate with me directly without hesitation if you should so wish.

(The following is a paraphrase of the text of a letter by Mr. Joseph Stalin under date of November 4, 1941, to the President of the United States, as released by the Department of State of the United States)

THE AMERICAN AMBASSADOR, Mr. Steinhardt, through Mr. Vyshinsky, presented to me on November 2, 1941, an *aide-mémoire* containing the contents of your message, the exact text of which I have not yet received.

First of all I would like to express my sincere thanks for your appreciative remarks regarding the expeditious manner in which the conference was handled. Your assurance that the decisions of the conference will be carried out to the limit is deeply appreciated by the Soviet government.

Your decision, Mr. President, to grant to the Soviet Union a loan in the amount of one billion dollars subject to no interest charges and for the purpose of paying for armaments and raw materials for the Soviet Union is accepted with sincere gratitude by the Soviet government as unusually substantial aid in its difficult and great struggle against our common enemy, bloodthirsty Hitlerism.

I agree completely, on behalf of the government of the Soviet Union, with the conditions which you outlined for this loan to the Soviet Union; namely, that payments on the loan shall begin five years after the end of the war and shall be completed during the following ten-year period.

The government of the U.S.S.R. stands ready to expedite in every possible way the supplying of available raw materials and goods required by the United States.

I am heartily in accord with your proposal, Mr. President, that we establish direct personal contact whenever circumstances warrant.

STALIN SPEAKS

RADIO ADDRESS BY J. V. STALIN, CHAIRMAN OF THE COUNCIL
OF PEOPLE'S COMMISSARS OF THE U.S.S.R., CHAIRMAN OF THE
NATIONAL DEFENSE COMMITTEE
(Full Text)

Moscow, July 3, 1941

COMRADES! CITIZENS! Brothers and sisters! Men of our army and navy! I am addressing you, my friends! The perfidious attack on our fatherland started on June 22 by Hitler Germany is continuing. In spite of the heroic resistance of the Red Army, and although the enemy's finest divisions and finest air-force units have already been smashed and have met their doom on the field of battle, the enemy continues to push forward, hurling fresh forces into attack. Hitler's troops have succeeded in capturing Lithuania, a considerable part of Latvia, the western part of Byelorussia, and part of the Western Ukraine. The Fascist air force is extending the range of operations of its bombers, and is bombing Murmansk, Orsha, Mogilev, Smolensk, Kiev, Odessa, Sevastopol. Grave danger overhangs our country.

How could it have happened that our glorious Red Army surrendered a number of our cities and districts to Fascist armies? Is it really true that German Fascist troops are invincible as is ceaselessly trumpeted by boastful Fascist propagandists? Of course not! History shows that there are no invincible armies and never have been. Napoleon's army was considered invincible but it was beaten successively by Russian, English, and German armies. Kaiser Wilhelm's German Army in the period of the first imperialist war was also considered invincible but it was beaten several times by Russian and Anglo-French forces

9

and was finally smashed by Anglo-French forces. The same must be said of Hitler's German Fascist army today. This army had not yet met with serious resistance on the continent of Europe, only on our territory it met serious resistance. And if as a result of this resistance the finest divisions of Hitler's German Fascist army have been defeated by our Red Army, it means that this army too can be smashed and will be smashed as were the armies of Napoleon and Wilhelm.

As to the part of our territory having nevertheless been seized by German Fascist troops, this is chiefly due to the fact that the war of Fascist Germany on the U.S.S.R. began under conditions favorable for the German forces and unfavorable for Soviet forces. The fact of the matter is that troops of Germany, as a country at war, were already fully mobilized, and the 170 divisions hurled by Germany against the U.S.S.R. and brought up to Soviet frontiers were in a state of complete readiness, only awaiting the signal to move into action, whereas the Soviet troops had still to effect mobilization and to move up to frontiers.

Of no little importance in this respect is the fact that Fascist Germany suddenly and treacherously violated the Non-aggression Pact she concluded in 1939 with the U.S.S.R., disregarding the fact that she would be regarded as aggressor by the whole world. Naturally, our peace-loving country, not wishing to take the initiative in breaking the pact, could not resort to perfidy. It may be asked how could the Soviet government have consented to conclude a non-aggression pact with such treacherous fiends as Hitler and Ribbentrop? Was this not an error on the part of the Soviet government? Of course not! Non-aggression pacts are pacts of peace between two states. It was such a pact that Germany proposed to us in 1939. Could the Soviet government have declined such a proposal? I think not a single peace-loving state could decline a peace treaty with a neighboring state even though the latter were headed by such fiends and cannibals as

Hitler and Ribbentrop. But that, of course, only on one indispensable condition, namely, that this peace treaty does not infringe either directly or indirectly on territorial integrity, independence, and honor of the peace-loving state. As is well known, the Non-aggression Pact between Germany and the U.S.S.R. is precisely such a pact. What did we gain by concluding the Non-aggression Pact with Germany? We secured our country's peace for a year and a half and the opportunity of preparing its forces to repulse Fascist Germany should she risk attack on our country despite the pact. This was a definite advantage for us and a disadvantage for Fascist Germany. What has Fascist Germany gained and what has she lost by treacherously tearing up the pact and attacking the U.S.S.R.? She has gained certain advantageous positions for her troops for a short period but she has lost politically by exposing herself in the eyes of the entire world as a bloodthirsty aggressor. There can be no doubt that this short-lived military gain for Germany is only an episode while the tremendous political gain of the U.S.S.R. is a serious and lasting factor that is bound to form a basis for development of decisive military successes of the Red Army in the war with Fascist Germany.

That is why our whole valiant Red Army, our whole valiant navy, all our falcons of the air, all the peoples of our country, all the finest men and women in Europe, America and Asia, finally all the finest men and women of Germany condemn the treacherous acts of the German Fascists and sympathize with the Soviet government, approve the conduct of the Soviet government, and see that ours is a just cause, that the enemy will be defeated, that we are bound to win.

By virtue of this war which has been forced upon us, our country has come to death grips with its most malicious and most perfidious enemy—German Fascism. Our troops are fighting heroically against an enemy armed to the teeth with tanks and aircraft. Overcoming innumerable difficulties, the Red Army and Red Navy are self-sacrificingly disputing every inch of Soviet soil. The main forces of the Red Army are coming into action armed with thousands of tanks and airplanes. Men of the Red Army are displaying unexampled valor. Our resistance to the enemy is growing in strength and power.

Side by side with the Red Army, the entire Soviet people are rising in defense of our native land. What is required to put an end to the danger hovering over our country, and what measures must be taken to smash the enemy? Above all, it is essential that our people, Soviet people, should understand the full immensity of the danger that threatens our country and abandon all complacency, all heedlessness, all those moods of peaceful constructive work which were natural before the war but which are fatal today when war has fundamentally changed everything. The enemy is cruel and implacable. He is out to seize our lands watered with our sweat, to seize our grain and oil secured by our labor. He is out to restore the rule of the landlords, to restore Tsarism, to destroy the national culture and national state existence of Russians, Ukrainians, Byelorussians, Lithuanians, Letts, Esthonians, Tartars, Uzbeks, Moldavians, Georgians, Armenians, Azerbaijanians, and the other free peoples of the Soviet Union, to Germanize them, to convert them into slaves of German princes and barons. Thus the issue is one of life or death of the Soviet state; for peoples of the U.S.S.R. the issue is whether peoples of the Soviet Union shall remain free or fall into slavery.

Soviet people must realize this and abandon all heedlessness, they must mobilize themselves and reorganize all their work on new, wartime lines, when there can be no mercy to the enemy. Further, there must be no room in our ranks for whimperers and cowards, panicmongers and deserters; our people must know no fear in fight and must selflessly join our patriotic war of liberation, our war against Fascist enslavers. Lenin, the great founder of our state, used to say that the chief virtue of the Soviet people must be courage, valor, fearlessness in struggle, readiness to fight together with the people against enemies of our country. This splendid virtue of a Bolshevik must become the virtue of millions and millions of Red Army, of Red Navy, of all peoples of the Soviet Union.

All our work must be immediately reconstructed on a war footing, everything must be subordinated to interests of the front and the task of organizing demolition of the enemy.

Peoples of the Soviet Union now see that there is no taming of German Fascism in its savage fury and hatred of our country which has ensured all working people labor, freedom, and prosperity. Peoples of the Soviet Union must rise against the enemy and defend their rights and their land. The Red Army, Red Navy, and all citizens of the Soviet Union must defend every inch of Soviet soil, must fight to the last drop of blood for our towns and villages, must display the daring initiative and intelligence that are inherent in our people. We must organize all-round assistance to the Red Army, ensure powerful reinforcements for its ranks and supply of everything it requires, we must organize rapid transport of troops and military freight and extensive aid to the wounded.

We must strengthen the Red Army's rear, subordinating all our work to this cause; all our industries must be put to work with greater intensity to produce more rifles, machine guns, artillery, bullets, shells, airplanes; we must organize guarding of factories, power stations, telephonic and telegraphic communications, and arrange effective air-raid protection in all localities. We must wage a ruthless fight against all disorganizers of the rear, deserters, panicmongers, rumormongers, exterminate spies, diversionists, enemy parachutists, rendering rapid aid in all this to our destroyer battalions.

We must bear in mind that the enemy is crafty, unscrupulous, and experienced in deception and dissemination of false rumors. We must reckon with all this and not fall victim to provocation. All who by their panicmongering and cowardice hinder work of defense, no matter who they are, must be immediately haled before military tribunal. In case of forced retreat of the Red Army units, all rolling stock must be evacuated, the enemy must not be left a single engine, single railway car, not a single pound of grain or gallon of fuel.

Collective farmers must drive off all their cattle and turn over their grain to the safekeeping of state authorities for transportation to the rear. All valuable property, including non-ferrous metals, grain and fuel, which cannot be withdrawn, must without fail be destroyed. In areas occupied by the enemy, guerrilla units, mounted and foot, must be formed, diversionist groups must be organized to combat enemy troops, to foment guerrilla warfare everywhere, blow up bridges, roads, damage telephone and telegraph lines, set fire to forests, stores, and transports.

In occupied regions conditions must be made unbearable for the enemy and all his accomplices. They must be hounded and annihilated at every step, and all their measures frustrated. This war with Fascist Germany cannot be considered an ordinary war. It is not only a war between two armies, it is also a great war of the entire Soviet people against German Fascist forces. The aim of this people's war in defense of our country against Fascist oppressors is not only elimination of the danger hanging over our country but also aid to all European peoples groaning under the yoke of German Fascism.

In this war of liberation we shall not be alone. In this great war we shall have loyal allies in peoples of Europe and America, including German people who are enslaved by Hitlerite despots. Our war for freedom of our country will merge with the struggle of peoples of Europe and America for their independence, for democratic liberties. It will be a united front of peoples standing for freedom and against enslavement and threats of enslavement by Hitler's Fascist armies.

In this connection the historic utterance of British Prime Minister Churchill regarding aid to the Soviet Union and the declaration of the United States government signifying readiness to render aid to our country, which can only evoke a feeling of gratitude in the hearts of the peoples of the Soviet Union, are fully comprehensible and symptomatic. Comrades, our forces are numberless. The overweening enemy will soon learn this to his cost. Side by side with the Red Army, thousands of workers, collective farmers, and intellectuals are rising to fight the enemy aggressor.

Masses of our people will rise up in their millions. Working people of Moscow and Leningrad have already commenced to form vast popular levies in support of the Red Army. Such popular levies must be raised in every city which is in danger of enemy invasion, all working people must be roused to defend our freedom, our honor, our country, in our patriotic war against German Fascism.

In order to ensure rapid mobilization of all forces of peoples of the U.S.S.R. and to repulse the enemy who treacherously attacked our country, a State Committee of Defense has been formed in whose hands the entire power of the state has been vested. The State Committee of Defense has entered in its functions and calls upon all our people to rally around the party of Lenin-Stalin and around the Soviet government so as to support self-denyingly the Red Army and Navy, demolish the enemy, and secure victory. All our forces for support of our heroic Red Army and our glorious Red Navy! All forces of people— for demolition of the enemy! Forward, to our victory!

CHAPTER I

WHAT WE ARE DEFENDING

By Alexei Tolstoy

THE PROGRAM of the National Socialists has not been exhausted in Hitler's book. This contains only that which could be confessed. The further development of their program harbors within itself such delirious, sadistic, bloody aims that to confess them would be disadvantageous. But the Nazis' conduct in the occupied countries somewhat reveals the "secret," the hints are all too obvious—slavery, starvation and brutalization await all who do not say in good time and firmly: "Death is better than Nazi victory."

The Nazis are self-assured to the point of hysteria. After conquering Poland and France, essentially through bribery and diversionist decomposition of the military might of the enemy, after conquering other, smaller lands that fell with honor before an immeasurably stronger adversary, the Nazis hastily began to materialize the further development of their platform. Thus, in Poland, in concentration camps which confine Polish workingmen and Polish intellectuals, as early as the spring of this year mortality reached seventy per cent; today it is wholesale. Poland's population is being exterminated. In Norway, the Nazis picked several thousand citizens, put them aboard barges, and "without helm and sails" let them drift on the ocean. During the offensive in France, with a particularly sadistic relish the Nazis bombarded small undefended towns filled with refugees, "combed" them in a strafing flight, crushed with tanks all

19

that could be crushed. Then came their infantry—out of the shelters the Nazis dragged half-dead children, distributed chocolate among them, and posed for the photographers with them, in order to be able to distribute, where they would do the trick, such documents testifying to German "humaneness." By the time they reached Serbia, they no longer gave away chocolate nor posed with children for the cameras.

All these deeds flow out of the general National Socialist program, namely, the conquest of Europe, Asia, the Americas, all continents and islands. Exterminated are all the defiant, who are unwilling to reconcile themselves to the loss of their independence. In the legal and material sense all peoples are being converted into speech-endowed animals and are working on terms dictated to them. If the Nazis find population numbers in one country or another excessive, they reduce them by extermination in the concentration camps or by some other less cumbrous method. Then, having arranged all this, like the Lord, in six days, on the seventh day the Nazis, as behooves the premier race with blond elongated heads, begin to live well, eating sausages to repletion, clinking beer mugs, yelling stein songs about their superman origin. . . .

All this is not out of a fantastic novel in the style of H. G. Wells—it is precisely so that they are determined soberly to develop their program in the Reich Chancery in Berlin. It is for this that they are spilling rivers of blood and tears, for this cities are burning, thousands of ships are blown up and sunk, and scores of millions of peaceful populations are dying from hunger.

To smash up the armies of the Third Empire, to sweep off the face of the earth all Nazis with their barbarously bloody designs, to give our country peace, repose, eternal freedom, prosperity, every opportunity of continued development on the road of the higher human freedom—such is the lofty and noble mission that must be carried out by the Russian and all other peoples of the Soviet Union.

The Germans calculated on breaking into the U.S.S.R. with their tanks and bombers, as they did in Poland, France, and other states, where victory was secured in advance by their preliminary undermining work. On the frontiers of the U.S.S.R. they hit against a wall of steel and their blood has spurted far and wide. The German armies, driven into battle by the red-hot iron of terror and madness, have encountered the powerful strength of an intelligent, courageous, freedom-loving people which in the course of its thousand-year-old history has many times expelled by sword and bayonet the invaders of the spacious expanses of its native soil—the Khazars, Polovtzi and Pechenegi, the Tartar hordes and Teutonic Knights, the Poles, Swedes, Napoleon's Frenchmen and Wilhelm's Germans. . . . "They all have flashed before us."

Previously, the people of my country rose to the struggle, understanding full well that they would receive no thanks from either the Tsar, the whipper-in, or the boyar. But ardent was their love for their land, for their untender fatherland. Inextinguishably there burned in their minds the faith in the coming of the day of justice when they would cast off their hunched backs all parasites, when Russian soil would be their soil and they would plow it up for the golden harvest from ocean to ocean.

In the War for the Fatherland in 1918–20, the White armies pressed our country from all sides and she—prostrated, famished, dying out from the typhus epidemic—after two years of a bloody and seemingly unequal struggle, broke the encirclement, drove out and exterminated the foe, and began to build a new life. The nation drew strength in toil illuminated by a great ideal, in its faith in happiness, in the love of the native land where sweet is the smoke and sweet is the bread.

So, on what mercy from the Soviet side can the Nazis reckon now as they drive the German people to face the Soviet steel fortresses hurtling into battle like a hurricane, the belts of Soviet fortifications roaring with their monstrous muzzles, the numberless warplanes, the Red Army bayonets?

> *Or are there not enough of us? Perhaps from*
> *   Perm to Taurus,*
> *From Finland's chilly cliffs to fiery Colchis,*
> *Or from the shaken-up Kremlin*
> *To the immobile Cathay's walls,*
> *The Land of Russia will not arise,*
> *Its shield of steel all sparkling?*

The Russian has this characteristic—in life's difficult moments, in the years of trial, he easily renounces all that he has become accustomed to, that by which he has lived day by day. Behold, here was a man—so-so; suddenly it was demanded of him to become a hero, and he is a hero. . . . And how can it be otherwise? In the olden times of the recruit impressment, the boy destined for head-shaving had his fun for three days, he danced and, leaning his head on his palm, sang heart-rending songs; he bade farewell to his father and mother, and there he was, a different man—austere and fearless, guarding the honor of the fatherland. He followed Suvoroff's charger across the glaciers of the Alps as he kept his precarious foothold by digging his bayonet into the ice; at Moscow he repulsed the attacks of Murat's cuirassiers; in a clean undershirt, shouldering his musket under the deadly bullet fire at Plevna, he stood awaiting the order to storm the inaccessible heights.

Three fellows came together from different villages to serve in the Red Army. Whether they were good or bad before this, no one knows. They were assigned to the tank corps and sent into battle. Their tank lunged far ahead into the midst of the enemy infantry, was crippled, expended all its ammunition. When the enemies had crept quite close to the disabled tank to take its crew prisoners, the three chaps came out of the machine. Each of the three had one last cartridge left, each raised his weapon to his temple; they had not surrendered. Glory to them, the proud fighters, cherishing the honor of the fatherland and the army.

A pursuit pilot related to me: "The enemy planes swirled about me like a swarm of bees. My neck hurt from turning my head so much. So great was the excitement that I was shouting at the top of my voice. I knocked down three and tried to get into a clinch with the fourth one. Above—sometimes the sky and sometimes the ground, the sun—now on the right of me, then on the left. I was somersaulting, diving, climbing up. So, I took aim at one enemy, and suddenly from under me an interceptor plane shot up, hung for a split second before my nose, I saw a man's face—strong, bearded, in his eyes hatred and a plea for mercy. . . . The interceptor turned upside down and smoke began to pour from it. Suddenly I could not move my leg, as though I had sat on it too long; this meant I was wounded. Then something hit my shoulder. My machine-gun cartridge ribbon gave out, I had nothing to fire with. I started away; my left arm hung lifelessly. The airdrome was far away. If only everything does not go dark before my eyes from loss of blood, I was thinking; yet, a dizzy film spread over my eyes, but I was already sitting down upon the airdrome, without my landing gear, on the ship's belly."

For more than half a century now I have watched my native land in its struggles for freedom, in its surprising changes. I recall the deathly quiet of Alexander III; the impoverished village with its wasteland, thatched roofs, and willows on the shore of a steppe river. I peer into the past and in my memory there arise the clever, clean-cut, unhurried people preserving

their dignity. . . . Here is the father of my childhood playmate—
Alexander Sizoff, very handsome with his curly blond beard, a
powerful athlete. When of a holiday in the village the mighty
Russian tug-of-war got under way in the deep snowdrifts, Sizoff's merry eyes watched through a small window; by and by
he would come out, stand in the gate, and when entreaties for
help addressed to him became particularly insistent, he pulled
on his gloves and effortlessly felled the whole human wall. In
a threadbare, undressed-sheepskin coat, his neck wrapped in
a scarf, he trod a hundred versts in a blizzard behind a cart of
corn, taking to the city his entire year's meager yield. Today
his grandson, most certainly, throws himself like an angry falcon at the German bombers.

I remember how in a hut with a warm stove, where a young
housewife sat at the loom, where a calf slumbered on a pile of
straw in a corner, we children gathered on benches around
the table, listening to a tall one-eyed old man resembling a horse
and telling us fairy tales. He was an itinerant beggar, moving
from village to village, spending the night wherever allowed.
The young housewife behind the loom whispered to him: "What
for are you telling them terrible and more terrible things all
the time? Tell them something happy." He replied, "I know no
happy tale, my dear; never heard it, never saw it." With his one
terrible eye fixed on us, he continued, "They, mayhap, will see
and hear something happy. . . ."

I remember the year 1914 when millions of people had received weapons into their hands. The intelligent people understood that its foremost and sacred duty was to drive the enemy
from its soil. Straight out of their railroad trains the Siberian
corps leaped to the bayonet attack, and there was nothing
fiercer in that war than the Russian bayonet charges. It was
only because of the ignorance, stupidity, utmost mediocrity of
the Tsarist high command, because of the general looting and

thievery, speculation and treason, that the Russian people failed to win that war.

Twenty-five years passed. From ocean to ocean rustled the golden collective-farm fields, orchards bloomed, cotton fluffed up where but a short time before there only drifted sterile sand. Streams of smoke ascended from scores of thousands of shops and factories. Perhaps the same grandson of Alexander Sizoff, the same kind of noble athlete, went underground to stir, titanlike, singlehanded, hundreds of tons of coal per shift. Thousand-ton hammers, shaking the earth, began to forge arms for the Red Army, the army of a liberated people, the army of freedom, the army which is a defender of this world's peace, of higher culture, of flowering and happiness.

This is my birthplace, my native soil, my fatherland—there is not in life a more ardent, deeper, and holier feeling than my love for you.

CHAPTER II

TO THE FRONT!

Moscow on June 22

AN UNOBSERVANT PERSON might not have noticed anything. Flooded with the June-afternoon sunshine, the city—the capital of the Soviet Union—was unhurried in the Sunday manner, as it had been since morning. Along the boulevards rolled the light small carriages with citizens born in 1940 and 1941. In Pushkin Plaza, in the heart of the city, brisk trade was going on in white lilies, tulips, and peonies. People were carrying fresh lilacs. Everything looked very ordinary. No hurly-burly, no haste. . . .

Only after gazing for a while could an attentive eye discern some kind of general preoccupation which had placed its stamp on the entire life of the huge thriving city. The people's faces looked as though they had suddenly become handsomer, touched with a simple and severe decisiveness. There also appeared restraint in gestures and speech, a more direct look, a firmer step, a sharper line of the lips.

With all his unprecedented perfidy, the enemy, who counted on catching the U.S.S.R. unawares, had miscalculated from the first minute. The Soviet people knew that on the other side of the border there raged the flame of an all-European conflagration. Ever nearer to the U.S.S.R. fell its brands. Faithful to every letter, every word of their treaties and compacts, the Soviet people were preserving their neutrality and composure,

29

busy with their work. But they knew that an hour might strike when all international decencies would be cast aside, all laws of human conscience would be forgotten, and the enemy, having bared himself shamelessly, would attempt to push his swinish snout into the Soviet garden. That day came. The people were made ready for it by the writings of Lenin. Stalin used to warn his nation, calling upon it to maintain its mobilization preparedness so that no enemy stratagem might succeed. For the sake of this day and of what would follow, people sometimes skipped sleep, sometimes denied themselves a good deal, learned how to cherish every moment of their labor, every kopeck of the national funds, which now came to the fore as the public savings of the national-defense rubles.

Beautiful as ever but solemn, wrathfully concentrated was Moscow on this day, June 22.

In the streets of Moscow on this day we envisaged the tall, stooped figure of Maxim Gorky who in his muffled voice would have reminded the country one more time of the great feeling of love for the fatherland, of the duty to defend it valorously from the enemies. Concern about this day, about the degree of preparedness with which the country would meet it, had not left Gorky until the last moment of his life. With his entire life, with every line that he wrote, he strove to prepare the people for this day.

And come the day did—a day of great clarity. Everyone knew what to do, how to comport himself. Many Muscovites were outside the metropolitan limits this day, in the country, but many were in the city too. Those who were not summoned to the city by suddenly pressing matters and duties remained at the resorts, on excursions, aboard the vessels plying the Moscow-Volga Canal. Those who had to arrived at their posts in good time. There was no stampede, no unscheduled interruptions of work, of the movement, the pulse of the giant city.

Toward the evening we toured the streets of Moscow once again. Performances went on at the motion-picture theaters and the public crowded about box offices, buying up all available tickets. In the Park of Culture and Rest named after Gorky, the walks were filled with promenaders. An especially great throng surrounded the parachute tower, whence every second there blossomed out the great silk convolvuli of the chutes, only to wilt as they neared the ground.

We visited the suburbs and the center, the stores, the factories, bars, and railroad stations. There was the same feeling of strictly focused composure. In the trolley cars today the people were somehow particularly considerate: as though they had all become dearer to one another, united in one profound aspiration that permeated all hearts—to repel, to exterminate the foe, this plague of Europe. At the factories, where just before there resounded sincerely and angrily the speeches at the meetings, there now reigned, equally expressive, the deep silence of the people working with inspired zeal at their benches.

Pasted up on the walls of buildings, there were posters reproducing the text of V. M. Molotoff's radio address. In front of these the people stood, conversing not too loudly—as stern, composed, and self-assured as the whole city. Overhead a radio loud-speaker was distinctly explaining how every street, every home, the entire city was to conduct itself from now on. The orange-colored sunset clouds were vanishing from the sky. The day of June 22 was coming to a close in Moscow. Bluish twilight was gathering under the branches of the fir trees by the Kremlin wall. And facing each other, motionless as though made a monolith of granite, stood the sentries in the niche of the Lenin Mausoleum before the walls of the Kremlin. They stood silent, preoccupied, unshakable, as they stood yesterday, as they will stand always.

Patriots of the Fatherland

The courtyard of the mobilization point. A young man is seated on the bricks by the fence. Next to him is a woman, apparently his wife, and opposite them stands a man in a long blouse, a bricklayer, one may suppose. He has gray, firm eyes and a broad smile.

"Ooh, how many buildings I have put together!" he drawls. "A goo-ood many! The best people of the country reside in my buildings; of the Heroes of the Soviet Union alone, maybe at least a hundred and fifty. I can call off their names for you."

"You must have worked all right, haven't you?" asks the young man.

"Yes, I've done my share! Now I am thinking: here I was building homes, and now the enemy has come. So, what, shall I let him destroy my buildings? Is it for that that I built them? Was I a Stakhanoffite for that?"

"To the front, then?"

"Without fail! Smack Hitler in the eye!"

In another part an old man with a long gray mustache has brought three of his sons. By his speech we can tell that he is a Siberian. We come nearer. That is so. The old man is informing those around him:

"We are from Siberia, near Tomsk. In the First World War we marched against the same German in East Prussia. We campaigned well, if only. . . ."

"Your armaments were poor, they say."

"They were poor, fellow, very poor. We did not have enough rifles, not to mention artillery. I had to go into battle, straight at the barbed wire. I asked my sergeant major: 'Ivan Maximich, how about a gun for me?' And he looks at me with tears in his eyes—he loved his country—and answers, 'There is none, Yegor Yegorich, my dear man. As soon as somebody dies, you pick up that comrade's rifle and charge!' "

"And is that how you went into battle?" the old man is queried with awe and respect.

"That's how we went. Your neighbor had a gun, and you had hopes. And we beat them pretty smartly. And now, look, I have brought three sons to give to the Soviet people. If I had thirty more, I would give them also. Who am I now? I am a most honored person in the country. I am a worker, a mechanic at the Stalin Automobile Works. Who was I before? I was in the oil mill in Omsk, producing oil for a merchant, at twelve rubles a month. But now the whole country belongs to me. So, what do you say, won't we defend it, eh? Now we don't have to worry about armaments!"

"Have no fear! We shall defend it and drive off any Fascist no matter from what swamphole he may crawl out," a firm voice declares.

This is the young man who was sitting by the fence, now passing by the group. He was summoned by the commissar. He is on his way to the mobilization point, already he has received some sort of assignment. He is calm and proud. He kisses his wife lingeringly, sends regards to friends. Then, before crossing the threshold, he turns to his wife once more and says:

"We shall win, Grusha, I give you my word."

Here they are, two of the episodes observed at a mobilization point in Moscow of today.

Moscow is marvelous these days. Proud and self-confident even before, now it is as though it has blossomed out with pride, filled to the brim.

The fatherland is mustering its defenders. Fascism will be smashed and destroyed to the end.

Farewells

Broad shadows have overspread the grass and the road. On the hillock, around the table, on the benches, on the benchlike earthen mounds encircling the village homes are seated collective farmers who have gathered for the meeting. Speeches are none too long; it is clear to everyone what is to be done.

"The war against the Fascist reptile will demand of us not only courage and the straining of all our energies, but also a multitude of products, for our beloved Red Army must have everything on time and of the best quality. And this means fellow *kolkhozniks* that we must work as if we have been mobilized ourselves, as if we are at the front!"

A lean *kolkhoznik* of rather low stature, wearing a small cap but also a pullover and Red Army boots, enumerates in the thorough businesslike manner of a good husbandman what and how all forms of work are to be carried out in the field and garden, on farm and in the forest—"in a word, all that comprises our collective-farm plan."

After the meeting an old woman with serious blue eyes says meditatively: "What is there to say but that our work must be co-operative, selfless?"

Early in the morning the bell of the artel sharply pierces the quiet, summons to work; at noon it reminds about lunch, and toward the evening when the gnarled shadows of old willows lie across the country road, this farm herald permits all to take a rest. And there will be not the slightest deviation from this established order of labor life, started over a decade ago.

. . . Along the platforms of Moscow's suburban railway stations people are standing in thick files. Holiday-like appear the variegated, light-colored and motley kerchiefs of the women. The smaller figures of children and adolescents dart among the adults. Restrained conversation, restrained gestures, as if the people do not want to violate the solemnity of waiting. Yes, they are waiting for the trains which will rush to the front their fathers, husbands, sons, brothers.

To one's mind come the send-offs for the sons of the people during the Civil War. Grimly, without superfluous words and sighs, burning with iron will power and thirst for victory, the workers and peasants went to the front, to fight for the young Soviet republic.

Here are the send-offs to the front again, and the whole nation has come to the broad road, a living wall, along which the Red Army echelons are leaving, one after another, to the front, an expansive front—from the Baltic to the Black Sea. From the smallest to the grownups everyone understands that the sacred frontiers of the fatherland have been attacked by an enemy who is cruel, treacherous, armed to the teeth—the mad wolves of the Hitlerite Fascist band. Everyone—those leaving for the front, and those taking their places in the rear, be it a woman, young girl, or even an adolescent—all, all see before them the bloody face of Fascism, the murderer of peoples, the inhuman exterminator of women and children. The people, master of the socialist state, fearless fighter and creator, such is the people now seeing off its sons going to battle the blood-thirsty enemy of all progressive humanity. This is why the Soviet people are calm. Boundless, all-conquering love for the native land fills the people, the fiery battle cry, "For the Fatherland, for Stalin!" resounds from the breast of the nation, fierce confidence in ultimate victory looks out of the eyes of millions of people.

Solemnly and calmly the people is seeing off its sons—the defenders of the fatherland. Here is a mother silently embracing her son, with quiet tears, pressing his blond head to her breast. Friends clasp each other's hands firmly.

A young wife is bidding farewell to her husband at a small station. Her head in a white silk kerchief rests on his shoulder, her arms about his neck, as he hastily and tenderly strokes the luxuriant black hair, which broke out of the kerchief, and her flaming cheek. The pain of saying good-bye has so seized them that they no longer have the strength to speak. . . . Next to them two other spouses have at last separated their arms and lips, the husband has already ascended the platform of the coach; but after a glance at the woman in the white kerchief, he quickly jumps back to the ground. Gently he pulls his comrade's sleeve, and with a tender, pitiful gesture takes the woman by the shoulders. She raises her eyes to him as if to say, "But you understand." And the friend's glance replies, "Yes, I understand, I understand, but we must go, it's unavoidable." The two men board the coach together. The one who has just interrupted the other's farewell stares at his own wife with a long look filled with love and controlled sadness. Suddenly he purses his lips jestingly, as if teasing, draws his fingers along his lower eyelids, as though ordering his wife: "Go ahead, wipe them, wipe your tears."

And how many such farewells does one see, and they are all equally restrained, equally heroically simple. These are no mere send-offs for people who are close and dear, these are send-offs for companions-in-arms: "When you go away, I shall take your place, we shall struggle, we shall beat the enemy, each of us at his post!"

The Train Goes to the Front

The chief of the echelon issues his order:
"Get set!"
All voices are silenced in the yard of the school which houses

the mobilization point. The people line up. They march briskly to the station, without even looking back, remembering each rounded corner, each street of the native city.

The train is already waiting at the station. Preparing for the long journey, the engine is already letting off smoke, gathering up steam. Railway workers have gathered to send off the echelon. Young people from the neighboring locomotive repair shop have brought things to read. Performers from the town have sung, told some funny stories, and upon leaving have shaken the fighters' hands warmly. One railwayman who had come with an accordion, stretched out the bellows and began to play a slow meditative tune, then changed the tempo, and quickened, merry sounds issued forth.

One of the groups leads off with:

"Bravely, O comrades, in step."

The old revolutionary song is being sung thoughtfully, with serious faces, by strong youthful voices.

The time of the train's departure nears. The commander signals for the men to go to their coaches. The fighters enter, look around, lay down their knapsacks, take their seats. Passing by, a girl stranger presented the crew with a bouquet of lilies of the valley. It passes from hand to hand, the simple Muscovite present. Then it is affixed at a window. The unpretentious decoration makes things cozier, warms up hearts.

The platform has become empty. The locomotive lunges forward, and the engineer smoothly glides his rolling stock. A warm breeze hits faces. During the first minutes aboard the moving train the men remain silent, stand in the doors, look out of windows at houses, gardens, crossroad small stations en route, all swimming past ever faster.

As they see the train approaching, children, women, old people, everyone living near the tracks flocks toward it.

Someone yells: "Win, comrades! Smash the reptiles!"

A locomotive stands on a neighboring track. From its window pops a smiling girlish face. The girl waves a handkerchief, crying out something encouraging and tender. But the engine whistles and her words cannot be made out.

Someone says in the troop train: "Atta boy, girlie, she has turned a railroad engineer. This is to take our place."

"My wife," says Fighter Menshikoff, "has gotten a job at the factory as a ring spinner."

Farther and farther away from Moscow goes the train. All along the way friendly appreciative faces look at it. People look out of the windows of buildings and of trains coming to Moscow. Boys, who have been playing soccer near the roadbed, abandon the ball and running after the train cheer at the top of their voices, "Hurrah!"

Small and quick, their figures can be seen for a long time.

At a textile factory scores of women workers crowd the wide-open windows.

Standing by the tracks, a Young Pioneer unit salutes.

An elderly collective farmer, hatless, bows to each passing coach.

The train stood ten minutes at the first stop. The inhabitants of the small town turned out at the station. They surrounded the fighters. Strangers embraced them, shook hands with the fighters, wished them bon voyage and speedy triumph over the enemy.

"Quite a few have gone to the front from our town. If necessary, we'll send more. Have a pleasant trip, comrades."

It is as if the whole country is seeing its brave sons off to battle.

In the heated freight cars men sit on benches, alongside one another. This is the beginning of front-line friendships, fast-maturing but sturdy and dependable.

In one of the cars a group of fighters listens attentively to the news from the battlefields. A mechanic from the Sickle-and-Hammer Plant, now an artillerist, is reading aloud a newspaper report from the Special Baltic Military District:

"A wing of pursuits met the enemy in the air. A trio of Soviet planes courageously attacked nine fast bombers. The enemy lost his spirit and tried to escape toward the sea. The commander's pursuit ship tumbled down upon one of the bombers and in a few seconds the Nazi machine found its rest on the bottom of the Gulf of Riga."

These war incidents evoke memories of former glorious battles for the fatherland.

Komsomol member Vasily Zhukoff has been at three fronts already. "Now," he says, "there remains the final, the decisive front. We shall destroy the Fascist highwaymen, extract the poison fang of the Hitlerite gang, squash them. Then nobody will dare attack our country."

Two Zhukoff brothers, Ivan and Ignat, are already fighting in the ranks of the Red Army. Vasily, too, is riding to the front. He is a seasoned artillerist who knows his job well.

Younger fighters follow attentively the stories of their comrades. It is getting dark. A trackwalker waves his lantern and shouts:

"Fight, boys! Fight well and defeat the enemy!"

BOOK II

CHAPTER III

ON THE BATTLELINE

The courage of the fighters of the Red Army is unexampled. Our repulse to the enemy is growing and becoming stronger. Together with the Red Army the whole Soviet nation is rising to defend the fatherland.

J. V. STALIN.

Junior Sergeant Fedorkoff's gun on the firing line

The Early Bouts

SOVIET FRONTIER GUARDS received the first blow of the Nazi highwaymen. The insidious foe in his monstrous treachery pinned great hopes on the suddenness of the attack. But nowhere, not on a single sector of the front, did the Hitlerites succeed in taking by surprise the valiant sentinels of the Soviet land. Upon the enormous expanse from the Baltic to the Black Sea the frontier troops held down the pressure of the German hordes.

Everywhere the frontiersmen fought heroically, affording the advance units of the Red Army an opportunity to deploy. On an overwhelming majority of sectors, groups of frontier guards in fierce engagements with numerically superior German regulars did not permit them to establish themselves on the Soviet territory, throwing the enemy beyond the frontier. Only on some few sectors did the enemy make headway at the expense of heavy losses. The Fascists paid dearly for every inch of Soviet soil.

Reports from the army of operation contain numerous data characterizing the stubbornness, self-sacrifice, and combat masterfulness of the frontiersmen. Because of the circumstances of the border-patrol service, they again and again operated as isolated groups not only against the infantry but also against motorized-mechanized detachments; they maneuvered so as to resist the enemy even when their units were no bigger than the compact contingent of a solitary outpost. Waiting rooms of fron-

45

tier quarters were converted into unapproachable blockhouses against which the hostile assaults spent themselves. The frontier guards fought off the enemy until Red Army units arrived to aid them.

Shoulder to shoulder with the frontiersmen fought their womenfolk. They stayed on duty as telephonists, delivered ammunition, food, and water to the fighters. Alone at one of the outposts were the wife and children of Commander Dzus, the wife of Assistant Commander Bondarev, and the wife of Acting Chief of the Political Section Lepeshin. The Fascists broke into the building, but the women, without losing their self-possession, concealed themselves in one of the residential rooms. After the enemy set fire to the building and it became enveloped in flames, they abandoned the structure, crept toward the water, and hid in the thick reed growth. Staying there until morning, the brave women, observing all required precautions, came on to the road and soon met some Red Army men who sent them and the children to a safe spot.

At one outpost Acting Political Chief Bashmakoff, Corporal Mashin, Junior Sergeant Mamyshev, and Private Korabelnikoff were surrounded on all sides but accepted battle. For six hours the courageous quartet beat off the mad onslaught of the enemy, dealing him cruel blows. After presenting exceptional specimens of combat at close quarters, the frontiersmen broke out of the encirclement. Joining their own troops, the valiant four had not left the battlefield.

At another border post the man in charge was one Rumiantzev. With four Red Army men he met an invading German group which was about the size of a platoon and engaged them in fighting. Taking an advantageous position, the commander skillfully conducted fire and turned the enemy to flight. The Nazis withdrew beyond the frontier in such a hurry that they left behind the corpses of their fallen soldiers.

The enemy's calculation on his overwhelming numerical superiority was smashed against the iron stamina and valiant endurance of the men of the frontier. Examples of heroism and military art were displayed by Lieutenant Sukharev, commander of the "N" outpost. With only four men he engaged an entire detachment of the Germans. Conditions of that battle demanded inhuman exertion. In an extended struggle, after masterful organization of Soviet fire, the commander inspired his men by personal example, showing them how to fire without wasting a single bullet. In a few hours the battlefield was strewn with the bodies of Hitlerites. Only twenty remained of the Fascist detachment; these retreated beyond the frontier. On that sector the enemy did not succeed in crossing the border.

On the Border

Senior Sergeant N. Shabota of the frontier guards relates:

The camp was asleep. Suddenly the roar of motors was heard. The battle alarm was sounded and our unit was up instantly. The first enemy aircraft were over our native soil. The Fascists tried to bomb our camp and perhaps to break through into the depth of the country.

They succeeded in neither—the powerful fire of the antiaircraft batteries forced them to turn back.

Faster than ever we completed the eight-kilometer march to the border to meet the Nazi usurpers, to check without delay their advance.

By that time the Nazis had seized a settlement situated some four kilometers from the border. Our unit began to surround this from the east.

Under the fire of the enemy artillery we advanced for a few hundred meters toward the settlement. Ahead, about one hun-

dred meters from the settlement, there was an antitank ditch, behind that barbed-wire entanglements.

The subunit commander ordered me to take my group to the
antitank ditch and to keep the wire entanglement under fire. We
set forth at once to carry out our mission.

Noticing our movement, the Nazis concentrated strong artillery fire on the line of the antitank ditch. Their shells, landing
continuously, raised black columns of earth.

Presently the enemy artillery grew quiet but only to be replaced by the rat-tat-tat of a heavy-caliber machine gun. Another
similar machine-gun fired from the forest fringe.

"The sub machine gun of Comrade Grien must move forward and suppress the enemy machine gun," I ordered, pointing
out to the fighter his objective.

Machine-gunner Grien crawled to the spot, installed his
weapon, and no sooner did he fire his first volley than from
somewhere on the left one of our own heavy machine guns went
to work. The enemy firing point was suppressed. At the same
time, our artillery opened up smashing fire at the Fascist concentration on the outskirts and in the settlement proper.

It seemed as though we had practically attained our objective.
But no, the detonations of the enemy shells became more frequent at the breastworks, the Nazi cannons struck with earlier
force. It was as though the enemy had divined our scheme. Apparently, they were availing themselves of a new fire corrector.
But where?

I observed that crows circled without a letup over the forest
fringe where we had just suppressed the Nazis' heavy-caliber
machine gun. Evidently someone had come close to their nest.

The conclusion proved to be correct this time, too. There was
a new observer in the tree. The fire of our snipers removed
this one. This could be told by the ensuing confused firing of
Nazi artillery.

At last we smashed our way to the antitank ditch, although it was not given to us to utilize it in full measure. While we were breaking through on the left, a group of Nazis, about twenty of them, made their way to the ditch.

I gave the command to prepare for the attack. The enemy was literally within twenty paces of us. There he was, rising from the breastworks. Green shadows in camouflage cloaks and helmets entered the rye. They were making for us, without seeing us, without suspecting anything.

"Fire!"

Co-operatively the automatic machine guns and rifles went into action. The Nazi band was thinned out, the survivors fled.

Sharpshooters with automatics were executing the Nazis, goring some with bayonets. Two Nazis assaulted me. I shot at one point-blank. The other had scarcely managed to catch at the sleeve of my shirt when he was felled by one of our bayonets.

In the meantime, another group of the Nazi jackals reached the antitank ditch. It was our duty to knock them out of there. Shouting "Hurrah! For the fatherland!" we lunged into the ditch.

The Hitlerian warriors accepted battle . . . with bared heads, with their arms raised high, with their weapons dropped at their feet.

There were about fifty of these.

The People of One Outpost

The faith-breaking Nazi brigand focused an artillery blow of tremendous force on one outpost of the Kiev Special Military District.

Within two minutes the fighters of Lieutenant Gusev's subunit took up their defense posts, rushed to the blockhouses.

Under cover of their artillery fire, the Nazi troops began to outflank the subunit on the right. A German battalion was advancing against fifty-seven Soviet fighters.

The order was precise:

"No retreat. Engage the advancing enemy. Wait for reinforcements."

Groups of German soldiers appeared. On orders of Lieutenant Gusev the snipers fired accurately at the German officers. The enemy wavered and paused. The annihilating fire pressed the German battalion to the ground; the fifty-seven heroes were knocking out the hostile man power.

But the Nazi command introduced fresh forces into action. At a terrific speed, a battalion of German motorcyclists rushed at the tiny group of Soviet fighters. The motorcyclists were armed with light machine guns and were outflanking on the right.

The fighters lay calmly in their blockhouses, biding their time. Political Instructor Leonid Zhurikoff, a decisive, cool-headed individual, had splendidly organized the fire directed against the enemy. The attack of the Nazi motorcycle battalion had swallowed wrong. In impotent rage its remnants made another attempt to smash their way to the handful of defenders, but they were repelled with heavy losses.

Then the German command threw more than 200 soldiers into battle. Again the Fascists opened a hurricane of artillery fire. The quarters of the outpost and all surrounding structures were gutted. But the murderers' rejoicing was premature. The structures narrowed the field of Soviet fire. Now that they had burned down, a great open space was before the fighters and they could keep the entire surrounding terrain under their fire.

After a while the blockhouses caught fire. However, the fighters did not lose their presence of mind. Political Instructor

Zhurikoff, while directing the fire fighting, never for a moment weakened his observation of the enemy. His keen eye noted a movement of foliage. Further watching disclosed that somewhere near by, behind a cluster of trees, a German cannon had been concealed. Aiming directly, it was hitting a neighboring blockhouse. The political instructor fired at the crew of the German gun, only fifty meters away. After investing three cartridge ribbons, the entire crew was knocked out. Seeing that a German officer, the one who was in charge of that cannon, was speedily escaping on a motorcycle, Zhurikoff picked him off with a well-aimed bullet.

Ordering Kobeshkin, who was operating a heavy-caliber machine gun, to exterminate the enemies if they tried to reapproach their cannon, the Political Instructor rushed over to the observation post of Sharpshooter Sovanenko. Suddenly there was a staggering blow and an explosion. The Germans' heavy artillery had opened fire at the blockhouse. By a direct hit at the embrasure they had disabled the heavy-caliber machine gun and wounded three fighters.

German heavy artillery was also firing at the remaining blockhouses.

Seven fighters, Lieutenant Gusev, Political Instructor Zhurikoff, and the wife of Political Instructor Gorokhoff of the next subunit began to leave the outpost, making for near-by shrubbery. This was not a departure in the ordinary sense of the word. It was a death-defying plunge to break away from the Nazi chain that was choking the outpost on all sides. The first chain of encirclement was broken.

Zhurikoff's group crept on knees and elbows for some two kilometers. All this time the German heavy-caliber machine gun fired at them, aiming particularly at Gorokhoff's wife, for her white dress stood out prominently against the green grass. But it was too late. The fighters had outmaneuvered the German

soldiers and were moving toward the side of the Soviet cover-
ing-up troops.

Learning of the failure of its men, the German command
threw a cavalry squadron of 120 or 130 blades at the break-
through group of Soviet fighters. The Nazi cavalrymen attacked
on the run the group under Junior Corporal Petroff. The squadron was faced manfully, courageously. No, the Fascist command was obviously doomed to failure in its plan to destroy
the man power of the Soviet country, its brave, noble people!

They had apparently observed from the German command
position that the handful of Soviet heroes had repulsed the cavalry squadron and that with the aid of rearguard fire they were
proceeding to join their own. Then the German officers decided to destroy the smallest group, that of Political Instructor
Zhurikoff. The German command sent five tanks against it. Firing, the Soviet fighters retreated and disappeared in the forest.
But Zhurikoff could not forget the group under the command
of Junior Corporal Petroff. He maneuvered in such a way as
to divert the enemy fire to himself. Understanding this maneuver
and making use of it, Petroff and his fighters continued to move
out of the second ring of German encirclement. Eventually the
enemy also understood, but too late. In helpless fury he concentrated the fire of his machine guns on Petroff's group. Sharpshooter Sovanenko was seriously wounded. Four fighters carried him in their arms. This slowed up the group.

"Leave me on the field, comrades," Sovanenko said quietly.
"Leave a small machine gun for me. I will not live much longer,
but I can help you. I shall spend the cartridges on the Fascist
reptiles, and the last one on myself. Well, go away, comrades. . . ."

Under cover of the heavily wounded Sharpshooter Sovanenko's machine-gun fire, Corporal Petroff's group began to retreat for a break-through of the second encirclement. The Nazi

scavengers opened mine-thrower fire at the fatally wounded fighter. The fearless hero died the death of the brave. Gritting their teeth and vowing revenge, Petroff's fighters hurled themselves into a furious attack and cleared the way.

Meanwhile, the tiny group of Lieutenant Gusev and Political Instructor Zhurikoff, emerging at the clearing, bumped into a platoon of Germans marching on the highway. Both adversaries stopped. There was a moment of indecision, after which the Germans ran helter-skelter. One of the German tanks which were pursuing the Soviet fighters in the forest leaped forth from behind the trees; its crew, upon seeing the fleeing men, decided that these were the sought-after Reds and opened fire—at its own soldiers. Availing themselves of this development, the fighters moved away from the line of pursuit of the remaining enemy tanks which were approaching.

But the ring about the gallant fighters was growing narrower. Wherever they turned, they encountered the always more numerous enemy. Knowing the terrain well, they decided to wait in a swamp, two kilometers away from the outpost and 200 meters from the border. They spent some five days there. There was neither food nor water. After crashing through the top layer of the swamp, they put in long reeds and through these they drew black peaty water.

In such surroundings the bravest people would be justified in feeling that their destruction was unavoidable. But the Soviet patriots judged differently. The Lieutenant and the Political Instructor roused their fighters to the final charge for a breakthrough. Everyone was abundantly supplied with cartridges and grenades. Even before leaving the outpost, they removed the gas masks from their kits and replaced them with cartridges.

The Soviet warriors chose a route that was entirely unanticipated by the Germans—directly through the enemy troop dispositions. The unexpectedness and the daring of this decision brought success to the fighters. Again they emerged from the encirclement.

Not far from the village of "B" the peasants informed the fighters that nearby German reconnaissance was operating. Pretending to be working in the fields, the peasants were in reality scouting in the surrounding territory and were able to indicate to the fighters the way back to the Soviet positions.

ON RECONNAISSANCE

The Brave Scout Beliakoff

Guns thundered; the enemy was staging a fierce offensive. The Soviet units greeted the Nazis with their own hurricane of fire. This stubborn battle had lasted for several hours already; dozens of times the Germans passed into attack and each time fell back before the impenetrable rain of lead.

And now, apparently, their dash was played out. The enemy entrenched himself in a forest clearing and somehow, unexpectedly, ceased firing. Silence fell.

"That's strange," the commander thought. "Are the bandits preparing some kind of surprise?"

He summoned Sergeant Beliakoff.

"Comrade Sergeant, take along two fighters and ascertain the disposition of the enemy firing points."

"Aye, aye, it will be done!"

Donning green branches over their uniforms, the scouts crept away. They crossed the advance line of our infantry. Ahead lay the forest, in it the enemy. But in what part?

Beliakoff ordered the two scouts to halt and to camouflage themselves further. Carefully he climbed a small shrub-covered hill and began to scrutinize the terrain through his field glasses.

Nothing suspicious was discernible. The forest was silent, the fields deserted. But somewhere on his right there sounded a solitary rifle shot.

"It's there!" thought the Sergeant.

He nodded to the other scouts and they resumed their creeping advance. They crept, covered with greenery, using every bush, every hillock for concealment. Now they were very close to the enemy position.

At this moment the detachment they had left behind opened fire at the enemy to distract attention from the approaching scouts.

The Nazis remained silent for a few minutes, then replied.

The scouts crept ahead faster. By and by the enemy firing points stood out clearly. But not all of them. Somewhere ceaselessly, in short volleys, there rat-tat-tatted an invisible machine gun. Its whereabouts had to be determined.

Sergeant Beliakoff decided to creep still nearer to the enemy. He crept cautiously, slowly, his ear cocked for the slightest stir. Suddenly he heard strange voices, words he could not understand.

"The Nazis!" Beliakoff decided.

To be sure, some ten meters away, in a shell-made crater sat the enemies. Beliakoff sidestepped them and continued to move ahead. Near the clearing he paused. Now he was at the very position of the Germans.

After establishing the location of the firing point, Beliakoff began to backtrack.

He and his comrades had hardly crept twenty meters before rifle shots crackled after them. The enemy had discovered the daring men. A hail of bullets avalanched after them. The scouts returned the fire. The Germans were approaching, surrounding them in a gradually tighter ring. One of the fighters was killed. Two remained. They fired, striking everyone who showed up above the cover.

But there were only two scouts and two or three dozen Germans. The ring tightened. A bullet killed the other fighter. Beliakoff remained alone.

"You are lying, you will not take me!" the Sergeant said angrily.

Hiding behind a hillock, he continued firing. The Nazis came nearer still; they apparently wanted to take the scout prisoner.

"Surrender!" yelled one of the Germans in broken Russian.

"Take me!" taunted Beliakoff.

He took aim, then threw two grenades one after another. Columns of earth shot up; cries and groans were heard. Not a second was to be lost. Hurling one more grenade, Beliakoff impetuously rolled down the hillock and began to run away, taking cover behind bushes. But the enemy followed on his heels, anxious to take the scout prisoner at any price.

Again Beliakoff hid himself. The Germans searched about the clearing. Here and there they fired lone shots. At times the enemy soldiers passed quite close to Beliakoff but did not notice him—he lay motionless, covered with greenery.

By and by everything grew quiet. It seemed as if the Germans had despaired of locating the scout. Waiting a little longer, Beliakoff stood up and noiselessly began to make his way back to his own people, stopping frequently to listen. Not a soul around. Silence. . . .

He had hardly left the grove when three Germans set upon him from three sides.

With a neat shot Beliakoff killed one of them outright.

Another leaped at the Sergeant from behind, seized him by the shoulders, pressing with the full weight of his own body. Throwing the Nazi to the ground, Beliakoff finished him off with the butt of his gun.

Seeing the way the struggle was going, the third German made ready to shoot Beliakoff. Bending low, the Sergeant lunged at him, knocking his rifle out of his hands, and in the same instant pierced him with his bayonet.

Attracted by the shot, other Germans hurried to the scene of the clash. It was necessary to retreat very quickly. Sometimes creeping and sometimes running, hiding amid rocks, utilizing ditches, the scout struggled on toward his own lines.

His strength was ebbing when he heard the challenge:

"Halt! Who goes there?"

These were his own people.

The fighters surrounded Beliakoff, lifted and carried him. For some time he lay without moving. Then, turning in the direction of the forest where he had left the enemy, he said with a smile:

"Well, what do you say? Did you take me?"

Promptly and concisely Beliakoff reported to the commander the results of his reconnaissance.

The commander shook his hand vigorously.

"Thank you, Comrade Sergeant."

"I serve the Soviet Union!" snapped the valiant scout.

Reports of the Soviet Information Bureau

Scouts of the "N" Regiment, penetrating into the rear of the enemy, raided the staff headquarters of a German regiment and seized many valuable documents. On their return trip, the scouts had mined several sections of the highway which the Germans used to deliver shells. On the following day, the Soviet airmen ascertained that the mines had blown up eleven German automobiles.

Red Army scouts Zhilin and Chesnokoff discovered some sixteen camouflaged tanks at a forest fringe in the enemy rear.

Realizing at once that the enemy had prepared an ambuscade, the scouts decided to warn their command of the waiting trap. Red Armyman Chesnokoff, leaving Fighter Zhilin to observe the enemy, quickly made for the nearest Red Army detachment to report the Nazi undertaking. Shortly a wing of dive bombers commanded by Lieutenant Ilushin dropped upon the enemy who did not expect the raid by the Soviet aircraft. Not a single crew of the Nazi tanks got a chance even to start their motors. Every enemy machine was destroyed.

On June 28 a plane of the "N" escadrille took off to reconnoiter. Flying in a low-altitude strafing manner, the plane unexpectedly encountered a Do-17 Nazi bomber flying in the same manner. The plane's commander, Senior Lieutenant Lobanoff, fired a short volley and shot down the enemy bomber. The Nazi machine dropped to the ground like a rock, without firing a shot. Continuing on its way, the plane's crew subjected to their fire and turned to flight one more enemy machine, dispersed a concentration of infantry and auto vehicles, and after securing a number of valuable reconnaissance data, safely returned to their base.

A Nameless Elevation

Pointing with his hand to a small elevation in the distance, the battalion commander ordered that the enemy be knocked off it.

The battalion went into the attack. Lieutenant Posokhoff's platoon advanced in the van. Immediately behind and to the right operated a neighboring company. The fighters advanced carefully.

There was not a stir or a sound in the forest. The methods

of the treacherous enemy were well known to everyone. The platoon had scarcely emerged into the glade when several shots resounded simultaneously from three directions. Instantly, the fighters fell prone and camouflaged. The bullets did no harm. A brief order followed:

"Section Commander Snezhko, Red Armymen Yelkin and Oreshnikoff, reconnoiter the location of the enemy 'cuckoos' and destroy them."

The scouts soon vanished. Snezhko went to the left, Yelkin and Oreshnikoff to the right. The "cuckoos" raged. As soon as the scouts would appear in an open spot, bullets would buzz about them in a swarm. It was necessary to lie in the grass for several minutes at a stretch, without showing signs of life.

Soon Snezhko saw a large fir tree ahead of him.

"The reptile must be hiding there for sure!"

It was so. Camouflaged by branches, an enemy sniper was ensconced at the top of the tree. With his first shot Snezhko wounded him, with the second one he finished him off.

At the same time Yelkin and Oreshnikoff were tracking down other "cuckoos." The forest reared up like a great wall. An enemy rifleman might be hidden in every tree.

It was not easy to notice him. Ignoring the hazard, Yelkin raised his head and began to figure out where the enemies were hiding by the sounds made by their bullets in flight.

Soon the fighter reported to his comrade the results of his observation:

"The snipers are in two trees, over there, by the lake, between the rows of rocks. They are firing alternately. You shoot down the left one, and I'll take care of the one on the right."

The "cuckoos" were silenced forever.

The platoon continued its attack. From the elevation the White Guard Finns opened an intensive cannonade from their machine guns, mine throwers, and cannons. The neighboring company was subjected to the heaviest fire. The enemy sought to check the advance at any cost, in order subsequently to destroy the attackers section by section.

But the company commander had understood the scheme in good time. The fighters lay down and stoically endured the hail of fire, while Lieutenant Posokhoff's platoon continued to move forward. Section Commander Snezhko skillfully led his fighters. Bullets whistled all around, mines detonated. But the courageous warriors advanced bravely toward their objective. Thus they reached an open clearing.

"To be traversed in two double-quick runs!"

Harmoniously the fighters followed their commander. Half of the expanse of the clearing was now behind them. They were ready to fall prone before completing the crossing, but at this moment a mine, whistling shrilly, landed behind them. Snezhko looked back and ran a few more steps. The entire section followed him. They succeeded in running for quite a stretch, then dropped down, while a deafening explosion resounded behind them.

Red Armyman Yelkin chose his firing position near his section commander. He did not fire too often. Yelkin keenly peered into the shrubs which framed the elevation; against the green background he would locate a gray White Guard Finnish cap and, after making sure that it was on an enemy head rather than on a stick (the enemy is crafty!), he would aim calmly.

"One bandit less," Yelkin said each time as he began looking for a new target.

The White Guard Finns discovered the whereabouts of the platoon and began to slither like snakes toward the fighters, in order to surround them.

"Get your grenades ready!" ordered Lieutenant Posokhoff.

The first to apply "pocket artillery" was Section Commander Snezhko. He allowed two White Guard Finns to come within thirty meters and with a clean throw settled their fate. Right after Snezhko, Red Armymen Yelkin and Oreshnikoff hurled their grenades. The surviving enemies showed their heels.

By this time the neighboring company pulled up toward the elevation. A mighty battle cry was sounded:

"Forward, for the beloved fatherland, for the great Stalin!"

The White Guard Finns could not stand up under the tempestuous blow and retired to their former lines. The nameless elevation had been cleared of the enemy.

THE BAYONET CHARGE

A Decisive Engagement

Early in the morning units of the Red Army took their starting positions for the battle. The communications platoon of the headquarters battery had laid a field telephone line as soon as they had received their assignment. After fulfilling this urgent mission, the fighters were now resting.

Next to them was Lieutenant Potorochin's staff-headquarters platoon. Suddenly rifle and machine-gun shots shattered the silence of the southern midday. Some 200 meters away from the fighters a Nazi infantry unit appeared, more than 250 Germans. Some seventy Red Armymen were on hand. Colonel Zakharoff appealed to the fighters to greet the enemy determinedly and mercilessly. A new wave of rage and hatred for the perfidious foe was evoked in the hearts of the Red Armymen by the words of their commander.

Junior Political Instructor Kashin took over the command of some twenty-five fighters. He bravely led his group against the left flank of the Germans. On the right went forty-five fighters under Lieutenant Potorochin. A brief order, "Into attack, follow me!" and, inspired by the example of their commanders, the fighters advanced on the enemy.

Their helmets occasionally flashing in the sun, the Germans were moving through tall rye. Attacking from a height, the enemy had an advantageous position. But the Red Armymen courageously crept forward with their rifles and grenades, eager to close in on the attackers. They fired not a single shot, nearing the Nazi bandits in concealment.

The fire of the automatic weapons and mine throwers of the enemy was fruitless. The fighters crept along for more than 150 meters and when they were within from forty to fifty meters of the enemy, they stood up and with a loud "Hurrah!" charged. Finding the Red Army bayonet charge unbearable, the enemy ran. A few German soldiers, seeing the Soviet fighters quite near and running toward them with bayonets atilt, threw up their hands and surrendered.

The heroes chased the enemy for about three kilometers. They stabbed him mercilessly with their bayonets and fired at the back of his head, until the remnants of Nazi infantry disappeared in the woods.

All had shown themselves courageous fighters in that short but decisive engagement. Among those who distinguished themselves particularly were Junior Political Instructor Kashin, who with his revolver shot several Nazis, Junior Sergeant Beliayev, Red Armymen Volkoff, Grishin, and others. They exterminated the Nazi brigands without mercy. In cases where the enemy, refusing to accept battle, ran away from a Red Army bayonet, he was reached by a well-aimed bullet.

The enemy left more than 100 corpses on the field of battle.

The Crushing Blow

Violent fighting continued in the mountains for several days, relates Senior Political Instructor I. Deygen. The Nazis hurled into the attack the highly trained Alpine mountaineer division. With these marched the Hitlerite hangers-on—the White Guard Finnish Schutzkorps. The men of the Red Army greeted the bandits with withering fire. The river, across the rapids of which the Hitlerites attempted to advance, reddened with their blood.

Murin's company fought the Fascists courageously for a few hours, knocking more than one enemy section out of the ranks. When the drunken horde turned up at close quarters, the company fearlessly charged with bayonets and forced the attackers to roll back with heavy casualties. Matching the sharpshooters were the artillerists. When the Schutzkorps approached defending positions very closely, the artillerists fired at the enemy point-blank.

The mine-thrower subunit of Lieutenant Zhukoff and the machine-gun contingent of Sergeant Panoff especially distinguished themselves in this operation. Permitting the Fascists to come close, they had opened such fire that in a few minutes more than half of the enemy numbers was wiped out.

Our units ably repelled the Nazi pressure with successful counterattacks. The enemy seized elevation "N" which dominates a series of small and large mounds. Subunit Commander Filipoff was assigned to expel the enemy and occupy the elevation. Making use of every feature of the terrain, the courageous commander approached the enemy, unnoticed. The concentrated fire of the Soviet machine guns and mine throwers avalanched upon the Nazi fortifications. Then, shouting "For the fatherland! For

Stalin!" the fighters charged with bayonets and gained the elevation.

The earliest battles under the complex conditions of the North furnished many examples of mutuality and combat co-ordination of the Red Armymen. Artillerist Kryloff noted that an enemy machine gunner, having ascended the top of a crag, was keeping one of our subunits under his fire. Without losing a second, Kryloff rolled his own gun onto the highway and with a trusty shell knocked off the top of the crag and, simultaneously, the Nazi "woodpecker."

They, Too, Are "Warriors"

In a small forest, on a river shore—says the wounded Junior Sergeant, Shamil Dooniashev, of the infantry—I stood guard over an important objective. Everything was silent, not a shot was heard. After it grew dark, our sentries discovered the enemy who was secretly stealing toward us. The captain decided to let them come still nearer, then led the subunit in a bayonet charge. Shouting "For the fatherland, for Stalin," my comrades rushed at the Nazis. I remained at my post, though I could hardly control myself from running along to help my own.

However, they did not need my help. The German infantrymen evidently have weak nerves. The ranks of the Red fighters had scarcely appeared, flashing their polished steel, when you should have seen how the heels of the Hitlerite warriors flashed.

They did not bother us any more that night.

At the very break of dawn enemy aircraft were circling over our small forest. They began to dive at our subunit. It would have been unwise to remain, and we received an order to leave.

Then the enemy infantry showed up again. Under cover of

a hurricane of machine-gun and rifle fire, they emerged from their shelters, intending to occupy the position just abandoned by us. Their aircraft, having spent their supply of bombs, flew away. Our commander led us into a new attack.

But while still some distance away, we could see that there was no one to stab. Firing in disorderly fashion, the Nazis were running away. Almost without a casualty, we took their trenches, quickly picked off a few automatic gunners who made themselves at home in near-by trees. Then we saw running toward us some sixty persons in Red Army uniforms. They were pleading with us not to fire:

"We are your own men, comrades."

We did not understand: How did they manage to get themselves between the two lines of fire? Just the same, we did not shoot. When they were some fifty meters away from us, the group unexpectedly dropped down in a convenient spot and started throwing grenades at us.

By command we retreated into an orchard on the left flank. But there further unpleasantness awaited us. The cunning enemy prepared an ambush, intending to mow down the sub-unit with cross-fire. However, their nerves had once more played a trick on the ill-starred "warriors." We did not come very near before the Nazis opened fire and thereby gave themselves away. In an energetic charge we cleaned up the orchard. And this time it was not our lot to meet them face to face—the enemy knows all too well the meaning of the Red Army bayonet.

Not far from me fell a lieutenant stricken with a stray bullet. I picked up the officer and carried him farther away from the fire. Soon I met an ambulance cart. It took the lieutenant away.

Infuriated by their failures, the Germans started to plow up the orchard with their artillery shells. A fragment wounded me in the left hip. On one foot I hopped into a ditch. There a comrade bandaged my wound, stopped the bleeding. The nurses showed up in a few minutes.

I did not fight long but I could see well that the Germans were afraid to accept our bayonet charge.

Bayonet, Grenade, Rifle

Retreating to new positions, a Soviet fighting detachment concentrated in a grove before a forest.

Observing the retreat but failing to grasp its purpose, the Germans decided to begin pursuit of the fighters, assigning for this task a mobile group of more than 600 on bicycles, motorcycles, and in automobiles.

"Prepare for defense!" came the command.

Every tree became a fortress. Unexpected assistance was rendered by a light fog.

Thanks to a well-arranged defense, the enemy found himself at once under the cross-fire of rifles and machine guns. But numerical superiority was on his side. The Nazis struck at the right flank. Three German antitank guns opened fire.

Captain Meshkorudny, commander of the Red Army detachment, then ordered his left flank:

"Forward, with bayonets fixed!"

Advancing to meet the German mobile units, the Red Army bayonets gleamed.

One junior lieutenant, annoyed because the operations of his men were hindered by an enemy antitank gun, crept toward it and with a grenade exterminated its entire crew. The second antitank gun was disabled in the same manner. The next minute rifle fire destroyed six Nazi automatic gunners who marched in the first row. Precisely placed bullets stopped a German light automobile; when its door was opened, out fell a dead major decorated with three Iron Crosses.

Meanwhile, Captain Meshkorudny and his group of fighters pressed the enemies, showering them with grenades.

Nazi soldiers began to throw down their arms and flee. They fell under the bayonet blows, dropped stricken with bullets. Some German soldiers fell on their knees and, stretching out their arms, begged: "*Schiessen Sie nicht!*"

The enemy abandoned the third antitank gun to fate.

Pursued by our detachment, the Germans fled for twelve kilometers. About 300 Nazis were killed in this clash. Over 300 bicycles, a truck, a light car, and many weapons were captured. Among our trophies were secret documents.

Sergeant Stupichenko's Exploit

Following is a report by Battalion Commissar Y. Gorodskoy:

Sergeant Mikola Stupichenko was a sociable and merry man. The fighters liked to chat with him, they enjoyed his wit and friendly funmaking. Only once did the Red Armymen see the Sergeant's face beclouded—when the conversation turned to his parents.

"Dad and Mother?" Mikola said, as though asking himself. "I have none. . . . In 1918 the German occupants shot them. At that time the Germans sent practically our entire village to the grave. I was just about a year old then. . . ."

That conversation took place rather recently but much has changed since then. A black cloud moved over a clear June dawn. The German Fascists began a war against Sergeant Stupichenko's native land. The army unit seethed. Many impassioned words were spoken at the meeting—they were all from the heart, and heart to heart. When Mikola took the floor, those present pricked up their ears; many knew his history. Mikola did not speak long:

"I promise you, comrades, to finish with my own hands two German Fascists in the very first battle. This is my plan to begin with, we shall see what to do after that."

This brief speech evoked a veritable storm of an ovation. The fighters of Sergeant Stupichenko's section embraced him, which caused Mikola no small embarrassment:

"Let me go, fellows. . . . You certainly found some orator in me."

"Speechmaking is not the idea," they answered him. "You've touched our hearts. You spoke for all of us."

One dark June night the section took a firing position. Sergeant Stupichenko explained to his fighters their mission and at the end added:

"If they crawl at us, we'll greet them with a good morning."

A thundering duel opened the morning. German artillery unleashed an intensive barrage. Soviet artillery replied most persuasively. Mikola noted with satisfaction that the fighters of his section did not lose their heads; instead, in a businesslike manner, they masterfully made use of every fold in the terrain.

"Very good, fellows, very good," he would cry out in Ukrainian. Because of the roar of the cannonade, the Red Armymen could not make out a single word but they understood that the Sergeant was pleased and that they need not blush for their performance.

The Germans apparently decided that their artillery's work had been adequate and that the time had come for their attack. The enemy infantry poured forth in a torrent toward the approaches to this sector. Here the native soil was being defended by Sergeant Stupichenko and his fighters. All along the front line the same was being done by thousands upon thousands of other people—from privates to generals. Mikola felt as though he and his section were closely watched by the whole Red Army. Through the din of battle he seemed to hear distinctly the army's voice: "Make your stand well, sonny." Those words might have been spoken to him by his own mother whom he did not know.

The Nazis were tearing ahead. The automatic weapons in Stupichenko's section worked dependably. But the enemy ranks came and came. Mikola issued orders and rained hot lead on the enemy soldiers, who dropped to the ground, then rose again and advanced again, resembling lunatics who are subservient to someone else's malevolent will, who are directed by someone else's hand. They were commanded by a tall officer who continuously shouted his commands with such frenzy that his words turned into canine barking.

Mikola soberly evaluated the situation on his small sector. Although the Germans were sustaining heavy losses, there were three of them to every fighter in Stupichenko's section. It was clear that the Nazis wanted to break through no matter what their losses would be. If they were to come closer to the section's position, the struggle would be even more burdensome. It was necessary to meet the enemy halfway, to stun him so as to undermine his numerical advantage.

Firing and yelling, the Nazis were in direct proximity. The tall officer was running ahead of them, often dropping to the ground. For an instant Mikola plainly saw his face, perspiring and red. At the same time he was thinking: "The same kind killed my father and mother." After that, some fighters heard him while others sensed it in their hearts that the Sergeant exclaimed: "For the fatherland, for Stalin, forward!" Straightening up, Mikola led his section into a counterattack. Next turn was the bayonet's, and the fighters' bayonets were sharp and merciless to the enemy. Sergeant Stupichenko's section was famed throughout the regiment for their mastery of bayonet techniques. Mikola himself used to say: "In the bayonet business, one must work without kindliness, one must move angrily."

It was thus that the section battled. Hatred for the Nazi plunderers multiplied tenfold the strength of each fighter. The Red Army blow was so powerful and impetuous that the Germans paused. They were not given a chance to come to.

"Beat the Nazi thieves!" Mikola roared resoundingly. For a split second the overheated face of the tall officer flashed before him, then came the short Stupichenko blow—it was as though lightning pierced the enemy's chest; the officer lumberingly heaped to the ground.

The Germans wavered but, aware of their advantage in numbers, accepted battle. Stupichenko's section fought splendidly. There was not a fighter among them who had not downed one or two enemy soldiers.

Whirlwind-like, Mikola leaped at a stocky German infantryman who but a moment before had bayoneted a Red Armyman in the back. The thick-set German fell with a pierced heart. But now two soldiers set upon Mikola at one time. The Sergeant brought the butt of his rifle into play. One soldier dropped dead from Mikola's athletic blow. The other preferred to avoid an encounter. To speak plainly, he ran and his example was shortly followed by the few raiders who were still alive. All along the line, of which the Stupichenko section was a part, the same results took place. The Nazis were beaten back behind the border.

By midday the Major said to Sergeant Stupichenko in front of everybody:

"You fought excellently. Thank you!"

"I serve the Soviet Union," Stupichenko replied quietly.

COURAGE AND INITIATIVE

Swimming Two Kilometers

The battle was getting hotter. The White Guard Finns, having received re-enforcements, tried at all costs to drive the Red Army platoon from the position they occupied. Drunken soldiers were breaking through, but stricken by the accurate bullets of the Red fighters, they fell, as if mowed down, a few meters from the trenches.

Enraged by their failure, a White Finnish officer jumped out ahead, yelled shrilly at the soldiers, and led the bandits against the defending Red soldiers. A shot rang out and the officer fell.

Under the cover of machine-gun and trench-mortar fire, another officer, commander of the White Finns, again went into attack. At this moment, the Soviet guns suddenly went quiet; the commander and the gunners were wounded.

The situation became more complicated. The enemy was preparing to attack the trenches.

And then the commander of the detachment, Junior Sergeant Egoroff, ordered one of the fighters to take command of the detachment and himself crawled toward the silent guns. The enemy noticed the brave soldier and opened intense rifle and machine-gun fire at him.

Egoroff pulled his head into his shoulders and played dead. Egoroff deceived the enemy and in a quiet moment attained his goal.

"Roll the guns ten meters forward; fire at the enemy point-blank," Egoroff ordered the detachment, and himself seized the trigger handles. The enemy was enraged. By the time the guns were rolled up to the new position, two bullets slid over Egoroff's helmet.

At last the first shell was fired. It burst in the midst of the White Finns. Shapeless parts of machine guns, fragments of rifle butts and gray caps flew through the air.

The second shell was just as accurate.

The enemy virtually stopped shooting. Then there was a unanimous "Hurrah" and loud shouts of "For the fatherland, for Stalin."

The detachment went into attack and took the enemy's first line. The White Finns took cover behind the opposite slope, which was of no great height, and left behind about fifteen soldiers with automatics to cover their retreat.

Egoroff had to overtake the detachment, but it was very difficult. "Cuckoos" were scattered all around. He began making his way ahead very carefully. Meanwhile, the White Finns, having recovered from the attack, again opened fierce fire at the platoon.

"Why is our trench mortar quiet? It should be somewhere around here."

Looking closely, Egoroff saw the camouflaged trench mortar and two fighters several feet ahead of him, apparently out of formation.

Egoroff made a decision at once—he himself would open fire with the mortar; thus bombs began to fly to the elevation whither the enemy was heading. Egoroff worked accurately and confidently.

After every shot his hand instinctively flew to the gun. He looked around. The enemy is deceitful. An attack could be expected at any moment.

Thirty of the bombs shot by Egoroff had done their work. Thoroughly shaken, the enemy quieted down. The mighty "Hurrah" of Red Army men was heard once more.

"That means our men are breaking through again."

This time, not only the platoon but the whole company counterattacked. Toward evening, when Egoroff succeeded in safely reaching his own detachment, the enemy brought artillery into action. Shells were bursting close to the trenches. The fighters withstood the fire stoically. They were often covered with earth. Egoroff stuck his head out of the trench and saw that the company was retreating, not being able to withstand the overwhelming numbers of the enemy. He immediately formed a plan: "To cover the retreating regiment with my fire."

"To your stations," the Junior Sergeant commanded.

The first to open fire was Red Armyman Petroff. The other fighters followed him. The White Finns, taking advantage of the fact that the company was silent, tried to pursue, but their attempts were unsuccessful. Co-ordinated rifle and machine-gun fire from the trenches on the left flank brought confusion to the drunken White Finnish ranks and forced them to lie down.

Failure infuriated the enemy. Three times Junior Sergeant Egoroff shattered the enemy's plans; now they decided to vent their bestial anger on him.

Over the trench bullets began to whistle with renewed strength. The enemy began to surround the handful of daring men. Egoroff commanded: "One at a time; out of the trench toward the lake."

Soon the detachment reached the big lake. But what to do next? On three sides were the enemies; on the fourth, two kilometers of water hazards.

"Strip!" ordered Egoroff to the fighters.

And a minute later: "Follow me!"

The fighters swam, carrying along their weapons and uniforms. They swam for about an hour and were beginning to feel tired. Junior Sergeant Egoroff encouraged them:

"It's not far to the bank. A little more effort, comrades!"

At last their feet touched the weedy bottom. Recovering their breath on the bank, after a few minutes, the fighters went forward, with Egoroff as commander at the head of the detachment, together with the company, along the bank to meet the enemy.

Courage and Recklessness

The attack began about midday. Senior Lieutenant Alexander Kolomietz led his company to the ford, in order to force the river and drive out the German troops disposed on the opposite bank. The Nazis were visible in a quiet village at the edge of the forest. The well-known countryside, so familiar and dear; whitewashed huts with carved shutters, sunk in flowery gardens, freshly painted fences, paths covered with sunshine and bordered by grass, green melon beds, and fields stretching to the horizon. The bountiful Ukrainian land.

Alexander Kolomietz led his company out of the lowland and began to climb a small hillock. Kolomietz ordered Lieutenant Ryaboy to cross the river with his platoon and come out in the rear of the enemy. The platoon moved on. The enemy must have noticed this movement and began to march off, drawing after them Ryaboy and his Red Army men. The platoon entered the village without a single shot.

"What is this? Does it mean the enemy isn't here?" thought Ryaboy.

It was quiet in the village. But Kolomietz noticed through his field glasses what Ryaboy hadn't seen: the enemy had entered the thick, tall rye, enticing the platoon ever farther in order to surround it. To delay longer was impossible. The Senior Lieutenant made his decision: to attack the enemy overwhelmingly superior in numbers.

The company advanced to attack. Suddenly, from the rear the enemy opened intense fire on the attackers. The company fell to the ground. To go farther was impossible until the Nazis, shooting from behind, out of a window of a deserted peasant's house, were exterminated.

Kolomietz commanded Sergeant Tichomiroff. "Throw a grenade at the window!"

But the enemy had already opened fire from the attic, the roof, and the barn. The operation must be ended promptly. Otherwise, Ryaboy's platoon, which had crossed the river, would be exterminated, and then the enemy himself would advance to the attack.

"Set fire to the yard!"

The thatched roof flared up, the flames touched the walls, caught the fence. The Fascists wavered at the unexpected action of the fighters, fell into confusion, and fled in panic, firing over their shoulders.

"Company forward!"

The fighters began to pursue the Nazis. They raced through the garden, passed the meadow, the hollow.

"Our cause is right; forward!"

"Forward . . . forward!"

Here, in the war, you especially feel the strength lodged in this word.

Suddenly Alexander Kolomietz stumbled, slowed his run a bit, then fell on his face. Wounded? He tried to get up, made several steps, and fell anew. He crawled. He crawled, and continued to command. Forward, forward . . . we can't give the enemy a chance to collect its wits. We can't give them a chance to stop. This is the decisive moment. Kolomietz crawled, crawled, he came up to some scattered thorn bushes. He felt that he was getting weaker; his left knee did not bend any more.

"They have wounded me. The devil take 'em."

Through the bushes, where the Senior Lieutenant lay, one could see how the fighters advanced and one could glimpse their figures. Kolomietz could not move, but his voice was still strong.

He continued following the rapidly developing fight and to command it. After a while, Senior Lieutenant Alexander Kolomietz raised himself on his elbows and saw that his company had crossed the river and joined with Ryaboy's platoon and the attack continued.

Maxim Zukin, a Junior Lieutenant, received an order to turn back with his squad. Back? Yes. Parachutists had landed in the rear of the Soviet Army.

The order was brief:

"The squad is directed to liquidate this party."

It was necessary to do this quickly, before the Nazis succeeded in creating diversions in the rear and blowing up the columns moving along the highway.

Who knows where the Nazi parachutists have landed and where they have already succeeded in penetrating? They investigated the hollow, the copse, the ditch along the road—nobody was there. Then Zukin decided to surround the nearest village. The squad moved cautiously, straining their eyes and ears. The fighters did not trust tufts, stumps, noises, and the rustle of trees. Not far off Zukin saw on the highway a group in Red Army uniforms huddling against baby tanks. They also noticed the squad advancing toward them. One of them—a tall, broad-shouldered man waved his hand:

"Hi, come here!"

"Who are you?"

"Soviet. . . . Can't you see?"

"Our own," thought the Junior Lieutenant, and went nearer. Approaching, he noticed in the field, amongst the stalks, some soldiers, crouching there. As soon as the squad came up to them, Zukin heard a command in German. The Junior Lieutenant understood the crafty trick of the enemy. Keeping his head, he commanded:

"To arms!"

The fighters opened fire on the masquerading Nazis. The enemy light tank advanced against the two-story house, behind which the fighters hid. Zukin sent a Red Armyman to tell this to the ordnance commander, who was posted 500 meters away. After some minutes, the artillery opened fire on the baby tank. The shattered machine stopped.

But even then the German parachutists did not desist. They fortified themselves at a mill, firing upon Zukin's squad.

"The mill must be destroyed!"

A messenger dashed again toward the artillery commander. A minute went by, another, five, the artillery was silent. And the Nazi fire became increasingly fiercer. It meant the Red Armyman had not crawled to the guns; he was either dead or wounded.

Junior Lieutenant Zukin turned his command over to a captain who arrived at that time and, crouching, ran to the commander of artillery. Zukin was noticed. Bullets whistled over his head. He huddled and then ran farther. Showing the commander of artillery the disposition of the enemy's hide-out, the Junior Lieutenant returned. Before he had time to return to the squad, the mill was wiped out by accurate shots.

The report of the wounded parachutist found in the barn helped to establish that he alone remained alive of the fifteen Nazis who dared to descend on Soviet soil. The whole party was exterminated.

The operation took one hour.

Fights at the River

On one of the sectors of the western front a river separated the Nazi troops and units of the Red Army. There was a sudden and suspicious quietness on the enemy bank throughout the day. Every occurrence at the front is treated with particular suspicion. Tonight it was confirmed as a wise military tradition.

The Germans decided to force the river and with large forces to attack suddenly the Soviet fighters. At night a striking silence reigned, as if the heavy clashes which occurred in the morning had killed everything living.

And now in this silence, the enemy began the crossing. In trenches, in holes, at all strong points which fighters make quickly and skillfully, they were on the alert. The commander tensely observed the river. They were confident of victory although their detail was much smaller than the crossing Hitlerites.

The crossing acquired a deep significance.

"They decided to take us with smartness, but we, it seems, will outsmart them," said the battalion commander.

When the crossing was at its peak, suddenly, from somewhere among the clouds, there appeared Soviet bombers. The Nazis did not have time to think before the Soviet fliers began to smash their troops, weapons, machines, located on the river and the approaches to it. The blows were accurate and destructive. The roar of explosions increased on the river. The bombers sank many Nazi troops and the survivors began to retreat.

When the enemy drew off, the Soviet bombers returned to their base. The Red infantry from their hiding places greeted the courageous fliers:

"Swell guys!"

The infantrymen weren't heard in the airplanes and knew it, but it was hard to contain their admiration of the accurate and timely action of the air force. Accurate calculation was necessary in this operation. Everything was foreseen and checked. The bombers flew over at the precise moment when it seemed to the Fascists that the crossing was already accomplished. The bombers acted with lightning speed.

Toward dawn, the fighters counted the enemy's losses. A young scout, Sergei Seleznev, as if summing up the night operation, said:

"A great thing—courage."

Political Instructor Kemal Kasumoff

The fellows were already asleep, when in his quarters Political Instructor Kemal Kasumoff heard a knock. It was late. The small riverside town was quiet. A man standing in the street said something and Kemal hurried to his room. "Alarm," said he to his wife. "They are calling me."

In a few hours, Political Instructor Kasumoff went into battle. His detachment left Ungen. The commander of the detachment was on leave, and Kasumoff took charge.

On the left was the silver ribbon of the Prut; cannon boomed, machine guns chattered. There was firing in the rear where Ungen was. In the town was his family: a little boy, eight years old, a little girl, six; and his wife, a comrade, a good wife, who had come with him from Baku.

The first night of the war passed, after that, the first day, and then the second night. The troops that crept from the other bank were driven back and shattered.

The fighters sat in a tight cluster. A young soldier was telling something very interesting and funny. They listened to him with pleasure, diverting their attention momentarily if a plane droned in the sky.

Kasumoff went up to his people. He knew each of his subordinates well, young sappers full of life, their habits, tendencies, even little traits of character. The storyteller said something, and Kemal thought: Markutsa will laugh immediately.

And without looking, he felt how clear-eyed Yakov Markutsa was beginning to smile.

"Comrades," said Kasumoff, and the fighters jumped up. "Comrades," repeated the Political Instructor. "Who wants to go with me?"

He was silent for a minute, and added, "A serious job awaits us. I warn you—a great danger threatens, perhaps death. Volunteers are needed."

"I'll go," quickly said Markutsa and again smiled, this time shyly.

"I will go," repeated Tsedin.

"Me, me," said others.

Kasumoff looked over them all. There wasn't one who had not said, "Me!" Only Sergeant Sotnikoff, Komsomoletz, said: "I beg you to take me."

All? All were not needed, too many. Kemal chose six. He called them out one by one—Sergeant Peter Sotnikoff, Private Alexander Tsedin, Private Semyen Artamanoff, Private Nicolai Buchtiaroff, Private Vasily Christichenkoff, Private Yakov Markutsa.

There was a cemetery, where Kasumoff met the detachment of Lieutenant Zveruk. Combining, both groups moved toward the bridge in order to blow it up.

Quietly, crouching, they walked. The hostile bank was quiet, as if no one was there.

Three hundred paces remained. Suddenly machine-gun shots struck. They hammered on the right, left, in front. A mortar bomb whined, then another. Evidently, this bridge, a good crossing, was guarded in expectation of a visit from the Soviet sappers.

Thirteen men crept forward toward the bridge, dragging three boxes of explosives. Three hundred paces took two and a half hours. The men huddled against the ground, closely, as if drawn to it by a powerful magnet. They raised their heads for a second only, to see forward and to look at a neighbor—was he lagging, was he wounded?

The fire from the Rumanian bank grew stronger, became unbearable. The enemy was enraged because destruction threatened the bridge, because soon the means of crossing over to Soviet soil would be taken away from them. But though their wrath was great, though they wished to save the bridge, yet not one man came out from behind the bushes, tufts, and invisible trenches. Only thirteen men were moving toward the bridge, and yet against this handful, they did not risk to attack from the other bank.

The sappers already were crawling on the bridge, devoid of any kind of cover, except darkness. In front were Kasumoff and Zveruk.

"Far enough? Shall we stick the stuff in?" asked someone.

"No," answered Kasumoff. "Better get still nearer to them. . . ."

And they crawled right up to the Rumanian sentry box. Having prepared the explosion with Zveruk, Kasumoff began to lead his people away with the same caution with which they had advanced. On the bridge only one fighter from Zveruk's detachment remained. He lit the fuse and quickly crawled back. He had scarcely rejoined his comrades, when suddenly the explosion boomed, smote the air, and the bridge, as if cut down, settled in the water.

When on the following evening, Kasumoff summoned the sextet of yesterday's heroes, they thought he wished to discuss with them the results of the operation. But Kasumoff said: "Today we will go once again. Another bridge—there are many tanks and infantry there. An attack is expected. The bridge must be blown up."

Soon Kasumoff and his sextet, with explosives prepared, were already within forty meters of the bridge. The winding Prut formed a bend here. Soviet territory jutted out, rimmed by a ribbon of water. Therefore, when the Germans surrounded the crawling soldiers, they struck from three sides. A mass of metal descended upon the little detachment. Again the sappers clung to the ground and crawled, but this time it was decidedly harder.

The bridge was wooden; it was necessary to make their way underneath. The sappers surmounted three arches, and fifteen meters from the shore they placed the explosives. Kasumoff took back five men and left Tsedin to fire the charge. Tsedin waited several minutes, lit the fuse, and quickly turned toward land. The fuse was short and Tsedin thought that he would not succeed in getting away, that the explosion would go off before he reached his native shore. But he succeeded and lay down, feeling the earth under his feet. Immediately the explosion was heard, machine-gun fire began.

The crackle of machine guns fused into one continuous roar —so great was the power the enemy used to take revenge on the brave men for their achievement. It was evident that this time the Fascists had decided not to let the sappers escape alive. The machine guns were firing from sixty or seventy meters away. The fighters lay quietly, because any movement, even crawling, would bring on inescapable death.

Finally, the firing stopped. The cunning Germans decided to wait with shooting until the Red soldiers stirred and showed themselves. But Kasumoff guessed this maneuver. Quietly, he gave the order to lie down and not to stir, under any circumstances. He himself lay down, turning his head to one side, looking to the sides and behind, to the opposite shore.

This lasted two hours. For a hundred and twenty minutes a psychological battle went on between the German machine gunners and the soldiers of the Red Army. The Germans had the advantage. They were hidden and had the machine guns. But the Red Armymen and their commander won. Their endurance, will power, and composure won.

In the morning, Kemal went off into a wood by himself and sat there on the trunk of a tree felled by an air bomb. He thought of his own, of the people closest to him, of his wife and children.

A messenger arrived and broke up his thoughts. He called Kasumoff to the commander of the detail and a new task was given him. Again evening, again a bridge, the third one, this time a railroad bridge. And again in the evening, taking his old sextet and two more—Feshin and Yudin—Kasumoff went to the bank of the Prut and again worked under fierce fire and again blew up a bridge, depriving the enemy of still one more hope of crossing to the Soviet bank.

Night filled the world. Kasumoff stood bending in the entrance to the tent and listened. A vice-commander in the political division, holding a paper, was saying:

"Comrade Political Instructor, here is an address in Ungen, where you are to go. There in the cellar of a house where a Stakhanovite weaver lives, the wife and children of Political Instructor Kasumoff are taking shelter from bombings. You will have to take them to a safer place, farther from the front. Understand?"

"I understand," said Kasumoff and his throat went dry. He understood, he was ordered to go to Ungen and to conduct to a safe place the wife and children of Political Leader Kasumoff. "May I go now?"

"Go."

Kasumoff went off to fulfill his mission.

Disregarding Life

It was a fierce and unequal fight. At dawn, a large part of the Nazi detachment went into attack. The enemy strove by a brief attack to occupy an important height on the approach to the town. He unleashed a storm of fire that lasted almost half an hour.

Lieutenant Lopushenko's company held the height. From the first days of the war, the Lieutenant had won the affection and respect of the fighters.

"Hold the height at any price," ordered the battalion commander.

"Aye, hold the height at any cost!" briefly repeated Lopushenko.

And he made the decision—to permit the enemy to approach so as to fire point-blank. Already the Nazis were not far off. They wanted to shoot, badly, but the soldiers awaited the order.

"Fire!" the voice of the commander was heard.

The machine guns began to shoot. Fragmentation mines fell on the heads of the enemy. The enemy did not hold out against this defense and began to give ground. But, after a while, he decided to repeat the attack. But this time, too, the Red troops repulsed the attack of the numerically superior adversary. The height was held.

Only after the clash did the Red Armymen notice that their brave commander was hit. It was necessary to send him to a hospital. But it didn't take three days before the Lieutenant again appeared at the front-line position. He refused to stay put in the hospital.

"Permit me to assume command of the company," the Lieutenant asked his commander.

"But you are hurt, you need medical attention!"

"I am ready to fulfill any task," answered the Lieutenant.

The valiant officer again returned to the front-line position and led his company against the enemy.

In one of the fights, Red Armyman Artamonoff was wounded. He categorically refused to go to the hospital.

"I shall remain in the ranks as long as my strength lasts, until we defeat the Nazis," he declared.

"But you can't shoot, you have an injured hand," they reasoned with him.

"I was a cook, I can bake bread. Send me to the front as a baker. I will prepare tasty food for the fighters." The Red Armyman did not yield.

Artamonoff won. He remained with the detachment.

Through the Enemy's Encirclement

The broad-shouldered, bull-necked Junior Lieutenant Sukin, resembled a man ashamed of his strength. It seemed as though he did not know where to put his great, heavy, leaden fists. In his time, he was forbidden to indulge in boxing.

"I have a frightful punch," Sukin used to say, as if justifying himself, "a deadly punch. . . ."

So the athletic Peter Sukin had to be satisfied with weight-lifting and such. These days Adjutant Sukin does not indulge in sports. At the front one could see him everywhere, wherever the regiment commander usually was. And here it is known the colonel appears where the fight is the hottest.

A fierce fight was on. Sukin found out that a machine gunner on the right flank was wounded, and taking advantage of this, the enemy was pouring forward. Sukin ran to the right flank. After some minutes the rat-tat-tat of the machine gun was resumed. Very few of the enemy escaped.

When the fight ended, the Junior Lieutenant carefully took the wounded machine gunner on his own broad back and, on all fours, pushing the machine gun ahead of him, reached a safe place.

"Cuckoos" appeared in the woods. Here and there automatics rattled.

"Permit me; I'll 'comb out' the woods," asked Junior Lieutenant Sukin. And, in truth, he "combed out" the woods so well that a good many of the enemy "cuckoos" were silenced forever.

Junior Lieutenant Sukin acquired military popularity.

The commander of the regiment was notified that the liaison with one of the detachments was broken. The report said that the enemy had surrounded it. The colonel decided to break the ring with the help of the artillery. But how let the commander of the detachment know that artillery fire was the signal to break through?

Who will go through to him?

The colonel said this quietly. He did not address anyone in particular, as if taking counsel with himself. But standing near by Junior Lieutenant Sukin overheard the commander's words.

"Permit me, Comrade Colonel."

The commander of the regiment glanced at his adjutant and said, "I'll give you two hours for this operation. Take an automatic and any horse."

Shortly Sukin disappeared from sight.

When bullets began to whistle frequently over his head, the Junior Lieutenant dismounted, threw the bridle to the orderly who was with him, and went on, hiding behind bushes and trunks of trees. From a treetop an automatic began to rattle off. Sukin answered in short order. He had to crawl for more than a kilometer.

The appearance of Sukin among the encircled soldiers was received with great joy. He delivered the regimental commander's order and crawled back. Soon Sukin returned to his detail. "Your order is fulfilled," he said to the colonel.

The regimental commander glanced at his watch. Fifty-five

minutes had passed from the time that Sukin had received his order.

The artillery opened fire and broke the ring. Warned by Sukin, the fighters arose and, running into the underbrush, broke out of encirclement.

A Suvoroff Stroke

The Russian armies reverently preserve the traditions of the famous general, Suvoroff—quick action and attack. These traditions are kept alive in the battles with Hitlerite Fascists.

For a distance of several kilometers the highway is cluttered with military trophies. About ten freight trucks, about the same amount of guns of different calibers, antitank guns, machine guns, mortars, supply wagons, hundreds of rifles, mountains of shells, and bullets—all these military weapons are piled up in a monstrous disorder.

Here a large combination of German-Rumanian troops was shattered. Within several hours the heroic units of the Red Army waged a fierce fight with the enemy. In this battle three German regiments perished.

Hundreds of Fascist corpses and dead horses are strewn around, on both sides of the highway. Here, too, are scattered the "trophies" of the enemy: Soviet matches, sugar, tobacco, and perfume, all stolen in the border villages. Near the partly destroyed machine guns, among dozens of corpses, lies the body of a Rumanian captain. Alongside of him there are an open suitcase and a guitar. In the suitcase—powder, perfume, lipstick "Tezhe," and some women's underwear stolen in a Soviet village.

The two-footed swine robbed without mercy. This is the tradition of the Fascist army. And next to the two-footed swine wallow ordinary pigs, cows, ducks, chickens, and geese which were carried by the provision wagons. All this was also stolen from the peasants. The field of battle tells the story of the terrific devastation to which the German-Rumanian troops were subjected.

How did this happen?

An infantry and artillery enemy regiment had invaded Soviet territory. Soviet scouts established accurately the location and the strength of the enemy. The enemy's force was numerically superior to the Red Army force operating on this sector of the front. The enemy was moving along the highway in column formation extending for several kilometers. In this column there were large numbers of artillery, heavy trucks, and supplies for battle.

The enemy column was given the chance to pull into a hollow unhindered. This put it in a disadvantageous position. The enemy did not suspect that in a few hours this sunken road would become the valley of death for all the hundreds of soldiers and officers of the German-Rumanian troops.

Evening drew near. Suddenly, a rain of deadly metal descended on the head of the column. The Red artillery opened up a point-blank fire at the enemy from a short distance. Scouts in armored cars went out ahead and also fired at the enemy point-blank. Commander Mishak and Senior Lieutenant Dolgy headed this heroic detachment of scouts. The courageous infantry of Major Vrutsky cut the enemy down from the flanks with machine guns, cannons, and rifles. Volleys of the artillery barred the enemy's way out. On the highway, insane panic began. The drivers of the seven-ton trucks, which pulled the heavy artillery, tried to turn back, but collided with the other machines which cluttered the road. The maddened horses tore at their reins and crushed the enemy soldiers. Their corpses, disfigured and torn, wallowed under the wheels of their own trucks and guns. The terrified artillerymen, not heeding the command of their officers, abandoned the guns, threw off their equipment and shoes, and ran wherever they could. The Soviet fighters surrounded the enemy with a ring of fire. The well-aimed fire of the snipers smote the Fascist officers, who tried to organize in this chaos some semblance of defense. Red Armyman Sukor got into the rear of the Nazis and mowed them down with the deadly hail from his machine gun. Then, moving up still closer, he destroyed the Nazis with hand grenades. The bandits surrendered, to one fighter! The corpses of the enemy were piled up near the silent cannons.

But the enemy guns weren't silent long. The Red artillerymen, having arrived in time, turned the guns on the running enemy and opened up a destructive fire on them from their own cannon. Senior Lieutenant Kudryavtsev and a group of fighters threw themselves on the German-Rumanian regiment, who tried to defend themselves. Covering the Fascists with hand grenades, the fighters began to fire at them from rifles. And when the supply of bullets was exhausted, Kudryavtsev led his detachment in a bayonet attack. The remnants of the regiment turned to flight.

When the operation ended, it was dark. On the field of battle lay hundreds of wounded and dead. About two hundred soldiers and officers were taken prisoners. The colonel, lieutenant colonel, captains, and dozens of junior officers surrendered to the Red fighters.

The captive Rumanian colonel said sorrowfully:

"The attack of your Red troops was prepared ideally. It stunned our details and produced a complete panic. Only a few minutes after your sudden attack, I understood the destruction of our regiments was inevitable. But I could not understand from where Red Armymen suddenly appeared. After all, the German air scouts, after very carefully examining this section, were very positive that your troops were not here. We were moving along calmly, and suddenly, as if from beneath the ground, your soldiers struck. The lightning attack from the front and the flanks paralyzed our details. I saw that destruction was inevitable. It was impossible to orientate myself in the circumstances. It seemed to me that we were surrounded by large forces of the Red Army. Only afterwards did I find out that our regiments were destroyed by lesser forces."

Only twenty-four hours have passed since the destruction of the Fascists in the "Valley of Death." On the roads to the rear was carried the greatest part of the trophies. Very important operative documents and secret orders of the Fascist headquarters fell into the hands of the Soviet commanders. The Red Army fighters seized fifty-three cannons, eighty seven-ton trucks, four machines, 600 wagons, 1000 horses, baby tanks, numbers of rifles, machine guns, shells, bullets, and supplies.

BEHIND STEEL ARMOR

Tanks Lead the Fight

Simple rank-and-file men, not at all conspicuous at first glance, and, until the war, not distinguished by anything unusual—now these rank-and-file Soviet tank drivers show extraordinary feats of courage. Their courage is based not only on devotion to the fatherland, personal valor, but on the exact knowledge of tank technique, tactics, and sober appraisal of the enemy's strength.

The enemy threw his best tank regiments to the border. Many of them are already destroyed, and many found their graves in the rivers, the ponds, or on the battlefields. In the tank battles the tank drivers of the units led by Commander Bogdanoff proved their fearlessness.

The scouts took the first blow. The commander gave orders to feel out by an attack the strength of the enemy, his possibilities, the strength of his tank armor and tactics. Senior Lieutenant Iosif Mandel, commander of the scout detachment, led his tanks first. Soon they went into battle. The Senior Lieutenant ordered the tankists to hold off the attack of the enemy until new forces would join them, while he sent one tank with a report. This order was carried out. The tankists did not give ground; unshaken and determined, they stood at their posts.

The commander of the detachment sent a motorcycle scout, Arcady Pentin, to find out what forces the enemy had concentrated. Pentin, using bushes and hillocks for cover, made his way to the rear of the enemy. He had to pull a motorcycle with him and have a machine gun in readiness.

Pentin, after getting the necessary information, decided to make his report to the commander as quickly as possible. He rose, started the motorcycle in quick order, and huddling to the motorcycle, as if a part of it, he flew to his detail. There was machine-gun and rifle fire, but too late. The Germans were confused by this sudden occurrence. The impetuous courage of this Soviet fighter was stunning, and they did not begin shooting right away; after the first moments of surprise there was firing at Pentin's motorcycle from all sides.

Soon Pentin arrived and reported the results of his reconnoitering. He was shaking. Blood streamed down his face. He was wounded, but carried out his task with honor. Pentin refused to leave the field of battle. "It's nonsense," he smiled. But his strength was ebbing. The commander put him into an automobile and Pentin was taken to the rear.

Meanwhile, the tanks went into attack. "Keep calm, and aim the shots accurately, carefully; change your positions quickly.

Shoot from one place, let the enemy approach closer. Aim at the motor and caterpillar tracks until the strength of the armor and the ease in puncturing are found out." All this Commander Peter Ivanuk told his tankists. The front tanks, methodically, as if underscoring the calm of the people, began firing at the enemy. Junior Lieutenant Peter Praschin had already partly destroyed, set on fire, and put out of commission eight of the enemy tanks with his well-aimed shots. The Germans began an intense fire at Peter Praschin's tank. The turret was carried off by a shell. Praschin jumped out of the broken tank and transferred to the next tank where the commander was killed. He replaced him. Again he went into battle. Three enemy tanks with broken caterpillars, stricken dumb, went up in flames. The Fascists were hunting Praschin again. This time they succeeded in knocking the Soviet tank out of formation. But Praschin fought on. He leaped out with a machine gun in hand, collected about ten fighters and tankists, and led them against the enemy armored cars and motorcyclists. Praschin went the roundabout way. He hid, fired at the enemy. Wounded, for a moment he fell, but was up again—ran, fell again. "Eh, it's a pity," he said. "My leg is injured. . . ."

Ivan Olkhovsky, the head mechanic, who fought the enemy as fearlessly as his commander, ran to him. Olkhovsky lifted Praschin and carried him. In dangerous spots he crawled, never letting down his weakening commander. Olkhovsky carried his commander through the fire to the rear.

Peter Ivanuk meanwhile decided to attack the enemy medium tanks. The attack began suddenly and rapidly. Immediately, nine other Fascist tanks and forty motorcyclists were out of commission. Through the din of motors and the noise of battle, the tankists received the calm and confident order: "Forward!"

Senior Lieutenant Mikhail Matukhin made his way to the rear of the enemy. This successful maneuver upset the plans of

Lieutenant I. Pirozhkoff, commander of a heavy tank,
who destroyed a whole column of Nazis with his machine

the Nazi tank units. Matukhin set on fire one tank after another and jumped out of his own only when it was completely enveloped in flames.

The tankists fought with great determination and heroism. Unsparing of their own lives, they defended every inch of their native land.

The commander ordered the tank crew to leave their machine. Birulin left his machine last and blew it up.

Tank Drivers in Battle

The dark-blue overalls of the tank drivers were dusty, saturated with oil, and covered with soot and clay. In some places they were burned, in others, torn by Nazi bullets.

In stubborn fights with the enemy, the Soviet tank men are covering themselves with undying glory.

Near the town of N a division of German riflemen was concentrated. Supported by artillery, they were preparing to attack. It was necessary to hold off the enemy at all costs. The higher command entrusted this task to the tank regiment under leadership of Senior Lieutenant B. Mikheyev, one of the patriotic Mikheyev brothers, whose names are known throughout the whole land.

The commander explained the task to the fighters and ordered:

"To the machines!"

The tanks lunged into action. They were supported by a battalion of infantry, which had already been three days in continuous fighting. Breaking through the brush to a wide field, dug up into shallow trenches, the tank of the mechanic leader, Ivan Ampilogoff, pounded upon the enemy infantry. The Fascists did not have time to come to, before their first ranks were mowed down by machine-gun fire and squashed by the caterpillar of the heavy tank.

From behind the bushes at the clearing of the wood, there was the continuous firing of the machine guns. The thunderous bursting of shells began. An enemy airplane appeared and, circling over the tank, began to drop bombs.

The battalion commissar, in command of the tank, ordered: "To firing stations!"

The tanks opened fire. The first shot from the tank cannon shot down a Fascist machine gun. The rapidly moving machine squashed the second machine-gun nest.

The German cannon were still from thirty to forty meters away. It was hitting point-blank, but the strong, dependable armor of the Soviet tank remained untouched. However, one of the shells obstructed the lookout hatch. The tank went blind, as it were. Ampilogoff continued driving the machine though he did not see anything ahead of him. He zigzagged and did not give the Fascists an opportunity to aim accurately.

Another sizable shell struck the machine and it caught fire.

"Get out of the tank!" commanded the commissar. After he himself got out, he started shooting from his automatic at the pressing enemy.

Ampilogoff tore off the fire extinguisher and, under the enemy fire, directed its foamy stream at the fire. The fire extinguisher helped. The flame died down. Then the leader threw himself back into the tank and led it out of battle.

Twenty minutes at least were needed to put the tank in order. Again the fearless vehicle threw itself into the fight.

The Fascists noticed the rapidly moving tank. Its fire mowed down a good many enemy soldiers. The tank brought down two machine guns and a gun. The enemy decided to take this tank into "pincers." Cannons fired at it from the front; from the flanks, machine guns fired; the infantry surrounded it.

The tank was aflame again. The fighters' clothes were burning. The commander and turret gunner jumped clear of the tank. Ampilogoff, turning around sharply, began to run down the pressing enemy with full force. Two comrades, firing and throwing hand grenades at the enemy, were running alongside of the machine.

They did not surrender the tank to the enemy. They led it in the direction of their own detachments.

Tankist Birulin manifested valor and stoicism. At the very beginning of the battle he was entrusted with the destruction of a large-caliber German machine gun hidden in the woods. Fearlessly the tank went forward, running down Fascists with the caterpillars, mowing them down with cannon shots, and crushing them with felled trees. Within less than fifteen minutes, all the machine-gun nests of the enemy were annihilated.

The tank broke out to the outskirts of the wood and there Birulin saw that the enemy surrounded the infantrymen. The commander ordered the tank to move to the rescue of the infantry. The fight, however, was joined by the Nazi tanks. One of them was going straight at Birulin.

The fight was short. With two shots, the Soviet tank men knocked off the enemy machine's caterpillars and set it on fire. The tank broke the enemy ring. Braced up by support, the infantrymen dashed into a bayonet charge and pushed the enemy off.

Major Bandurko

Wounded three times, he was at last taken to the hospital against his wishes.

"*Nichevo*, he'll be back soon," smiled the commanders, telling the story about him. "He is that kind; three wounds aren't going to keep him down—an Ilya Muromets! [a legendary Russian hero]"

They talk with such warmth about this common favorite that we feel as if we really see before us Major Maxim Artemovich Bandurko—a man of tremendous height, of rare physical strength, calm and jolly, with a sly twinkle and good-natured Ukrainian humor.

In 1928, when he was twenty-two years old, he came to the Red Army. His whole life was tied up with the army. That is where he got his education, that's where he was brought up and where his character formed and he prepared for many years for the decisive hour when he could use all these qualities for the glory of the army.

The detachment of light tanks under the Major's command in the very first fight came up against a regiment of medium tanks. The situation was bad. But Bandurko quickly made the only correct decision. He distributed his tanks along the outskirts of the wood and from carefully disguised positions opened fire at the moving German tanks.

Major Bandurko showed his celebrated calmness in the very first fight. He opened fire at the German tanks precisely when they entered the zone of the most intense fire, not a second before or after.

The medium and heavy German tanks have solid armor. Not just any shell from a light tank would penetrate this armor but only those aimed accurately. Here then the sharpshooters, taught by the commander, proved their skill. They struck at the most vulnerable spots of the German tanks: into the lateral armor, the motor, the caterpillar. They fired in such manner that the shells hit with the greatest destructive force—at right angles to the armor. Several German tanks went out of order.

And that is how Major Bandurko refuted the short-lived legend of impenetrable German armor.

Meanwhile, the Fascist tanks began to fire and their shells landed closer and closer. The Major ordered a change in position. The tanks moved along the edge of the wood and, from the new position, again opened fire.

Having come up against such resistance, the Germans were forced to change their direction. They retreated and began to look for a roundabout way.

One of their last shells struck Major Bandurko's tank and wounded him in the head with several fragments. Quickly bandaging his wounds, Bandurko got out of the tank and began to relate the first tank-battle experience to his comrades.

"It is necessary to direct an accurate fire from stationary position or from brief halts," he was saying. "It is good to camouflage yourself, let the enemy approach, and suddenly and accurately open fire—and success is on our side. The most important thing is to keep cool. While the Germans are firing, while the shells are falling within from 100 to 150 meters, don't change your position. Be calm—shoot from position. But when the shells begin to fall right near you, quickly and secretly change your place and then fire immediately! Change place faster than the enemy; fire faster than he; strike faster than he!"

On the fifth day of fighting, the detachment was going to a new gathering point. The detachment was moving straight ahead in full formation with turrets turned toward the enemy. Major Bandurko was covering the rear of the departing detachment and made an ambush at the road. His tanks were camouflaged to such an extent that one could be close upon them without seeing them.

Hardly was the camouflage completed when six German tanks appeared on the highway at the edge of the forest. The place of ambush was well chosen—both sides of the highway were bordered by marshes. The Germans were in a trap.

"Fire!" ordered the Major, and a volley from the Soviet guns descended upon the enemy tanks from the shortest distance.

Three tanks caught fire immediately, the rest were able to fire several shells and tried to turn on the narrow road but failed, caught by the new volleys from our cannons.

The Major was unlucky—he was wounded again by a fragment from a German shell. This time, he didn't even give himself a chance to bandage his wound, but gave an order: change the place of ambush immediately.

"First of all, change position, and then everything else."

The position was changed immediately. German airplanes, which came flying to the place of battle fifteen minutes later, carefully bombed the empty forest.

On the eighth day of fighting, Major Bandurko's tanks, hiding in the wood, guarded the highway near the town of P, not allowing the enemy to move through. Carefully camouflaging the tanks, as usual, the Major sent out a group to reconnoiter.

The Germans, secretly concentrated within three kilometers, were betrayed by their nerves and began to fire at the group of scouts prematurely, thereby revealing themselves. Within fifteen minutes the first German tanks appeared on the highway.

"Look out, this is not a drill!" said the Major to the turret gunner, Junior Sergeant Tertichny. "When you are drilling, you can get all excited, but in battle, you have to be cool, understand?"

The first of the German tanks was struck by a shell directly in the motor and caught fire.

The Major transferred fire to the second tank. The first shell fell short, but the third and fourth turned the machine over. The fight continued. An enemy shell broke into the turret and wounded Major Bandurko for the third time. He led the broken tank away from the field of battle, changed to another, and parried other enemy attacks. Only after that was it possible, though almost by force, to send Bandurko to the hospital.

"*Nichevo*, fellows, I'll come back soon," said the Major, parting with the fighters. "We'll turn better heat on the Germans yet!"

Four Tankists

Comrades in battle . . . here they stand alongside the tank. Black overalls, sturdy muscles. Wind-bitten, sunburned faces. Tall, blond Vasily Gubarev, tank commander. Good-natured and shy Radio Operator Belevtsoff, the youngest member of the crew, is checking up his apparatus. Uncommunicative Artillerist Isakoff is cleaning his dusty boots, and the ever-jolly turret gunner, Pertakhiya, having adjusted a small mirror, is shaving. Only an hour ago enemy planes dropped bombs here. The air shook with explosions and the earth groaned.

But even in war pauses occur. Very seldom days—more often hours and minutes. And so this is a quiet minute, and one feels like sinking into the soft and fragrant grass. The fighters write letters to their relatives and friends, read newspapers.

Suddenly there comes an end to this pause. The crew of Vasily Gubarev's tank is ordered to move ahead. All are as quiet as before but their faces become more stern.

Gubarev's tank, together with all the other tanks, comes out on the road. Avoiding hollows and gulleys, he goes rumbling ahead. The tankists are glued to the lookout slits but the enemy does not reveal himself. Suddenly the platoon commander turns sharply off the road to the right and rushes to some buildings. This is the signal that the enemy is on the right.

Hardly have the tanks scattered before the enemy opens fire upon them. Gubarev's tank makes fast spurts ahead. Artillerist Isakoff notices a camouflaged cannon at a short distance and fires. The shot goes over. Gubarev, at the controls, driving the tank, commands:

"Cut the distance!"

The second shell shatters the cannon. Taking advantage of confusion in the enemy ranks, the tank platoon throws itself ahead, breaking and crushing the battery. A hut by the road catches fire. When the roaring flames die down and the smoke begins to disappear, the tankists see that another enemy battery is hiding in a distant orchard.

The tanks concentrate their fire on the orchard. Soon, fire from there ceases. Gubarev receives an order to direct his tank into the orchard. The crew of the tank sees behind the smoking ruins two smashed guns and one good one. Contorted, flattened bodies of the dead are lying around.

It is necessary to reconnoiter further, and the crew moves on. The machine is going at low speed. Suddenly its armor shakes from a strong blow. The stern of the tank is hit by an enemy shell.

Gubarev changes to second speed, steps on the accelerator to give the tank gas. What happened? The tank does not move, but steeply turns toward the enemy. The crew realizes that the shell struck at the caterpillar and it fell apart. It is clear that it will not move again.

"Will we be surrounded?" asks someone.

"Yes. We are being surrounded," Gubarev replies coolly. "We will fight!"

With antitank guns firing at your machine and German infantrymen crawling out from hiding, what valor and fearlessness are needed to say these courageous words!

Artillerist Isakoff fires several times in succession, and the enemy guns are silenced. Intense machine-gun fire of the Soviet tank compels the enemy infantrymen to lie down. Five German soldiers with automatics stealthily begin to make their way to the rear of the tank. Belevtsoff, with an accurate shot, brings down three of them. Two crawl ahead and succeed in crawling up on the tank. They bang at the hatch and in broken Russian yell:

"Come out of the tank like good boys. . . . We have enough fighting supplies to make short shrift of you."

Silence ensues. After a few minutes, there is again a knock at the hatch.

"We'll give you eight thousand rubles. Surrender!"

"We are fighting, not shopping for bargains, you scoundrels," Pertakhiya burns up! He knows German and understands from the conversation of the infantrymen that the enemy decided to take them alive at all costs.

"We will hold out as long as our strength lasts," says Vasily Gubarev.

Through the slit he sees that on the right two guns and a wagon with ammunition are being rolled up. The German soldiers are carrying boxes with shells. Time must be gained.

Gubarev orders Isakoff: "Fire!"

One shot, another, a third.

Gubarev, observing everything closely, remarks:

"One of the guns has disappeared."

The unequal fight between the crew of the Soviet tank and the Nazis lasts about seven hours. The strength of the tankists is waning. Worried, they wait for their tank to catch on fire again. That would be better than to fall into the hands of the enemy.

Night is approaching.

An enemy shell again strikes at the turret. It fails to burst, but makes an opening over the triple glass. This is the final moment of life for the ever-jolly turret gunner, Pertakhiya. Yes, it is time to abandon the tank. Without ceasing fire, the crew begins to take the machine out of formation.

"Open the hatch," orders Gubarev.

He takes the spare machine gun and disks. Belevtsoff takes hand grenades and helps the weakened Isakoff to crawl out.

Unnoticed, they crawl to the hollow and lie down. For a long time the valiant tankists can hear the rat-tat of the machine guns and automatics. Afterwards the shots stop and mounted German officers gallop around in search of the tankists.

ANNIHILATING FIRE

The Fearless

Of the calmness of Lieutenant Leitinsky, the fighters say:

"On the field of battle he feels at home."

The Lieutenant is an extraordinary fighter, courageous, determined, exceptionally quick-witted.

In battles with the Finnish White Guards, he was wounded seven times. As the wounds were healing in the hospital, he was very sad and begged the doctors to release him from the hospital as soon as possible, assuring them that he was all well. He was anxious to get back to the front; at the front he very often found himself in difficult situations, but never lost presence of mind or spirit. In skirmishes with the enemy he was always victorious.

That is why young fighters, looking at this tall, broad-shouldered man, say:

"Eh, what a good fight Lieutenant Leitinsky puts up!"

The Lieutenant's composure, courage, and daring show up with particular clarity these days when the glorious Red fighters battle the hordes of Fascist robbers.

Large forces of the enemy suddenly seized and occupied advantageous firing positions. The robbers settled in a thick forest and from it sent frequent machine-gun volleys at the detachment of Lieutenant Leitinsky. The enemy was obviously stronger numerically. But this did not distress the commander. This decision was reached quickly: we have to push the enemy out of the wood. And to do this, it was necesary to emerge from the brush and cross the road under fire.

In a moment the Lieutenant was on the road, just as fast ran across it, and disappeared behind a hillock. His example was followed by the rest of the fighters.

The commander ordered the machine gunners to open hurricane fire at the enemy, so that, in the meantime, he could carry the cannon out of the brush. Taking six fighters with him, he skillfully made his way under hail of fire to the brush, and dragged the cannon with him to the hillock.

He was the soul of the artillery detachment. He helped the observers and, together with the fighters, brought up shells. One after another, machine-gun nests on the enemy side were silenced. Toward evening, the enemy was driven out of the wood.

The fighters usually imitate their commander. They fight the enemy ruthlessly.

The Red soldier, Boris Baryshnikoff, had to bring up bullets to the machine guns and to maintain communication between the commander and the firing points.

He operated well. He appeared where prompt help was needed. He found out from the fighters whether they had water or whether the machine gun had burned through; under a rain of bullets, he delivered water and relieved comrades. He carried out the commander's commissions clearly, intelligently, faultlessly.

And with what valiance and initiative machine-gunners and Komsomol members Pitchkin and Ivanovsky operated!

They noticed that a group of about eighty Hitlerite bandits came out on the outskirts of the wood, hid themselves in the rye, and began a stealthy approach toward their comrades.

"Ah, the scoundrels!" angrily said Pitchkin, and, assisted by a comrade, quickly pulled away the machine gun to a place where it was most convenient to meet the treacherous enemy.

The Nazis apparently thought that they would catch the fighters unawares. But they had miscalculated! They had but to stick their heads out of the rye when the machine gun began its work. None of the bandits got up. All of them were killed on the spot.

"All of us," said Machine Gunner Gavrilo Bubir, "took part in battle for the first time. It was our baptism of fire. The enemy will find out our strength yet! He will be smashed!"

Three Days and Three Nights

The batteries of the N-sk detail established themselves on a firing position and subjected the enemy to intense fire. The artillery had the task of smashing the maximum amount of firing points and of not allowing the Germans to advance farther.

Toward evening, the commander noticed that a fire started a few kilometers away, in Village N, occupied by the Germans. One house caught fire. After a moment, another burst into flames. Within a minute and a half, the fire enveloped ten peasant homes. They all burst into flame in a strictly consecutive order. It was evident that the Germans had sent a tank along the village street and it fired these homes with a flame thrower.

"The usual thing," said Commander Sirnikoff. "The village was pillaged and the Nazis don't need it any more. And they are planning to distract our attention with this fire. That means that we can expect a tank attack. Well, then, we will give them a proper reception."

As soon as he had reached this conclusion, Sirnikoff there and then ordered Artunian to get ready to repulse a tank attack. Fifteen minutes passed and, some four or five kilometers from the firing position of our artillery, four heavy German tanks appeared.

"Fire!" ordered Artunian.

Howitzer batteries spoke up. Shells fell precisely and were soon detonating in close proximity to the tanks. The Germans turned about and quickly disappeared in the hollow behind the rye field.

A half-hour later, enemy tanks again showed from the rye field. This time a whole tank column was going into attack. It appeared and disappeared in the hollow and was difficult to fire at.

Artunian decided to wait. He allowed the column to approach within a kilometer and then opened up a hurricane of fire. Heavy and light guns fired at the Nazi machines point-blank. Artillerists acted in harmony and accurately. Already the head tank was taken out of formation. A well-aimed shell cut short the movement of the second one.

A quarter of an hour of fierce fire and the howitzers smashed a few more tanks. The rest of them, unable to withstand the fire, began to retreat.

All night and the following day, the detail, with the support of the artillery, held on firmly to the section of the front in the station area.

The enemy regrouped his forces. Artillerists for a long time could not feel out the new positions of the German artillery. Then the commanders set off to the area of front observation posts for a personal reconnoitering of the enemy's firing positions. Toward evening, they came out onto a high embankment, covered with shrubs and trees. The adjacent country was seen well from here. On the right ran the highway, on the left, the railway. It was peaceful. The German artillerymen were quiet, not showing their presence in any way. It seemed as if the front had moved somewhere far away.

Such was the first impression, but the observers knew very well that this silence was deceiving. The enemy crouched, waiting for the opportune moment to open fire.

The German trench-mortar battery began to shoot; apparently the observers were noticed. Sirnikoff saw clearly where the fire should be directed and conveyed his order to the firing posts. Fedoroff's howitzer battery immediately opened fire. Accurate facts obtained by the commanders' scouting expedition made the Soviet artillerists' job easier. The German trench-mortar batteries were smashed.

The night passed. The artillery duel was still going on. Three days passed, during which the N-sk detail bravely and confidently held the front in the region of station N. The Germans undertook repeated attacks. But each time the infantry, supported by artillery, inflicted cruel losses on the Germans.

On the third day of the battle the Germans began an artillery barrage at noon. It seemed that toward evening they would again desperately attempt to occupy the station. For five hours the German artillery almost ceaselessly shelled the Soviet observation posts, batteries, and infantry detachments.

Toward evening, the enemy commenced their attack, throwing a strong infantry formation at a small section of the front. The valiant Soviet infantrymen again repulsed the German infantry with a determined counterattack. Co-operation between the infantry and artillery contributed to the success of the counterattack. Here the battery of Fedoroff acted with distinction. Light guns and howitzers poured shells on the attacking German infantry, causing heavy losses. The battlefield was covered with enemy corpses.

Notwithstanding the strong artillery fire, which the Germans concentrated upon the Soviet batteries, Fedoroff did not abandon his observation post. This guaranteed an excellent correction of fire. One after another, the firing posts of the enemy were silenced. Suffering a heavy loss of men and equipment, the German infantry began to fall back.

Night approached. All waited for the enemy to throw tank detachments into the fight. Fedoroff's batteries did not stop firing at the enemy's positions. They laid a powerful barrage. In the event that individual machines from the German tank column should break through, the artillerists prepared to fire upon them point-blank. The Fascists did not risk moving their tanks under the murderous fire of the Soviet artillery. The curtain of fire was again maintained by the valiant artillerists.

All attempts of the Germans to attack the Soviet positions suffered complete failure.

The fourth day of cruel, stubborn fighting began. The N-sk detachment bravely and strongly held a decisive sector of the front.

Artillerist Evgeny Zoliavin

Early in the morning the commander of an antitank battery received an order by telephone to prepare for battle. It had just been learned that the Nazis intended to undertake an attack with strong tank forces.

It was from the highway leading to the west that the enemy must appear. Pines were murmuring. A light wind was rocking their curly tops. On one side was a solitary farmhouse and farther off a village over which towered a windmill. The mill stood motionless, its sails tied, inactive. People at war don't need the mill to grind the grain, but to observe the enemy from its height.

Of course, the enemy had an observation post on the mill and perhaps even machine guns. Lieutenant Zoliavin measured the distance to the mill with his eye. He approached one of the men at the first gun, Krapivin.

"Well, are you ready?"

"Everything is in order, Lieutenant."

Evgeny Zoliavin checked the preparation of Krapivin's gun.

"A good cannon, Comrade Lieutenant," he said.

"You'll have to prove that on the backs of the Nazis," smilingly answered Zoliavin.

From far off came the muffled roar of motors. Zoliavin knew this meant that the enemy tanks were approaching. He looked forward, but saw nothing, despite the deepening roar. From the observation post sounded a command:

"At the enemy's tanks! Fire!"

The sight operator of the first gun, Krapivin, squeezed up against the sight. He aimed calmly but quickly, with short economical movements that are the result of long practice.

"Number-one gun—fire!"

The shot roared. A second, a third. Shells flew toward the unseen enemy but fell exactly where his tanks appeared.

"Three tanks hit!" they were informed from the lookout post.

Thus began a fierce battle. The Nazis poured like lava, trying to smash the opposition of the defenders. Six tanks appeared in front. The Red artillerists sent shell after shell to meet the enemy. The six leading tanks hit by accurate shots stood motionless in black piles of twisted iron.

The Nazi tanks turned back.

Nevertheless, after a while shells began to burst near the battery. The Nazis had decided to destroy it with their guns. An artillery duel began.

At a distance, behind two pines, Lieutenant Zoliavin noticed a Nazi cannon, and showed it to Krapivin. The latter did not take his time. With well-aimed shots he put the enemy's gun out of action. Immediately, the shelling of our positions stopped.

The Nazis, seeing that the tanks could not go through, began to bombard the village with incendiary shells. The peasant huts went up in flames. Under cover of this smoke screen, the Nazis hurled their infantry into the battle.

Lieutenant Zoliavin's platoon greeted the infantrymen with shells. The Nazis, breaking into the burning village, instantly converted the mill into their own observation point.

The battery was confronted with the mission of eliminating the enemy's observation post. The mill was brought down with accurate fire.

In the middle of the battle, communications suddenly broke. The order came: "Act on your own." This meant that Lieutenant Zoliavin became individually responsible for the fate of the artillery platoon. He had to act at his own risk and peril. But each artilleryman understood the seriousness of the situation and each strove with tenfold strength and ardor.

Then, through the gun sight, Krapivin espied a tank moving along the road. It was obviously trying to hide behind the farm buildings. Zoliavin gave an order to bombard the farm. Like a cockroach scalded with boiling water, the tank crawled out of hiding. Standing on the road, it opened fire at the battery, but its shells fell short.

"But ours will get there," said Krapivin, and with straight aim sent three shells at the tank. The Nazi tank caught fire.

The enemy threw infantry into the attack. Then Nazi chappies appeared in dark uniforms and puttees. Dashing into attack, they took off their packs, threw them on the ground, and advanced running.

"Shrapnel," commanded Zoliavin.

Shells burst over the heads of the Nazis, showering them with hot lead. The shrapnel cleared the field of Nazis. They retreated with great losses.

But after waiting a while and receiving reinforcements, the

enemy again went into attack. On this sector, he sent into battle great forces and began a fierce shelling of the Soviet artillery positions. The Soviet guns were red-hot from firing.

Yes, this was a hot fight! It was necessary to bring up shells in the midst of fighting. At the guns themselves very often only three men remained; the rest were bringing up shells. The enemy intensified his fire, but the heroes of the War for the Fatherland, the brave artillerists commanded by Zoliavin—not for a second were they shaken, defending every inch of their native soil.

Lieutenant Evgeny Zoliavin and his artillerists were given the name of "Tank Destroyers."

Rostislav Chizhoff's Return

Junior Military Technician Rostislav Chizhoff had not returned to his artillery detachment. He was considered missing or killed. But no one thought that Chizhoff could be taken prisoner.

"He would not give himself up alive," the artillerists said of him. "If he doesn't return, it must be that he is dead and has given his life for the fatherland."

Chizhoff had decided to bring to the battlefield an army kitchen with prepared dinner and attached it to a truck. At this moment the artillery unit occupied a new position, and the enemy cut off Chizhoff from his comrades and surrounded him. Yes, everyone saw how a bomb dropped by a Nazi plane had fallen on the road and torn it up. Earth and dust had obscured the horizon and it was difficult to see. Perhaps this bomb had destroyed Chizhoff.

Rostislav Chizhoff remained surrounded by the enemy. But after three days consumed by fights with enemy tanks, three days of new, bitter struggles for Soviet soil, Rostislav

Chizhoff suddenly appeared, totally unexpected, among our tankists and artillerists. He was in his usual oily, dark-blue overalls, without a hat and helmet; his smile seemed to say to all: "Well, here I have returned and you thought I was dead." Chizhoff with military brevity reported his return and began to tell the detachment the story of his three-day wandering in the enemy's rear. But the commander interrupted Chizhoff:

"First, rest up. Are you hungry?"

Chizhoff stretched out his hand for bread. Only now he realized that he had not eaten for three days and that weakness had permeated his whole body. He went aside and lay on the hard grass that was crumpled, cut up, and mixed up with earth by the caterpillars of the tanks; paying no attention to the roar of explosions, he slept soundly.

Now he tells about himself, while the fighters lie among the nut bushes behind the hillock.

"We are people who cling to life!" says Rostislav Chizhoff.

He had remained in the rear of the enemy and decided not to give himself up alive as a prisoner, but first he would try to get out. It is never too late to die; one must know how to live, to win. He would never have fallen behind his detachment. But attaching the kitchen to the automobile, he got stuck on the way, the motor went dead.

Chizhoff quickly opened the hood, discovered that the spark plug had gone bad. He decided to fix it there. At that time he saw that our tanks were going off to one side, and an enemy bomber began to circle over him. From somewhere to the side Chizhoff and the vehicle were being fired upon by a machine gun. He lay on the ground and with one hand, gropingly, connected the wires.

It was an unusually hot day, but Chizhoff did not feel the heat. He was face to face with death. But he did not want to abandon the automobile and kitchen. Most of all it hurt that hot soup and well-prepared meat should fall to the enemy! These Nazi dumbbells might think that the Soviet artillerists had lost their heads for a moment and forgotten about dinner and the kitchen. It seemed to Chizhoff that he particularly was at fault in that the machine had gone wrong and the kitchen got stuck. So it was his fault that the fighters' dinner would remain for the enemy. Chizhoff decided at all costs to take away the kitchen and to put the machine in order.

Armored cars, tanks, and tractors with cannons passed Chizhoff. Zlotnikoff, the commander of a detachment, paused:

"Well, can you mend it?"

"Yes," answered Chizhoff, "I'll catch up with you."

"We are occupying a defense line behind that wood."

Chizhoff remained alone. Bullets whistled over his head. The bomber appeared again and began to circle. "I must hide," thought Chizhoff. He crawled to a ditch dug out along the road, and lay quietly behind a shrub. The Nazi plane dropped a bomb; it fell near the machine, destroying the motor. Then Chizhoff destroyed the chassis and the kitchen. At that moment hostile tanks appeared.

He was cut off from his own. Chizhoff hid behind a small bush and decided to wait until the Nazi troops passed by. He counted the tanks, automobiles, infantrymen. Now was the time to inform the commander! Chizhoff was a changed man. Up until that minute it seemed to him no one needed him; they could count him among the missing, or prisoner. He again had a goal in life. He must reconnoiter the enemy's rear and inform the commander to break through at any cost—by crawling, hiding, cunning, to find hidden paths in the woods.

Chizhoff went to the village where the enemy troops were quartered. The local population helped him to determine the force of the enemy on this sector of the front. It was getting dark. He sat down in the rye until night came and went toward the wood. He made his way out on a path. By a roundabout road, he thought, I may be able to reach our tanks. The whole night long he followed this path, using only a compass. Toward morning, Chizhoff understood that the path through the woods was leading him astray. It was necessary to go back and take the road through the village. He must travel only at night.

By day he lay in the bushes and counted each approaching automobile or tank. Toward evening he crawled up to the front line and carefully inspected it. The following day, toward daybreak, he found himself far away from his detachment. Now it was necessary to hurry, not to tarry anywhere. Only one more day to lie in the rye, motionless, not to reveal his presence. He wanted to eat, but there was nothing around him except some unripe ears of corn.

"*Nichevo,* I'll be patient," thought Chizhoff.

He lay tightly squeezed in a furrow. Above him floated an untroubled sultry sky; groans and cries reached him from the village. The Nazi beasts were settling accounts with the inhabitants. He gnashed his teeth. He was alone and powerless. But he would return to battle. Not one drop of our blood shall go unavenged!

Chizhoff recalled the tankists, chauffeurs, technicians, all were close to him, like kinsmen. He remembered his childhood years, his father, his mother, the town of Kirovograd where he attended high school. His father—a professor, head of the department—continues to live and work in his home town. His father very much wanted that, until he received his higher education, Rostislav should go through the practical school of life. He would work as a technician. With this intention, Rostislav entered the Red Army which turned him into a fighter, a staunch warrior. He must prove it in action by getting to his detachment with valuable information—after successful reconnaisance.

With these thoughts he lay out the whole day, not stirring.

Only three times he turned from side to side, carefully and gradually. At night he again went along the road. Toward morning he approached the river. But he had to leave the crossing for the following night.

During the day he succeeded in spotting a small boat. The river was wide. At night he made his way to it. Chizhoff saw a small fishing boat without oars. He began to row with his hands, the boat moved slowly, but Chizhoff was tireless. Already the goal was near and it was necessary to call upon all of his strength. After three hours he arrived at the opposite shore and crept along the bushes. Weakness was overcoming him. He lay down, but after an instant again got up and walked ahead, crawling in places, clutching at grass, bushes, stone.

Thus Rostislav Chizhoff reached his detachment and informed the commander of all that he had seen. Now he is again in a machine, again with the Soviet artillerists and tankists, he goes into battle for his native land.

WINGED WARRIORS

Air Scouts

Early in the morning, Captain Rudevich, commander of a long-range bomber, received orders to prepare it for flight, but without his customary load of bombs.

Immediately, intense work began around the plane. Small, stocky radio operator-gunner Balalykin checked his weapons in a businesslike manner. Notwithstanding his youth, he was already taking part in his second war. The veteran Balalykin had tested his machine guns first against Finnish planes.

"Why aren't they hanging up any bombs?" he asked in surprise.

"Because for some reason there is no order for it," answered Rudevich.

Captain Darello, the navigator, came. He occupied himself in studying the weather. Everything indicated favorable conditions for flying. The ceiling was good, you could fly as much as you wanted over enemy territory. A lieutenant colonel approached the plane and introduced himself:

"I am Lieutenant Colonel Ivanoff. Your craft is placed at my disposal," said he. Leading the men aside, he explained the task. The plane had to fly as long as possible over the field of battle so as to obtain a general impression of troop activities at the front and the situation in the enemy's rear.

"That means scouting," disappointedly thought Balalykin; and, as if guessing his thoughts, the Lieutenant Colonel warned him:

"Don't accept battle when you meet the enemy in the air. Everything must be done to see as much as possible of what is happening on the ground."

When the Lieutenant Colonel minutely instructed the crew, it became clear to the men that their flight this time was more responsible than their usual combat. And the faces of all became sterner, more serious, when the Lieutenant Colonel refused a proposal to fly with only one gunner-radio operator. Junior Sergeant Bashuk was summoned.

The Lieutenant Colonel skeptically looked over the young gunner-radio operator. It was evident that Bashuk was flying for the first time on a combat assignment.

"We need a second gunner to protect the tail. You must keep in mind that the plane is flying alone, without an escort of fighters."

"We will carry out the assignment, Comrade Lieutenant Colonel," Bashuk said suddenly, and this came out so sincerely, warmly, that the Lieutenant Colonel thought: "This chap has some zip to him."

At seven o'clock in the morning, the plane of Captain Rudevich took off from the airdrome. Lieutenant Colonel Ivanoff sat in the pilot's cabin alongside Captain Darello. He saw the navigator for the first time, but already in the short time while Darello was marking the route on the map, Ivanoff was filled with involuntary confidence in this unprepossessing man. He did everything exactly, thoughtfully, and with a deep knowledge of the subject.

A big task awaited the navigator: the plane had to be elusive, often to fly in the clouds, in blind flight, hiding from the pursuit of enemy fighters, again to drop down in order to inspect the field of battle. Already in the first hour of flight, it came under the fire of large-caliber Nazi antiaircraft guns. Beneath the plane, black puffs of explosion floated. The battery, quitting the lower range, began to strike higher, but Rudevich quickly climbed still higher and got out of the zone of fire. The navigator directed the plane carefully, skillfully slipping away from the enemy's fire.

But then a sextet of Messerschmitts appeared on the right and on the left. They began to pursue the Soviet plane. Captain Rudevich strictly observed the order "not to engage in battle," dove into the clouds, and thumbed his nose at the Messerschmitts.

The scout was already some hours in the air over the front. From above a grandiose picture of the battle opened up. Lieutenant Colonel Ivanoff saw tremendously deep funnels, the aftermath of Soviet bombs, overthrown, twisted enemy tanks, corpses of Nazis thickly covering the field, burning woods and bridges at the broken-up crossings of the enemy. A feeling of great admiration at the excellence of our fliers in destroying the enemy filled the Lieutenant Colonel as he diligently wrote down his observation.

In the fourth hour of the flight, the machine stumbled into a thunderhead. All around were impenetrable clouds and downpour.

The effort of Captain Rudevich to climb up failed. The plane was driven toward the earth. Under it flashed the treetops. It was necessary to land. But underneath was the enemy . . . it was unthinkable to land.

"Try your hardest to gain altitude," the Lieutenant Colonel ordered Captain Darello.

A tense struggle for each meter of altitude began. The engines grew weaker, the plane did not respond to the controls, but Captain Rudevich possessed a stubborn will and the resisting machine righted itself and slowly went higher. Somehow gaining 200 meters height, they arrived by blind flying at the airdrome, having flown over the front and rear of the enemy for about a thousand kilometers in the course of four hours.

The next day the weather was "rotten"; clouds disappeared, the sky was clear. To fly alone was dangerous; therefore, Captain Rudevich's plane took to the air with an escort of fighters. Flying over the enemy's positions, the fighters recognized two flights of Messerschmitts on the ground. The Soviet hawks dived like stones and in a strafing maneuver set on fire two enemy fighters. The rest began to take off. An air battle got under way.

Lieutenant Colonel Ivanoff saw two Nazi fighters going to attack the Soviet plane from both sides. These were small, white, stumpy-winged machines resembling white moths. The one flying from the left began to fire with its cannon at close range. Fragments penetrated Lieutenant Colonel Ivanoff's leg, but he did not feel the pain. All his attention was absorbed by the scene of the air battle. A Soviet heavy bomber was bravely repulsing the enemy pursuits pressing it. The forces were unequal, the superiority was on the side of the enemy. Accompanying light planes were diverted by other Nazi planes. The bomber entered into an individual engagement.

Gunner-radio operator Balalykin from afar watched the white Nazi moth flying to attack the plane on the left. And when the enemy shots burst from its cannon, Balalykin from the same distance fired at the enemy point-blank. The "white moth" burst into flames and dropped to earth like a flaming torch. All this took place so quickly that the enemy flier could not jump with his parachute.

Gunner-radio operator Bashuk observed the enemy. He noticed a pursuit coming up on his tail. That was when Bashuk, this fellow who was never fired on before, came in useful! The Nazi flew up close, the strong rattle of cannon fire was heard, but in the same instant Bashuk caught him in the sight and the second "white moth" was wrapped in flames.

The remaining enemies flying to attack the Soviet planes, seeing the sad fate of their two airmen, sidestepped, not accepting battle.

Blood poured from the stricken leg of Lieutenant Colonel Ivanoff. He somehow bandaged his leg with a towel, which by chance happened to be in his field kit, but blood continued to trickle.

"I'll fix things up a little better for you immediately," attentive Navigator Darello said solicitously.

He pulled up the wounded leg of the Lieutenant Colonel to the ceiling in order to reduce the loss of blood. Thus Lieutenant Colonel Ivanoff flew, holding up one leg to the roof of the pilot's cabin. It wasn't very convenient, but the Lieutenant Colonel, forgetting his wounds, thought feelingly of Navigator Captain Darello.

They landed, on their own airdrome, with a seriously damaged landing gear. They landed without mishap. The veteran Balalykin hopped out of the plane. He was wounded by fragments in the face, the left side, and hip. But, feeling nothing, he cried out in cheerful excitement:

"How we went after them! That is how it would be well always to strike the scoundrels!"

Bashuk's face also was bloody, but he too smiled happily, helping his comrades carry the wounded Lieutenant Colonel out of the machine.

"He didn't get away from me either! Did you see how I greeted him? Did you see?"

Yes, we saw, dear Comrade Bashuk. The whole country saw your achievement. Now in your crew there is no one who has not been under fire—there are only heroes!

A Flying Day

Bending over the map, Senior Lieutenant Morozoff and Lieutenant Dietz are studying the record of the flight. They are to bisect the front line, and to plunge into the enemy territory to reconnoiter over the airdrome near a Rumanian town.

The flight will pass over hills, valleys, copses, rivers. The flight will be difficult. In their imagination the fliers have already flown over it, picturing possible obstacles, and in thought overcame them, as they planned what they will do on the flight.

When everything was ready, they informed the commander of the detachment and received permission to start. Soon the two fighters took to the air and were out of sight.

They cut across the front line.

They passed over Rumanian territory. Both airmen scanned the air, attentively watching the ground, comparing the terrain with the map and once more checking the plan of flight with the actual situation which unrolled beneath them.

Their goal was already near.

Here are the ground features marked on the map.

Here a sharp turn must be made.

Here they are already over the airdrome.

Below, they obviously had not expected guests; planes stood peacefully on the ground.

Senior Lieutenant Morozoff and Lieutenant Dietz swooped down with all their fire power on the enemy's stationary machines. Flames quickly gutted one spot after another. The enemy could not extinguish them; they grew. At the edge of the airdrome a cloud of thick black smoke ascended.

The fighters change to the return course.

The assignment is fulfilled; the airport is destroyed.

In daylight Senior Lieutenant Morozoff brought the whole link to the well-known airport. Skillful approach to the objective. . . . An impetuous attack. . . .

Lieutenant Nagorny is shooting up the enemy's patrol links, caught on the ground. From above someone is visibly trying to jump out of the cabin; he falls; one of the enemy planes catches fire.

The enemy is infuriated with failure. All of his antiaircraft batteries open frantic fire. The sky is studded with shell puffs. The tracks of tracer bullets, like rain coming up from below, lace the air.

Over the flying field already run two Messerschmitts. But too late, too late. Morozoff's flight, having fulfilled its mission, quickly departs.

Morozoff liked the town which he visited twice in the course of two days.

A lot of greenery; nice orientation. Easy to calculate the

approach to the objective, he tells his comrades, recounting his impressions of two flights.

At sunset Morozoff with Nagorny and Dietz had to visit this town for the third time. The goal: the same airdrome. But this trip was not so quiet as the former ones. The enemy watched, in the air. Scarcely had they crossed the front line when the enemy's interceptor PZL-23 appeared.

Nagorny was the first to attack, Dietz second. Not accepting battle, the Hitlerite tries to escape; he is cunning, and dodges about. "Well, brother, first learn how to fight and then creep into it," says Morozoff with anger, and goes at the enemy's tail. A short volley. . . . One second, another. Somersaulting, the PZL-23 cuts into the ground.

The link continues according to the laid-out itinerary. And though the enemy expected an air attack and took appropriate measures, Morozoff's fighters subjected the air base to their fire again. On the spot of the morning fire, there was no longer visible the gutted-up building, nor the big transport plane which stood near by. The fire left only a spot of burned earth.

Now the twice-fooled and twice-beaten enemy opens antiaircraft fire, even fiercer than in the daytime.

White, black, and yellow puffs of explosions again and again appeared near the plane.

One machine was jarred high up and turned on its side but the pilot succeeded in righting it.

Maneuvering, Morozoff's fighters broke through this fiery curtain without casualties.

However, the link of fighters took longer than expected and at the airdrome they were anxiously looking at their watches. It was already getting dark, and the sky, still orange in the west, was already covered with twilight in the east.

But over the hills covered with the blue mist of twilight, almost pressing against the ground, one after another three shadows slid by. Another minute, and Senior Lieutenant Morozoff is reporting the results of the flight to the commander of the detachment. He finished his report and said to the mechanic:

"Cover up the holes in the center plane."

He goes to rest.

One Day

It is fast growing light on the horizon. In the flames of dawn against the background of the rising sun, the planes are already sharply outlined. The sun lights up the endless field and everywhere near the planes and under their wings sit pursuit pilots, on the dewy grass. They are awaiting a signal. A word of command, the signal rocket, and the fighters, like hurricanes caught by the wind, instantly are up in the air and rush into battle, at the enemy.

Up went the signal rocket. The sparks had not died down before the plane of the pursuit pilot, Podkriatoff, was up above the green field, quickly climbed and disappeared from sight. Far off was heard the racket of the engine, and then it was quiet, and the fliers remaining on the airdrome began to wait for Podkriatoff's return.

An hour passed. Pursuit planes continually went into the air; somewhere battles were going on. Then the fliers came back, landed, looked over their planes, and excitedly told each other about their skirmishes with the enemy, about battles and dogfights. Rockets flew up and again over the field was heard the roar of engines; pursuits flew into battle, but Podkriatoff had not returned yet.

This was a big and intense day for battles. Telephone bells shrilled every minute. The sharp racket of the machine guns was loud in the air. The grass waved under the wings of the planes,

and over the airdrome passed rapidly the shadows of the departing and returning pursuit planes.

"Podkriatoff did not return?"

"No."

Darkness came. The faces of the fliers were growing gloomy
and when night came, all were sadly quiet, remembering their
courageous friend.

Everyone hid his own thoughts but vowed to take revenge
cruelly on the black Nazi scavenger birds for Podkriatoff.

Night passed; a new day came, and again, as yesterday,
planes flew and returned.

And suddenly, out of one of the returned planes jumped
Lieutenant Alexander Podkriatoff, alive and unharmed. The
gladdened fliers embraced him, shook hands with and congratulated him.

Podkriatoff briefly recounted what happened to him.

After he had left the airdrome, Podkriatoff got into a fight
with two enemy interceptors. The fight was over enemy territory. The vultures fiercely attacked the Soviet flier. Machine guns
were whipping at the fuselage. After a few minutes, Podkriatoff's plane was hit in many places. The roar of the motors, firing weapons, glitter and sparkle of the propellers—everything
was tangled up. Finally, Podkriatoff made his way to the
enemy's tail, like lightning, and struck it like a dagger. The
Fascist interceptor listed on his wing, spun clumsily, and
crashed. At this moment, Podkriatoff felt that his own machine
was not responding, and he had to land, without losing any
time; else, destruction.

For the last time, Podkriatoff threw himself at the other Nazi
interceptor, whose pilot, after he saw how his companion had
perished, decided to withdraw from the fight and flee.

When the enemy plane disappeared, Podkriatoff came lower
and looked for a landing place. But what should he do? This

was enemy territory. There was no time for long deliberation. The plane was losing altitude. Suddenly Podkriatoff saw a strange airdrome not far off, devoid of men or planes. Obviously, the enemy had changed bases and flown over to another airdrome. Podkriatoff decided to land on this deserted enemy field. Silence. . . . In the grass fresh marks left by aircraft were visible, but not a soul was around. Podkriatoff convinced himself that he surmised correctly and, without losing a second, picked a good deal of thick grass and camouflaged his plane.

Twilight came. It turned dark and during these hours Podkriatoff repaired his machine. With sunrise, he went up and the motor hummed triumphantly in the morning air. And that is how he returned to his own base where his friends gave him a warm reception.

Podkriatoff scarcely had finished telling of his adventure when high in the sky appeared an enemy plane, roaring above, looking over the location and seeking out Soviet airdromes.

"Permit me, Comrade Commander," Podkriatoff interrupted his story, "permit me to go up."

"You have my permission."

The grass shook under the wings of the plane. Podkriatoff soared into the air and quickly drew near the Nazi plane. High up in the sky was heard machine-gun fire, and before the eyes of the grounded airmen, the enemy plane swerved sharply to the side, careened, and began to fall. Helplessly whirling its wings, the Nazi plane fell and with extraordinary speed cut into the ground and a column of smoke went up over the debris.

The government has now rewarded the first heroes of the War for the Fatherland. In the decree of the Presidium of the Supreme Soviet of the U.S.S.R., one can read the name of Flying Lieutenant Alexander Petrovich Podkriatoff, awarded the Order of the Red Star for his exploits; yet, we have told only about one of the fighting days of this fearless airman.

The crew of Lieutenant Orobiowik off's (right) plane set down route of the flight it is about to make

Pursuit Pilot Kuznetsoff

A fighter plane was flying over the town. The little machine circled in the sky with a sharp, angry buzzing—like a bumble-bee over its hive when an enemy has disturbed a comb full of honey.

Junior Lieutenant Alexander Kuznetsoff looked around carefully, seeking the enemy who might dive suddenly and thievishly from behind a small cloud. But everything was quiet around him. Below lay his native land illuminated by the rays of the sun, breaking through the windows in the clouds. Over this land not so long ago walked a prospecting geologist, Alexander Kuznetsoff, studying its very bowels.

He drilled this earth to find out its structure, the depth of subsoil water; in those places people built factories; the buildings stood sturdily on the earth, beautifying it and giving joy to men.

About fifteen Nazi planes suddenly appeared at an altitude of 2000 meters. Near them curled puffs of exploding antiaircraft shells. Kuznetsoff went against the enemy, attacking for the first time in his life, his heart filled with anger. Instantly, the air was broken by the blue trickles of tracer bullets, and suddenly and strangely, the map case hanging on Kuznetsoff's chest disappeared as if carried off by a strong gust of wind. The Nazi planes turned back and flew away from our fighter plane. Kuznetsoff overtook the enemy plane on the left and gave it a long volley of shots. The Nazi began to smoke but still continued his horizontal flight. Looking at his instruments, Kuznetsoff saw that his fuel was almost used up—he could not fly farther. He looked with vexation at the disappearing enemy.

"Not one did I bring down . . . not one," sadly thought Alexander, coming down to his airdrome. He felt ashamed to face

his comrades. Silently, he looked over his machine and saw
that it was punctured in many places. The feeling of annoyance
with himself for the failure of his first attack was replaced by
fierce anger.

"You wait! I will repay you for this!" thought Alexander
as he prepared for a new fight.

On the following day, Kuznetsoff was on patrol duty again.
Some enemy planes soon appeared.

In a matter of moments, up went the roaring, quick-winged
interceptor. But the Fascists disappeared quickly. Kuznetsoff
gained altitude and circled over the town, going above the
clouds and down again, looking attentively through the
windows. Again no one! He had to land as he had fuel only for
fifteen minutes.

When he had already let down his landing gear and was
circling over the airdrome, he noticed explosions of antiaircraft guns firing at enemy planes. Again he retracted his gear
and rushed up. "In fifteen minutes I will succeed in making at
least one attack," he decided and went after the Nazi carrion
eagles, who had meanwhile turned west. He noticed one Nazi
lagging behind his formation, flying at the same altitude of 500
meters and two Soviet fighter planes pursuing him. Kuznetsoff
was getting closer, squeezing all the reserve fighting strength
out of his new, powerful motor.

The distance was growing shorter. The German plane was
now within a hundred meters. Kuznetsoff went a little higher
and, aiming at the cabin, fired all the machine guns at once.
The Fascist became covered with smoke, then a bright-red flame
appeared, but the flier continued on his way. Suddenly he cut
down his speed, planning for the pursuer who was flying at
high speed to pass right over him so that he could hit Kuznetsoff
in the tail.

But Alexander quickly divined the enemy's trick and he, too, slowed down. The Fascist turned to the left, Kuznetsoff after him. He stubbornly drove the enemy down to Soviet territory, fatal for this bird of prey. From the flaming plane, the gunner-radio operator had already jumped, but the pilot continued to maneuver the burning plane; horizontally, at times lunging to one side. Kuznetsoff "sat on his back," not easing off a minute. When the enemy was eighty meters above the ground, Kuznetsoff fired his last volley into the plane. The hood came off and after it the pilot fell out and plunged like a stone into the fir trees, his parachute failing to open. The plane fell not far from him with a dull explosion.

On this day Alexander ate with great gusto—never was the black bread so tasty! He ate one portion of dessert, then asked for another helping of compote, but he did not have time to bite through the last apricot stone when the command sounded: "To your planes!"

The apricot pit still in his mouth, Kuznetsoff ran to his machine. When he came up over the town, the Nazi robbers were already running away from the interceptors. Kuznetsoff raced after them. He singled out the one on the extreme left. He cut the gas, somewhat raised his plane, and let the enemy have it from all his guns. The Fascist sharply pulled up the nose of his machine, which caught fire. At the same instant, Kuznetsoff felt a strong blow on his leg.

Avoiding the burning enemy plane and descending, Kuznetsoff was feeling his leg—it was all bloody and the boot was torn to shreds. He wanted to press his right foot on the pedal but it would not work.

He took a last look at the enemy burning and falling to the ground, and let out his landing gear as he flew straight over the airdrome.

At a tremendous speed, the interceptor was running over the field. The wounded flier, carefully pressing the pedal with the left foot, led it to the edge of the airdrome, describing a half circle to the left. Bleeding profusely, he stopped his machine ten meters away from the camouflaged planes.

Kuznetsoff was carried out of the machine.

"Went too close to the Nazi," he began to say. "Lost my head. I should have let him have it from 400 meters. With a cooler head . . ."

"Never mind, you'll have another chance to correct your mistake," said his comrades as they tenderly placed him in the ambulance.

Nikolai Terekhin

"To your planes!" was the command.

Over the small landing field soared a hissing signal rocket. The frightful fighter planes rapidly climbed up, took their course, and disappeared in the distance.

The weather was murky. Broken clouds were floating low. One had to peer sharply in order not to miss the cruel and tricky enemy. Senior Lieutenant Nikolai Terekhin, the escadrille commander, watched the air attentively.

Somewhere in the vicinity, Nazi bombers were passing, en route to bomb the flourishing city. They intended to drop their deadly load upon the inhabitants of the town, upon women, children, old people. The German bombers must not approach the town.

Terekhin's escadrille hunts in the vastness of the sky. It seeks out the enemy to destroy him. And now a keen delight flashes in Terekhin's gray eyes. His firm hand lightly dips wing tips, giving the signal to the rest. Senior Lieutenant Terekhin and his comrades hurl their obedient fighting machines upon the enemy.

Five Heinkels, just emerged from the clouds, experience a relentless, fierce pursuit and retribution. The Senior Lieutenant sees how the Nazi gunner-radio operator, jerkily turning his small black head, aims the fire of the machine guns on him. Terekhin notices that several enemy bullets hit his machine. But he has enough self-control, in spite of enemy fire, to approach the bomber much closer, and only then strike at him point-blank. Bull's-eye! Terekhin sees very clearly the bestial face of the Nazi, twisted with hatred and horror.

"Now's the time!" Terekhin decides.

He presses firmly the trigger of his machine guns. The fiery swords of his tracer bullets lash the bomber, killing the Nazis. A raging fire starts over the fuselage. The Heinkel falls down, out of control. Terekhin looks around. He sees two more Heinkels also in flames and smoke, shot down by Terekhin's comrades. Victory! Senior Lieutenant Terekhin's heart contracts in sweet excitement.

But he has to return to his own landing field. His engine misses; something is wrong with the rudder—it works poorly. On landing, the fighter plane suddenly is thrown to one side. Only Terekhin's coolness and skill avert disaster. Comrades, running to the plane, congratulate Terekhin on his victory; he smiles shyly. His white teeth gleam in his sunburned face. Boundlessly brave in battle, on the ground he is unassuming, quiet, and kindly. This further increases respect and love for him.

On the next day, Senior Lieutenant Terekhin went up again. His task was again to intercept a group of German bombers and to annihilate them. As yesterday, the weather was murky and it was difficult to find the enemy amid the gray clouds. But exactly as yesterday, Senior Lieutenant Terekhin located a group of German bombers and attacked them. Tempestuously, he dashed at the bomber nearest him; he fired point-blank and instantly killed the gunner-radio operator. Short, accurate volleys followed. The bomber dropped and flames from the explosion shot up from the ground.

But ahead there were still two German bombers. They were fleeing. He cannot let them escape! Terekhin follows the vultures. He directs his fire at the nearest bomber. Suddenly, his ammunition is exhausted! Now the enemy can get away. But this mustn't happen! The enemy must be destroyed at any cost. Nikolai Terekhin throws his fighter at the Nazi bomber, like a battering ram.

A stream of gas from the escaping plane drives Terekhin to one side; with the wing of his plane he slices, not at the engine, but at the enemy's tail. He will always remember how the German bomber tore downward and how his own right wing twisted up and curled.

But the fighter was still under control. Ahead was the last enemy bomber. It, too, must be destroyed! Thinking of nothing except this, Nikolai Terekhin swiftly approached the bomber. The bullets of the German gunner beat upon his fighter plane. Terekhin opened the cabin door with a quick, deft movement, unbuttoned his safety straps, pushed his goggles off, and at once rammed his fighter against the bomber, which fell in fragments.

But Terekhin's plane also broke into pieces and Terekhin himself, with a split forehead, fell down. At 400 meters, when he regained consciousness, he opened his parachute, and saw how, beneath him, two German parachutists were landing and running away. But they won't get away! Terekhin rejoices when he sees the German airmen fall into the hands of the Red Army-men. He, too, was falling into the same hands. But for him these hands were gentle and kindly, the hands of his close kin.

Peter Kharitonoff

In the very first hours of the war, Junior Lieutenant Kharitonoff, a pursuit pilot, was in the air. His small light-winged plane bore itself to any altitude like a meteor. The flier peered ahead, seeking out the Nazi brigands.

Anger and hatred filled his young heart. He wanted to fly his marvelous machine to meet the enemy, but he had to guard an important post and, consequently, had continued to patrol his designated zone.

The first day of the war passed. Kharitonoff went up several times, but failed to meet any German planes. Every time he landed, the pilots, mechanics, and fighters noticed ill-concealed disappointment on his face.

"I met no one," he complained.

After some days Kharitonoff again went up on a patrol mission. It was a beautiful summer day. Below, immense collective-farm fields were ripening. Roads intertwined like narrow ribbons. The young flier looked lovingly at this countryside.

The long-awaited meeting occurred. A Nazi plane was making its way deep into our territory. When Kharitonoff saw the enemy, his eyes shone. His engine roared threateningly, the pursuit dashed at the enemy. This was not anticipated by the crew of the German bomber. The Nazis opened fire, but Kharitonoff, by a skillful maneuver, avoided the bullets.

"Now, I'll show you," whispered the flier, and discharged the first volley.

The Junkers quivered. The Nazi pilot apparently decided to turn back and get away from the Soviet pursuit. Kharitonoff, ceaselessly showering the enemy with lead, circled around the Junkers and did not permit it to slip away. But, as luck would have it, his ammunition was exhausted.

When Kharitonoff saw that the Nazi flier was trying to give him the slip, he gave chase.

"You won't get away, you Fascist riffraff!"

The pursuit approached closer and closer to the Nazi bomber. When Kharitonoff was very near, he cut down speed. Now the pursuit was almost brushing against the enemy, who opened fire.

Kharitonoff came close to the tail of the enemy machine. In a twinkling, the pursuit's propeller chopped off the bomber's elevator flaps.

The Junkers opened another burst of machine-gun fire. Now it was not at all alarming.

The Junkers lost altitude and dived sharply. By skillful gliding, Kharitonoff landed on his own airdrome. When his comrades learned the results of his dogfight, they congratulated Komsomol member Kharitonoff on an excellent debut.

The Junkers cracked up near by.

Stepan Zdorovtsev

Zdorovtsev worked on water transport and was interested in the profession of flying until he was drafted into the Red Army. Without interrupting his regular work, he finished summer school at the local aero club. He stood out among his fellow students by a keen eye, strong arms, and self-control. The diver's art also interested him, and there, too, he showed self-control, exceptional endurance, and a quick wit.

Several times, at the risk of his life, he gave help to people in distress in the river.

"Determined, self-sacrificing, responsive." Thus spoke his comrades of Zdorovtsev.

Then came the day when Zdorovtsev was called to the Red

Army. He asked to be enrolled in the air force, and in 1940 successfully completed his aviation training.

The letter he sent to his wife, Alexandra Grigoryevna, after being appointed to the fighter squadron, was full of exceptional warmth and great patriotic feeling:

"Today I got my 'hawk.' I love it as much as I love you and Galochka."

Love for their fatherland, unbounded devotion to the great cause of Lenin and Stalin, and limitless hatred for the accursed enemy, this is what drives the Soviet people to great exploits. These feelings filled Zdorovtsev, too. Having neither fear nor doubt, full of courage and daring, he soared up in his "hawk" to wreck and annihilate the Fascist carrion birds.

Soon his neighbors working in Stalingrad and all the rest of the Soviet people heard over the radio the story of the fearless exploit of an aviator, Junior Lieutenant Stepan Zdorovtsev, who waged a lengthy fight with enemy bombers trying to break through to an important military objective. Skillfully maneuvering, he poured a rain of bullets on the enemy until all his ammunition was exhausted. Then this self-sacrificing airman, confident of his flying skill and full of deep hatred for the Nazi monsters, determined to stop at nothing, boldly prepared to ram. The German pilot's nerves could not sustain this skirmish with the daring flier, and he fled. But there was no escaping the Soviet "hawk." Zdorovtsev caught up with the Nazi bomber and with his propeller sliced off the tip of its tail and destroyed the enemy, himself landing unharmed.

Mikhail Zhukoff

The War for the Fatherland caught the twenty-four-year-old Mikhail Zhukoff in a fighter plane. He was patrolling over an airdrome, guarding it from Nazi marauders. Zhukoff's fighter fiercely roared over the earth, seeking the enemy. A river shone below; over a bridge a long military column moved—thousands of Soviet people going to protect their native land. Looking up to the fighter circling in the sky, they marched calmly, confident that Mikhail Zhukoff would not let the enemy approach.

But the enemy was already creeping up, hiding in the clouds. High up, Mikhail Zhukoff hurried on, but all the same he had time to notice a black shadow darting under him—a Nazi flying toward the bridge with a load of bombs. Another minute or two, and a hundred persons would plunge into the river together with burning fragments of the bridge.

Zhukoff hurled himself down upon the enemy. The wind whistled piercingly, stinging his face. Nearer and nearer was the enemy plane—already the swastika, resembling a spider, was visible; there was something repulsive in this black brand of the Nazi slave owners. His hand involuntarily went to the machine-gun trigger.

The Junkers met Zhukoff with a downpour of tracer bullets. "If only I don't make a mess of it! If only I don't make a mess of it!" Zhukoff excitedly repeated to himself. Indeed, this was the first time he had seen the accursed enemy so close to him. He fired at the Junkers from all his machine guns. He aimed at the armored cabin, at his adversary's head, at the fuel tanks. He saw how stripes from his bullets showed white on the metal seaming. The enemy suddenly went into a spin, trying to escape from the deadly fire. This was victory. The great armored bomber scurried with all its energy away from the Soviet pursuit.

On the ground people gazed at the daring flier. Many commented with pride:

"What a hero!"

The enemy was fleeing. But Mikhail Zhukoff daydreamed of

seeing him dashed down and flattened on the ground. Day after day he flew with this insistent dream. He often met Junkers and Heinkels and scrutinized their thievish ways, studied their bandit tactics, and sought out their vulnerable spots. Zhukoff found out that the best place to aim at in a Junkers was from below at the blind cone, for the armored Nazi is mortally afraid when a Soviet fighter plane directs the piercing fire of its machine guns into his very belly.

Once six Junkers broke through to the Soviet airdrome. They came in close formation. Zhukoff fell upon them suddenly out of the clouds and showered them with bullets. So daring was this attack of one fighter against six planes that the enemies lost their heads and took to their heels.

On the following morning, eight Junkers appeared in the neighborhood of the airdrome. Interceptors immediately encircled them. As always, avoiding a direct battle, the Nazi pilots took to flight.

Possessed by fierce anger, Mikhail Zhukoff chased them. In terror, the Nazis began to drop bombs indiscriminately. A nearby explosion tossed Zhukoff's machine, but he continued at the enemy's heels. Wing Commander Gorbachevsky, an airman who knew no fear, flew a little ahead. On the left sped the brave Lieutenant Fedorenko. It's fun to enter battle alongside such friends!

The Nazi bombers darted into the clouds, interceptors after them. One of the Junkers went into a spin. Mikhail Zhukoff followed him, spraying him with machine-gun bursts.

Swiftly, inexorably, the earth rushed up. A deep lake pushed apart its shores, as if opening its maw to swallow the approaching enemy. The Junkers swerved to one side, trying to escape death, but Zhukoff with his machine guns pressed it down to the lake, and the bomber, losing control, plunged into the water.

The lake boiled and swirled angrily. A spout rose from the

water, then thick smoke—the tail of the enemy bobbed up and the Soviet waters closed forever over the Nazi plane.

By decree of the Presidium of the Supreme Soviet of the U.S.S.R., aviators Stepan Zdorovtsev, Mikhail Zhukoff, and Peter Kharitonoff were each awarded the title of the Hero of the Soviet Union, and given the Order of Lenin, The Golden Star medal.

THE MIGHTY GUARDS OF THE SOVIET SEAS

Pirates Sink to the Bottom

Warm days prevailed on the Baltic. It was seldom foggy. One could see far in clear weather.

War, severe, relentless war is going on. An observer cannot be seen from sea or from land. He is carefully hidden from the outsider's gaze. But should a strange engine hum in the sky, the flat meadow will speak with a thunderous voice, the rocky shore will shake with the blow of volleys; sea and shore will come to life. The Baltic at war is terrible in its wrath. Every ship is an arsenal of hatred for the enemy. In every Red sailor is concentrated a people's mighty anger that animates everyone in the land, from children to adults.

A ship is going full speed. Aboard stands a Red sailor with a rifle, peering at the vast sea, upon its formless green waves, at a distant, billowy desert. Danger may lurk in each billow. A mine, perhaps dropped by the sneaky enemy, a torpedo fired by the accursed pirate. There, far off, a breaking wave raises some dark spot. Is it perhaps the periscope of a hiding foe? Dozens of eyes scan this point keenly. No, this is no periscope. This is a piece of wood borne out into the open sea.

The acting chief of the political department is Malyavkin. At the stern near the depth-bomb racks is Anikin, second-class boatswain. The acting commander knows that Anikin is a dependable and courageous man.

"Everything ready?" asks Malyavkin.

"Everything is in order," reports the boatswain. "We will strike the German vermin dead; just let them come along."

They did not have to wait long.

"A torpedo to starboard," suddenly report two observers simultaneously.

"To starboard!" commands the Captain, a Baltic fighter decorated for his feats against the White Guard Finns.

"Aye, aye; hard astarboard," replied the helmsman. The ship turned obediently. The torpedo rushed by.

The second torpedo also rushed by alongside the ship. The third one—the ship again escaped collision by a skillful maneuver.

The commander decided to ram the pirate. The ship went at the enemy head-on. The submarine tried to submerge and save itself from the unsuccessfully attacked Soviet ship. On the surface only a swirl was seen, then a narrow funnel. The submarine disappeared. In the engine room the fighters heard distinctly something screech. The ship's keel went over something hard, the log line parted.

The boat was still there then. She was under the ship and did not have time to submerge deep. It would have to be bombed.

Anikin and his coworker Shilovsky, both under the command of Lieutenant Belous, were waiting for orders at the depth-charge post.

"Begin bombing!"

The commander's words coincided with dull thuds under the water. Depth bombs went down. A blow, then another. . . . The turbulent sea reared up from the storm of battle.

The whole ship shook from explosions underwater. The bomb struck its target. "Accept a Baltic present." The German submarine gurgled something and then choked. On the surface were swimming many multicolored shining spots. The enemy submarine found a certain grave in the Baltic. And there is plenty of room for others!

The ship turned to pass again over the place of battle.

Suddenly, there was a roar of an explosion. This was a mine which the vigilant Red sailors had rendered safe. It burst not far from the vessel. The explosion was so powerful that it raised a real tempest near the ship. A squall of water poured down on the decks. Several officers and sailors on the poop were thrown off their feet. Lieutenant Belous fell on the stern scuppers and received a serious wound. A wave carried him overboard.

The life of the officer was in danger. Red seaman Madrichenko jumped to the rescue. The wave was knocking him off his feet too, but in the very last moment he succeeded in adroitly catching the Lieutenant under the arms and pulled him up on deck. All this happened in a few seconds. No one gave thought then to the Red sailor's courage. The actions and behavior of the fighters were discussed afterwards when the details of the fight were recalled, but now everyone was too busy doing something. Perhaps there was another enemy somewhere and he had to be destroyed too. The Lieutenant was taken to the sick bay. With him went Anikin and Shilovsky, who received serious bruises when the mine exploded. Belous was unconscious for a while. When he first came to, he asked:

"And how is it there? Any other periscopes visible?"

Anikin and Shilovsky were bandaged up. They turned to the commander and asked:

"Permit us to go up on deck again."

"How do you feel?" asked the commander.

"Swell."

They resumed their posts by the bomb rack.

Another warm, quiet day hovered over the sea.

A tremendous billow was washing off the shadowy lights at the stern. The vast mysterious expanse was deserted. The ship was advancing on a new pirate.

Serious and threatening Red sailors look at this expanse. Their keen eyes will not overlook the enemy. They are watching for new periscopes!

Links of Victory

A peaceful, white night. . . . The clouds are tinted with the delicate colors of sunrise. The sharp-pointed tops of the churches and towers of an ancient fortress are silhouetted against the distance.

The sea is calm. Fiery are the wonderful colors of the water and the sky. A high-speed cutter, the chaser of submarines, dashes over the oily water. The cutter is manned by Soviet people and supplied with bombs. It flies over the sea like a cyclone, yet finds time to trace the submarines. Heavy, black, curling columns—then on the still waters appears a wide, oily spot. The submarine submerged for the last time. The sea is watched.

Far on the horizon appear the Nazi planes. Against them rises a flock of fast-winged red-starred interceptors. They are approaching each other. The antiaircraft shell explosions are heard. The vultures with swastikas turn back sharply, far from having reached their goal. The sky is watched.

At times one can see these alert little beetles press the big birds, force them down, dive under their tails, drop on them stonelike from above. . . . At times one can see smoke going up

from a Nazi plane writing out in the sky its last illegible auto-
graph. That's how Junkers-86 wrote for the last time in the sky
over the sea, destroyed by Antonenko, a decorated flier who
went through the school of war over the forests of Finland. The
enemy, it appears, is stricken similarly everywhere.

There is a young woman in the flying-base commandant's office. She is excited, often unnecessarily asks for a cigarette. She
has a request—not a request, a demand—of a patriot and
friend:

"I am from Sevastopol. I left on the first day of war. My husband is at another distant base. Give me work, anything you
want! I am remaining here and will wait for my husband."

The commandant asks if there are children, and assigns her
to work.

"Somebody in the dining room has to be relieved. Will you
take that?"

"Yes, but . . ."

"What else?"

"You see I have a friend. Her husband is here but he insists
that she go back to town and she doesn't want to." And, businesslike, she adds, "They have no children and she can type."

"You just wait," laughs the commandant. "Your husband
will return and will chase you back to town too."

She looks at him and in her eyes, moistened by understandable excitement, there is sincere wonder.

"Me? Six years ago we vowed, in case anything happens, to
be together; where he is, that's where I'll be."

Two Red sailors, mechanics, are at the edge of the airdrome.
Between jobs (plenty of those) they managed to revive an old
refueling machine. This veteran of the White Guard Finnish

war, snorting happily, runs toward our wonderful fighter birds, hungry after the fight, and feeds them fuel.

The fighters look at this clear and indispensable liquid. Behind it is rising the great land: Baku, Caucasus, Central Asia, Siberia, the Volga. This is the power of war supplies and the gigantic strength of millions of people! In this great war there are no petty tasks. The repaired gas-supply machine, the woman in the dining room, the cutter with the bombs, the sentries watching from bushes—these are all links of victory.

From the efforts of millions of people, as from fine links, is welded the strongest chain on which there will be raised over the earth the proud word:

"Victory!"

Gunnery Commander Kutsev

He inspects them all: the gunners, shell carriers, replacement men. He looks attentively into their faces. The gunnery commander would like to know their thoughts, to understand their feelings before the battle, their first battle with the murderous enemy.

The men of this gun detachment have been serving together for the last three years now. They have had time to get used to each other, become close to each other, and Kutsev really has no difficulty in reading their thoughts and in understanding their interests in life. He sees and is able to sense the most important thing: composure, confidence, and determination. This imbues the commander with a firm belief in the success of the operation to which his gang are to contribute.

Here it is, his celebrated gun. Even in the dark he is able to touch it and know every detail of the fighting apparatus. But the real test will come in a few hours. They are all prepared, trained during many months and years for a few minutes of battle. Their will, their accumulated knowledge and dexterity, have been made ready for these hours and minutes.

Today there will be a real test of the military education, and above all a real checkup of the qualities of the gunnery commander. He had taught every fighter, personally, preparing him for the fight. To each of the fighters he was not only an exacting commander, but a patient educator devoting all his attention to them, solicitous of their individual needs, an older brother. Now on the eve of battle, Kutsev is giving his final instructions, briefly and in a low voice.

"Everything clear?"

"We understand, comrade!"

In the morning the ship took its appointed course. The command awaited by the fighters and Kutsev all night long with unusual excitement was heard at last!

"Portside, load guns!"

Confident gestures. Familiar sounds of the working mechanics. But it is not the same—there is something new in the fighters' activity, something unusual. The artillerists experience a new sensation: anger toward the base enemy, a burning hatred impossible to control, fierce anger as if projected into the barrel of the gun with the shell.

The first shot at the enemy has already burst out of Kutsev's gun. Firing at the enemy position begins. On the robbers' nest, on the heads of the Nazis descend hundreds of tons of fire and metal.

Kutsev had time to say only two words directed at the gunner: "More precision." A great deal depends on each of these fighters in this battle. None lags even for a second; everyone uses the precious time to the greatest advantage. The fighters work with automatic precision. Everyone shows a new unexpected strength, skill, and exactness of movement.

The guns have never known such fast firing.

"Faster, faster," Kutsev whispers to himself.

In these exciting minutes Kutsev sees a new expression on the faces of the fighters. Stern determination marks these unusually serious faces, suddenly grown old.

The guns fire fast and accurately. The Nazi base is in flames.

Three Long Days

The newspapers published a short account of how three brave pilots, Yur, Levinson, and Kuznetsoff, after a fight with the Nazi pursuit ships, made a forced landing on the sea. The airmen battled the elements for three days and three nights, making their way to their base in a rubber dinghy.

This is a fuller story of their courageous exploit.

Their battle assignment had been carried out. Only burned fragments remained of the hostile objectives. Gaining altitude the bomber was returning to its base.

"Two Nazi interceptors on the left!" Gunner-Radio Operator Kuznetsoff suddenly reported.

The commander of the plane decided to accept battle. It was an unequal match—a solitary bomber against two interceptors. But was this the first time that the Stalinist falcons had to fight a numerically superior enemy?

Like hawks, the interceptors hurled themselves upon the Soviet plane, trying to come up on its tail. Lieutenant Yur, guessing the Nazi intentions, maneuvered cleverly. Gunner-Radio Operator Kuznetsoff pressed the trigger of his machine gun. A hail of lead descended on the vultures. Another second, and one Messerschmitt wreathed in flames plunged into the sea and sank to the bottom.

"That's the place for him! There is ample space at the bottom of the sea," said Kuznetsoff.

The second enemy plane, unable to withstand such fire at first, went off, but then rushed into attack concentrating a hurricane of fire on the bomber. An exploding shell damaged the right wing of the Soviet plane. But this did not upset the glorious fliers. Their machine-gun fire drove off several desperate attacks and they continued their flight, although the plane no longer had its former maneuverability.

The air duel had already lasted twenty minutes. The bomber was all riddled with bullets. Its radio was out of order, a quarter of the wing had fallen off, the left engine was jammed.

With every minute the machine was losing altitude. The Nazi interceptor continued its attack. Then Gunner-Radio Operator Kuznetsoff opened fire through his stabilizer at the enemy's tail. This decided the outcome of the battle. The overweening Messerschmitt twisted and clumsily turned on its wing, caught fire, and fell down like a stone. The sea waves closed over this Hitlerite bandit forever.

"Altitude seventy meters," Navigator Levinson reported to the commander of the plane.

Below was the sea. It was more than a hundred and fifty miles to their native shore. The damaged plane scarcely responded to the controls.

All the time they were losing altitude. Twenty . . . ten . . . five meters. It was no longer possible to fly. The fliers shut off the engines. The machine dropped to the water and, after a minute and a half, sank. In this period the crew succeeded in emerging from the cabin straight into the water, carrying with them the collapsible rubber dinghy.

The airmen remained afloat without food and water.

Their heavy-fur flying suits became sodden and dragged the

daredevils down. The long air battle had tired out the fliers. Their fatigue oppressed them.

"We fought off two Messerschmitts. Can it be that we will not find a way out of this?" exclaimed Lieutenant Yur. He gave an order:

"Open up the boat!"

Here the navigator reported a new mishap: the inflation apparatus had sunk and the oars were carried off by the sea.

"Blow it up by mouth!"

For a long while the three courageous airmen trod water, as they took turns inflating the boat. In order to float more easily they discarded their fur flying suits and their boots.

At last the boat was inflated. All clambered aboard.

Stars appeared in the sky and the navigator quickly got his bearings by them. Lacking oars, they rowed with their hands. The boat slowly moved forward.

The night grew cold. But these men in shirt sleeves sweated. Overcoming fatigue, they rowed and rowed, dipping their arms into the water up to the elbows.

Time dragged on wearisomely. They knew that only stamina, composure, and will power would help them reach their native shore.

Morning came. Hunger made itself felt. Cruelly, thirst tortured them. Their strength ebbed. But they could not give up. How many hours, perhaps days, like that were still before them? They had to conserve their energy, to struggle.

After midday a fresh breeze sprang up; the boat began to rock.

"If only we had a sail," the navigator said.

"Let's make a sail out of our suits," suggested Yur.

Quickly they tore up a pair of blue overalls, and tied them together where necessary. A man stood on each side of the boat and stretched out this crude sail. The breeze filled it and the boat went faster.

Thus they sailed for several hours. Before sunset the breeze died down and they reverted to rowing with their hands.

The second night came. The courageous trio continued their valiant struggle with the elements. Salt water bit into their hands; they felt as if on fire. The men were tormented intolerably by hunger and thirst. Moments came when they thought that they no longer had the strength to struggle, but those were only moments. The fliers chased away such thoughts.

The third day of the struggle passed. The sea freshened. The breeze strengthened. The dinghy began to ship water, threatening to overturn momentarily. They began to bail, but this did not help; besides, they had to save their lowering strength.

At length the shore appeared in the distance.

"Land! Our Soviet land!" joyfully exclaimed the heroes.

They tried to row faster, but nothing came of it. Their swollen arms scarcely rose above the water, fell back helplessly.

The third day was coming to an end, but the shore was still scarcely visible. Worn out with lack of sleep and by hunger, they still did not give up.

One more weary night went by. Now the shore was some eighty to one hundred meters away, which they lacked the strength to traverse. For several interminable hours the fliers tried to overcome this short distance, but the undertow carried them back. The shore slowly retreated.

But they had been noticed from shore! Already a rescue party was being prepared, when suddenly the sound of an engine was heard overhead. This was a Soviet plane. The dinghy in which three men were prostrated was noticed. The plane landed on the water and steered to the lone boat. Within several minutes the three brave falcons were on board the plane.

Airman Anatoly Krokhalev

Anatoly Krokhalev has his own peculiar diary. The diary contains nothing of a personal nature—no biographical details —no descriptions of intimate experiences. The diary contains notations like this:

"Two flights were made. We bombed objective T."

"Weather conditions bad—low ceiling. We sometimes flew very low. Bombed objective R—destroyed ammunition stores and harbor constructions."

"Bombed munitions plant and docks."

"Bombed objective P. Destroyed hawsers and an army transport."

"Brought down a Finnish pursuit plane."

And so forth. These short entries reveal airman Krokhalev. In general, he rarely speaks of himself but becomes animated when he mentions his comrades-in-arms—pilots, navigators, gunners-radio operators who are under his command and whom he has led in battle and leads once more against the enemy of our fatherland.

In these notes—laconic and precise—emerges the selfless work of the detachment commanded by Anatoly Krokhalev.

All this took place a year and a half ago when Anatoly Krokhalev had the honor of defending the sacred borders of our Soviet fatherland against the onslaughts of the Finnish White Guardists.

After a few combat flights made by Anatoly Krokhalev, the entire air force knew of the commander who daily achieved new victories for the glory of his people. It was then that the air-force newspaper at the front coined the slogan:

"To fly and bomb like the Baltic airman, Anatoly Krokhalev."

Krokhalev was the talk of the whole air force, which followed his flights and those of his subordinates, and rejoiced in their victories.

The enemy felt the strength of Krokhalev's blows. He took up heavy planes and flew them deep into enemy territory, destroying military objectives and man power.

They had to fly under extremely complex conditions. It was a bitter cold winter; the temperature dropped far below freezing, but orders must be carried out. The aviators fulfilled their military duties in spite of all hardships.

Once Krokhalev's detachment went out on an assignment. It already was returning to its base when suddenly Krokhalev felt as if his shoulder was burning. At first he thought he was wounded but he soon discovered that was not the case. The unbearable heat continued to make itself felt—his fur flying suit was on fire. Something should really be done about it, but under the circumstances it was impossible to leave the controls. In an attempt to put out the flames, Krokhalev pressed his shoulder tightly against the seat. The fur continued to burn; the searing pain did not diminish.

However, Krokhalev went on steering his plane along the mapped-out course, keeping careful check on the time because it was still necessary to take some photographs. Only when his task was completed did he turn his plane homeward. Never letting go of the stick, Krokhalev finally managed somehow to throw off his flying suit.

And only two hours later, having flown a long distance half naked in the terrible cold, Krokhalev successfully landed his plane at his own base.

Today, in the War for the Fatherland, once again the name of the Hero of the Soviet Union—Anatoly Krokhalev—resounds among those courageous and daring airmen who bring such disaster on their foe.

Once again Krokhalev pilots his plane deep into the enemy's territory. Just recently he was set the task of bombing the enemy's massed tanks. Nine Messerschmitts, like beasts of prey, threw themselves on six Soviet planes, just as our fliers approached their objective. The gunners-radio operators had their hands full. They raked the Hitlerite bandits with precise fire. The enemy failed to hinder the task; its tanks were destroyed by our bombers.

In this battle the Nazi pursuits attacked several times but their end was disastrous as demonstrated by several enemy planes suddenly tailspinning to the ground and finding their graves there.

And here is the latest report: in the Irbensk Straits navy planes under the command of Hero of the Soviet Union Anatoly Krokhalev destroyed a Nazi torpedo boat that had been damaged by Soviet ships. Following this flight, Krokhalev's men also smartly bombed a Nazi transport with its complement of men.

The Germans learned many a hard lesson in the Irbensk Straits. The Baltic sailors continually beat them there and in the present War for the Fatherland the enemy again has tried to reach the Straits. The Soviet Navy dealt the Nazi vermin a severe blow here and the Krokhalev group again finished the enemy.

Once again the Baltic fighters say:

"To fly and bomb like the airman Anatoly Krokhalev."

Krokhalev's sisters live and work in the city of Molotoff. They sent him the following telegram:

"Dear brother Tolya: We are proud that you are so fearless in your battles with the accursed Nazis. Bomb them to the very end—to complete annihilation. We swear that we will be worthy of you; we will work even harder. This will be our gift to aid the Red Army. Your sisters—Maria, Vera, Zoya, Evgenia."

On to Constanza!

Calm and impenetrable night reigns over the sea. Churned by the propellers, the water glints phosphorescently, foams, boils up in bubbles astern, noisily throwing up fountains of spray against the ship's side. Even more impetuous is the ship's progress. And it seems to Commander Melnikoff and to Artilleryman Khulga, who are standing on the ship's bridge, that the wind hasn't diminished at all—that it is sharp and fresh as before.

"It will soon be dawn," says the Captain.

"Lookouts to be reinforced." Lieutenant Khulga, the Captain, leans from the bridge as he issues the order to Red Navymen Ednovitzky and Doronin.

"As soon as land is sighted, report!"

"Aye, aye—report immediately."

Again the binoculars of the lookouts and the signalmen sweep the horizon's rim, the moonless sky, the becalmed waters.

"They are not expecting us," remarks the Captain. At that moment one of the observers reports:

"Land."

With the coming of dawn, the gray shore line stands out clearly. Now one can make out the lighthouse, the rooftops, and the camouflaged tops of the oil tanks.

The battle alarm resounded on the ship. Conversations ceased. Sailors and guns were on the alert. The task is clear and exact: destroy the German fuel tanks.

Senior Red Navyman Krapin pressed the button, as ordered, and the mighty gun salvo shook the air. The ship trembled slightly, momentarily careened to portside. The guns were immediately loaded again. Boatswain Kutsev was ready for the next shot two and a half seconds before the appointed time.

Flares illuminated the decks; shells whistled by. Pillars of flame rose on the shore and the fire's smoke began to blanket Constanza.

After a few shots, Khulga noticed weird disklike forms on the shore, undoubtedly camouflaged oil wells.

Khulga ordered guns trained on them. They went up in flames like giant bonfires.

At this time huge columns of water spouted between the shore and the ship—the Fascist batteries had opened fire.

Firing several shots at the Fascist batteries, Khulga again trained his guns on the round gray roofs of the oil wells; tongues of flame again shot skyward.

At the fifth gun Subbotin shouted joyfully:

"The oil cisterns are burning!"

Loud-speakers transmitted throughout the ship: "Cisterns are burning."

But again from the left side of the shore flames shot up. Two large enemy land batteries entered the fight. The explosions of their shells neared the ship.

Obedient to the voice of the Captain, the helmsman Leonoff masterfully shifted the wheel. The Nazi shells exploded away from the ship.

Battle orders have been fulfilled. The ship takes its departure.

Now the signalmen noticed that from the Constanza side three torpedo boats had started out, hugging the shore line and avoiding their own mines. Together with the coastal batteries they started disorderly shooting, but could not bring themselves to accept open combat.

Khulga left the tower. He knew that the enemy would try other methods, as well as artillery, against his ship.

"Trofimenko," he called.

The commander of the machine gunners stood before the Captain.

"Bring the sub machine gun."

The machine gunner understood. The commander was preparing personally to repulse the torpedo boats. In a minute there was a machine gun in Khulga's hands.

In the boiler room the sprayers whistle rhythmically, a yellow flame burns in the furnaces. Bathed in sweat, the boiler machinists silently listen to the sounds of the pumps, ventilators, to the motion of each sprayer. Here they are accustomed to understand one another without words, through economical hand gesture, by a look, a whistle.

Komsomol member Grebennikoff is in charge of one of the boilers. Steam unexpectedly began to settle—that means a pipe has burst somewhere. Grebennikoff instantly turns off the sprayer and lowers the pressure in the oil main.

The commander of the section, Bondarenko, orders him to open the manhole of the furnace and examine the pipes. Grebennikoff leaned over, his cheek on the floor: the pipe in the second row had burst. It was necessary to act fast.

An asbestos suit was brought down. Grebennikoff started to put it on, solicitously assisted by seamen Reznikoff, Kozloff, and Danilenko. When he was finally dressed, the doctor covered his face with vaseline and bandaged his head tightly, leaving only small slits for the eyes.

The water was drawn off and now he, Grebennikoff, had to penetrate into the red-hot interior of the furnace to plug up the broken pipe.

Grebennikoff, with the plugs, crawled into the steam accumulator. He located the opening of the first pipe by feeling with his hands, placed the stopper in it, and hammered it down. He held his breath and occasionally stuck his head out. Having caught his breath, he would crawl back. Finally, crawling on his belly, he penetrated into the water collector. Seaman Tarasoff was pouring water on him from the hose; the water would warm up and roll off the asbestos suit and his bandaged head in a hot stream.

In the accumulator steam formed from the water. Grebennikoff knew that if he fainted no one would be able to pull him out. He hurried. In seven minutes the pipe was plugged. The gauze dried immediately and when his head brushed against the walls of the boiler, he heard his hair crackle and his face became enveloped in steam.

The boiler was fixed.

The sun was already high above the sea.

"Scan the sky carefully," Khulga ordered the lookouts. He had barely finished speaking when one of the signalmen announced:

"Enemy planes to starboard."

Two planes were flying at high altitude. The sailors recognized them as twin-motored dive bombers.

"Open fire," Lieutenant Bespalko transmitted from the bridge.

The antiaircraft guns sounded together. The higher-flying bomber shook, went into a nose dive, and unable to get out of the line of fire, its black swastika flashed in the sunlight for the last time, plunged into the water.

The AA gunners now trained their fire on the second plane, and after the second salvo, it turned over and also fell into the water.

A moment of silence followed.

The signalmen watched the morning sky tirelessly. Soon a voice sounded again:

"Planes."

The planes glinted silverlike in the morning sunrays.

Vassilenko, a painter, and Khlynin, an officer of the line, immediately opened fire, barring their progress.

The planes turned from their course and discharged their bombs into the water.

The heat was terrific but there was no time to take off excessive clothes.

Again two Nazi planes appeared to starboard. The guns fired a few volleys and one plane was brought down. Air attacks continued steadily—the bombers swooped down like hawks—the guns thundered ceaselessly, with shells bursting in air.

The enemy planes could not withstand the hurricane fire and scattered across the sky. They began to attack the ship singly. Each time our fire drove them away.

Then the planes disappeared. The watches on the ship were carried on silently.

Khulga pointed out with a red flag the glimmering shadows of the bombers to the gunners. The noise of the volleys again swelled into a single sound.

The sailors delightedly watched the work of the AA gunners. One of the planes tried to come close, first from one side, then from the other—the gunners concentrated their fire on it. It swung around and resumed attacking. The gunners fired with fierce vigor. The plane jolted and went down. But others took its place. The raiders came to the attack from the sun's side. Khulga looked over his AA gunners. They were awaiting his command and Khulga raised the little red flag. The guns went off. The green balls flared up and went out in the blinding light of the east. The whole ship's antiaircraft artillery and machine guns now fired at the brilliant disk of the sun. The planes did not appear. The signalmen saw them after they had come out of the attack formation, on the side.

"They haven't succeeded, and never will."

No sooner were the attacking planes beaten off than white

threads of torpedo tracks became attached to the ship. The Captain turned the ship sharply and the torpedo passed, astern. Melnikoff again made a turn and this time another torpedo cut across the prow, along the ship's course.

Planes appeared overhead again.

A huge four-engined bomber, flanked by escorting fighters, led the formation. The gunners were ready but Khulga kept his little red flag down. He saw the gunners' impatience; their faces were dirty and sweaty and only the whites of their eyes shone out from their itching faces. Khulga carefully scanned the outlines of the machines and the wrinkled bridge of his nose gradually straightened out. It was one of our own heavy bombers. Tipping its mighty wings, it circled over the ship and signaled:

"You are in enemy submarine-infested waters."

The planes disappeared. The water again churned with traces of the torpedo boats. The artillery opened fire. The diving shells sent up smoky pillars of water. After the fourth volley, a column of black smoke shot up and the torpedo boat did not appear any more.

The ship victoriously returned to its native shores. Several days later the entire crew gathered on the quarterdeck and listened with great emotion to Comrade Stalin's radio speech. Then and there it was decided to send a letter to Moscow to him who inspired the men to battle and in whose name they scored their victory.

The letter began thus:

"Dear Iossif Vissarionovich:

"In encounters with the enemy we have tried our strength, tested our ranks. Our artillerists calmly and accurately trained their guns on the military objectives of Constanza, setting them on fire and demolishing them. Our antiaircraft gunners accurately fired on the enemy planes, dispatching three of them down to the bottom of our Black Sea. We faithfully carried out our captain's orders.

"Having listened to your speech, we all want to tell you one thing: in this struggle of our people against the Fascist barbarism, the Soviet sailors will take a place worthy of them.

"We are ready for the battle! Our ranks will not falter before any enemy forces."

How We Bombed Ploeşti

Captain A. Sovin and Lieutenant I. Chuproff tell of their battle encounters:

The sea was shrouded in thick clouds. It was impossible to penetrate them and it became necessary to fly the planes blind, by instruments.

When the enemy territory was sighted, the thick mass of fog ended but thunderstorm clouds appeared repeatedly. From the elapsed time, we judged that we had already arrived at our objective but nothing was visible as yet. To the left of the plane the rays of five searchlights cut through the darkness. No other objective was near. Therefore, our navigators' calculations were accurate. This was Ploeşti—the target of our bombs.

Here we decided to apply military cunning. Our bombers kept their course. The whirr of our motors going southward was detected from the ground. The Fascist AA guns laid a strong barrage in that direction. But we had already succeeded in turning, and made our way to the oil fields. The navigator, Major V. Libanidze, made the final calculations.

We began bombing. At such a moment one does not feel how or when the plane becomes free of its cargo of bombs, so keyed up are the nerves of each flier.

When Major Libanidze finished bombing, Senior Lieutenant Kordonsky began. The enemy's searchlights began to catch our planes, the AA guns opened fire. Shells were bursting very close. The bombs had already been released, so we could change our course and get away from the antiaircraft guns and search- lights. We did take our leave. Far below, the oil fields were aflame.

"Look what's happening there," said Libanidze, his voice sounding complete gratification. He could plainly make out the raging sea of fire.

During this whole flight, the navigator, Major Libanidze, working with his customary thoroughness, brought the planes exactly to their destination—Ploeşti.

Regarding the raids by Soviet planes on Ploeşti, one of the participants in the fighting, Navigator M. Kordonsky, relates:

All of us who took part in the bombing of Ploeşti had one wish—how best to discharge our responsibilities, to make the bombing blow most effective.

The navigators worked very hard on this flight. The weather was bad. We had to make our way through banks of clouds for a long time; the visibility was so poor that it was impossible to distinguish land from water. We had to work in complete darkness, not even daring to turn on the cabin lights lest we unmask ourselves.

When our planes were discovered by the enemy searchlights, Captain Sovin and Lieutenant Chuproff used masterly combat cunning, thanks to which we fooled the Fascists. It was very pleasant to work under the direction of such an experienced navigator as Major Libanidze. His calculations were absolutely right as to time and place.

We navigators and gunners-radio operators were able to ob- serve directly over the objective the results of our work. Un- fortunately, the pilots couldn't look down—they were too busy maneuvering, getting out of the way of searchlight beams and bursting AA shells.

Below us huge flames shot up, embracing a distance of about two and a half square kilometers. Those were the oil fields on fire, where we dropped our "gift" to the Hitler monsters.

"These are swell presents," delightedly said Gunner-Radio Operator Mikhail Nikitich Drobot. This fine expert was greatly cheered on seeing the results of our bombing.

Satisfied, we returned to our own shores, to our own airdrome. The next day we were flying again, and again bombing enemy objectives.

The Rout of a Nazi Landing Party

Our naval planes discovered a powerful caravan of Nazi vessels in a certain part of the Baltic Sea. There were transports filled with troops, tanks, and ammunition, a strong detail of torpedo boats, trawlers, and other convoys. Flocks of Messerschmitts hovered over them.

Our fliers reported the presence of the enemy to their headquarters.

The first blow to the Nazi caravan was delivered by the Soviet coast artillery. The men and officers of the Red Navy fired heavily and tellingly at the Fascist pirates. These blows grew stronger by the minute. Meanwhile, torpedo boats were rushing to the place of battle. As usual, they attacked the enemy suddenly and from a direction whence they were least expected. Launching impetuous assaults, the torpedo cutters struck one objective after another.

Soon great fires flared up on many enemy boats, the result of accurate artillery and torpedo shots.

The roar of engines filled the air, as our heavy bombers fell upon the Nazis. A squadron of light ships, which had hurried to the scene, now joined the battle.

Attack! Co-ordinated, simultaneous blows were struck at the Nazis from the shore, the sea, and the air. Here was manifested all the splendid training of the Baltic contingent—their energy, courage, and maneuverability. The blows continued all night— one after another, and one after another the Nazi transports vanished to the bottom. Soldiers, ammunition, tanks went under, but the Baltic attacks would not let up.

With each transport sunk, they became fiercer. Panic developed among the enemy fleet. Forced off their course, having lost their direction, the German boats got into one another's way, straggled in various directions. Some of them ran aground.

Like a hurricane the Soviet pursuit planes attacked them— the fire of torpedo boats and coastal batteries was merciless. More, and then again! Tons of fire and steel came from the bombers. Bombs, torpedoes, and shells accurately hit their marks, breaking their hulls and turning the ships over. Already thirteen transports with everything they had aboard were at the bottom of the sea. The same fate was meted out to two destroyers and a barge with tanks. The remaining transports and a damaged destroyer were enveloped in flames and a black curtain of smoke rising skyward hid the clear blue horizon.

News of the victory immediately spread to the naval base, to all the fortresses and ships, arousing new energy and heightening the desire for a speedy smashup of the maddened Fascists.

"We'll turn the heat on," say the sailors. "They'll find out what the Red Banner Baltic Fleet is like."

In this important engagement hundreds of Red Navy sailors and officers achieved a complete victory over the enemy without any losses to themselves.

HOW THE GERMANS FIGHT

They Turn Their Backs

Participants in the war recount the methods of the vanguard of the Nazi troops whose task it is to make "lightning breakthroughs" against their enemy.

"Everything depends on self-control and endurance," say our fighters. "Under no circumstances should one overestimate the enemy. It is essential to observe and understand his methods and then find the proper countermeasures."

In actual combat everything turned out to be somewhat simpler than we had expected. The attacking tactic of the Hitlerites is the same. It is mainly based upon psychological factors, on creating the impression that a huge, tempestuous, irresistible force—with great firing power—is attacking you.

How do the Hitlerites operate?

On the sector marked out for the break-through, they throw a detachment of motorcyclists. We have become acquainted with them. These are young men, almost boys, of eighteen or nineteen, wild and ready for anything but not particularly stable. Some of them stimulate their daring with alcohol.

At a good speed of 70 to 80 kilometers an hour—depending on the terrain—they rush on the roads and fields, keeping everything before them under a continuous downpour of machine-gun fire. The shooting is terrific—there are no words to describe it—the roar and noise are overwhelming. But there is not much sense to it. At such speeds the motorcyclist can see little of what is before him and actually his mission is very different; it is to arouse panic.

We have become adroit in picking them off their machines with accuracy and, what is even more important, with calmness.

It is a remarkable business. Such a seemingly terrific offensive lunge, and yet it is only necessary for about a dozen of the vanguardists to fall and these "lightning troops" turn back with lightning rapidity, stepping on the gas with all their speed. Note this, just in case: it is even easier to catch them with an automatic as they turn.

After the first such attack, we busied ourselves at night with our forward zone of defense. We dug a series of simple small ditches about half a meter wide, no wider (otherwise they are noticeable). In some places we felled trees and mobilized all kinds of techniques, all of them available to any guerrilla detachment, to any army unit, or any tiny village—stones, catapults, all manner of unpleasantness. We covered all roads, paths, and fields.

The next attack of the frenzied youths "did not materialize," as they say.

Regarding attacks of the infantry, the tactics are the same— an attempt at moral pressure. Wild firing from automatics, quick determined marching, sometimes on the run, and the savage, hoarse cries of *"Hoch! Heil!"* to brace themselves and intimidate the enemy. But again it's the same story. Firing, as it were, "from the belly"—shooting in different directions with the butt on hip, while on the march. The impression created is as if they fire with their eyes shut. What is the purpose of such fire? To give the impression of a tremendous squall of fire impossible to suppress—to induce collapse, panic, disorganization, loss of morale in their opponents.

The best means of meeting it is again—calmness, self-control, and steady and accurate shooting. You are undercover; actually, this savage shooting so terrible on the ears is not really very dangerous. You choose your adversary and plant a bullet in his breast. Always remember one thing: your one precise shot is worth hundreds of bullets of this theatrical squall.

And the outcome is the same: as soon as the Nazis are aware of a stubborn defense and steady fire, as soon as they see a dozen or two of shriekers fall side by side, they crawl back; "the attack did not materialize."

Then we pass into a Soviet, a Red Army counterattack.

It has become clear that the Nazis can't stand our counter-attacks. This horde, accustomed to the paralyzing effects of its "mighty blow," is unable to withstand an opponent who means business.

You make out rising figures. Don't forget to stop and plant a bullet in their backs. Sometimes they throw up their hands and in the same savage tone cry out:

"Schiessen nicht!"

All these cheap stunts with wild automatic and machine-gun fire of the motorcyclists are aimed mainly at destroying morale, disorganizing our fighters, bringing about terror and panic, making steady shooting impossible, routing detachments, and clearing the roads, cutting wedges in the enemy's position.

The deduction from this is clear:

Do not be influenced by this theatrical effect with its powerful but disorganized shooting. Meet the attack calmly and firmly, building obstacles in the defense zone.

You just lie still, as though you are watching them in the movies—we advise one another. Lie still, make your selection, and shoot. Don't think that this avalanche will stop only when all of them are stricken down. Not at all! If you knock out two or three dozen of them, the rest will drop prone and there's your chance, brother.

The Hitlerite soldiers are brought up in the certainty that such an attack with the fire of the automatics is irresistible. Perhaps that's how they took, by terror, the French and the Belgians, brave fighters but unstable. Our fighter is not like that. It is important for him to assimilate the enemy's tactics, to analyze what the enemy is attempting. Once this is understood, our fighter does his job with firmness and exactness. Our task, the Red Army's task, is clear: to understand and to smash the enemy.

"Don't Shoot, We Surrender!"

This is what M. Zagrebelny, member of a tank crew, relates:

At dawn the Nazi shells came down on our frontier parking spaces and garages. But the treacherous foe miscalculated. Our tanks and automobiles were not at all in the parking spaces and garages. They were in the neighboring forest well camouflaged and well hidden.

Hitler's cutthroats soon felt the power of our tanks on their own skins. Our tanks destroyed the Hitlerites like mad dogs. German bullets could not stop us. One of our tanks came right up to a Nazi gunfire. Three enemy artillerymen were killed; the remaining four lay on the ground with their faces pressed into the earth; we took them prisoners.

When one sector was cleared of the enemy, a tall man in a Red Army coat with a major's insignia came up and asked sharply:

"Where is your detachment?"

"There," unhesitatingly answered a Red Armyman. "Get in and I'll drive you over."

The stranger boldly strode to the tank in order to enter the hatch, but the Red Armymen, to whom the "major" appeared suspicious, wouldn't let him ride inside. They made him climb on top and as soon as the "major" got there, the machine raced to headquarters at fourth speed.

The man in the Red Army uniform, speaking Russian well, turned out to be a German diversionist sent by the enemy to destroy the communications of our unit. The vigilance of the Red Armymen helped to expose the foul enemy.

The Red Armyman, V. Tikhomiroff, tells how the Nazis dread our bayonet charge:

The German infantrymen "bravely" deal with the civilian population; they shoot men and women collective farmers, burn their homes, and drive away the cattle. Before retreating from one village, the German officers seized and forcibly led away ten young girls. Escaping from a small settlement, the Germans machine-gunned the peasant horses. But the "bravery" of the Hitlerites disappears when it comes to bayonet fighting.

Behind our detachment enemy shells were exploding while ahead the machine guns kept up their stormy fire. We were suffering losses but continued to press forward. However, the Germans did not accept the attack. When they were menaced by bayonets, they ran for all they were worth. Junior Lieutenant Nefedoff, with three fighters, captured a group of firing soldiers. These threw down their arms and loudly begged for mercy. They begged so abjectly that it was impossible to recognize the "heroes" who mowed down the civilian population.

During the attack we heard the following cries in broken Russian:

"Comrades, don't shoot. We are Czechs."

Standing before us were Czechs dressed in the gray German jerseys. One of them shouted to us:

"Comrades, we go against our will; we are covered by the German bayonet!"

After a ten-kilometer thrust, recounts a regimental-school student, Komsomol member I. Litovetz, we met a German detachment. We hid in the rye and crawled forward. About 300 meters away the Germans opened heavy automatic and machine-gun fire. We were also shot at from the trees where the soldiers and officers sat. A ferocious hatred for the enemy impelled us forward. No one feared death. Our machine gunners worked splendidly. At one point a whole swarm of Germans rose and tried to push forward but they didn't achieve any kind of attack —the heavy fire of our machine guns soon mowed down a large number of the Germans and pressed the rest down to the ground. Now we went into attack; here the Nazis, in spite of their superior numbers, immediately wavered. Our platoon charged into a ditch where some sixty Hitlerites had dug in. One of our contingents never ceased firing while others fell upon the men in the ditches from the flank. Out of sixty soldiers and officers, only one dared raise his flat bayonet but lowered it immediately. The rest threw down their arms and yelled in German:

"Don't shoot; we surrender."

Out of the black glossy helmets there peered terrified bestial faces; with trembling hands they threw off their equipment and little bags with biscuits.

"See what's in their flasks," ordered our commander.

We opened one flask and rum poured out of it. Alcohol is in the arsenal of the Hitler army, just as it is in any band of highwaymen.

At several points the Germans tried to run away. Our young military students caught them and finished them off mercilessly. Where the regimental school operated, we gathered more than fifty bicycles abandoned by the Germans, many automatic weapons, mine throwers, and a cannon. The prisoners were sent to the rear under guard.

Two Photographs

A German tank was damaged by a well-thrown grenade bunch. It stopped with torn-up caterpillar but continued firing. A shell, destroying its turret, nailed it to the ground.

Two of its crew jumped out but were immediately mowed down by machine-gun bullets. The tank stood some fifty meters away from the Soviet trenches, deprived of its crew, silent and harmless.

In the evening when it became dark over the battlefield, when the whole ground was covered with the smoldering hulks of the burnt, shot, and mine-exploded German tanks, our soldiers approached the machine they had damaged.

They climbed into the tank.

Amid the shells and machine-gun bullets they stumbled on something soft. When they pulled out their find into the light, it proved to be some cloth marked "Belostok."

There was a great deal of cloth—an awful lot of it. There was enough to make five suits for each member of the tank's crew.

A huge heavy roll of brown cloth, all of one color.

Enough for five brown suits apiece for each of the three men.

To be sure, no one needs five brown suits at once. But a thief does not stop to reason, a thief has no time—he must look quickly, otherwise time may come to turn back before his job is done.

It certainly must have been heavy and uncomfortable dragging around that bolt of material from the looted warehouse.

Presumably all three of them had to carry it, pausing frequently to catch their breath. But later there must have arisen the fateful question of where to put the cloth? To leave it in the baggage train was dangerous, for the enemy was already raiding baggage trains.

They decided to drag the whole thing into the tank. True, that wasn't altogether convenient, but that was all right—perhaps their marksmanship would be somewhat impaired, but the cloth would always be at their side—fifty meters of brown cloth of very high quality.

Dragged across the trap door with difficulty, it was finally placed in the tank.

It is much easier with shoes and ladies' slippers stolen direct from the stores. These are easy to carry and to stow away.

There appeared to be lots of room in the tank, as if it were especially adapted for hiding ladies' slippers.

Finally ladies' underwear was loaded in the tank—silk nightgowns, etc., unlike the cloth, of many different colors; but the main thing was that there were lots of it.

They stuck the underwear wherever they could; it was easy to handle and it scarcely wrinkled. Part of it they placed right on their seats. Thus they went into battle, seated on ladies' underwear.

And here are the personal kits of the crew.

They loved to have their photographs taken, these looters. They had their pictures taken in Denmark and in Holland, in Belgium and in Greece. They posed for photographs and they looted. They looted and they posed for photographs.

They were photographed in most military poses, either stiff and choking in uniform or half naked in accordance with their meager conception of ancient times, like a group of gladiators.

However, most of the photographs included bottles.

Standing up, bottle in hand.

Seated at a table covered with bottles.

Lying on the floor, next to bottles.

And now comes the last picture. It was apparently taken

before the start of a campaign. All three stand next to their machine; on the turret the tank's number—514—shows plainly.

The last picture: all three are smiling; they had been promised a merry campaign, a light military excursion.

Beg pardon, that isn't the last picture. The last picture is taken by a Soviet newspaper photographer.

He stands in front of the tank with its smashed and burned Nazi emblem. He snaps a picture of the knocked-out tank and of the two Red Armymen who destroyed it.

The Red Armymen hold the heavy rolls of Belostok cloth against the background of the tank. They have unrolled it so that everyone can see how much these three Nazi looters needed, these three Fascist thieves who now need only six feet of ground apiece.

According to the information received from the Soviet guerrillas, heroically fighting in the Nazi rear, the bestiality of the Hitlerites in occupied territory becomes more and more monstrous. On July 13, Nazi tankmen captured three Soviet scouts of a guerrilla unit. The young partisans refused to identify themselves or give any information regarding the whereabouts of their encampment. No amount of beating by a German officer elicited any information from them.

Partisan Alexander Samokhin was put under the tank caterpillar track and threatened with being run over if he did not disclose the detachment's whereabouts. The threat of a painful death, however, did not break the hero's spirit. Then the enraged Fascists tied the partisans' feet to the tank and let the machine go through the brushwood at top speed. The mutilated bodies of the heroes were picked up at night by the partisans.

The Storm Troop detachments sent by Hitler to the Eastern front play the role of executioners. After capturing a group of collective farmers from the "Free Labor" Village Co-operative, the Hitlerite cannibals beat them brutally with whips of steel wire tipped with lead. After they had lost consciousness, they were thrown into a heap, kerosene was poured over them, and they were set on fire.

A few kilometers away from the collective farm, the Fascists captured a field hospital in which lay twenty-three gravely wounded Red Armymen. The Storm Troopers questioned them in the hope of securing information regarding the disposition and fire power of the Red Army units. Failing, the infuriated Fascists tortured the wounded for two hours, tearing off their bandages and finally stringing them up on telegraph poles along the village street.

Reports of the Soviet Information Bureau

The heroic resistance of the Red Army arouses the greatest fury of the German Fascists. They try to wreak their fury on the wounded Red Armymen. German fighter planes, like hawks, aim even at lone stretcher-bearers collecting the wounded from the battlefields. In the town of Postav, a Nazi light bomber machine-gunned stretcher-bearers carrying wounded men, in spite of the fact that the German flier clearly saw their Red Cross markings. The Fascists are especially brutal with the wounded Red Armymen. Escaping from a nightmare of Hitler captivity, Sergeant I. Karasev reported the wild orgies of the Fascists over four seriously wounded prisoners of war. One of the wounded soldiers, who categorically refused to answer any questions of a military nature, had his hands cut off and his eyes put out by order of the commanding officer. The remaining three Red Armymen, weakened by loss of blood, were scalded

with boiling water and then gored with bayonets by the executioners.

The maddened Fascists criminally violate the international
law relating to the treatment of wounded soldiers. A wounded
Red Armyman, Zudin, snatched from Fascist captivity by Soviet
troops, told of the inhuman treatment meted to the wounded by
the Nazis. Together with Red Armyman Fedoroff, he was captured while in a field hospital. After refusal to answer questions
regarding the whereabouts of the Red Army units, the wounded
were beaten and subjected to bestial tortures. An officer personally tortured Fedoroff. He burned Fedoroff's hands through
with a heated bayonet, stuck him in the chest and back. Failing
to obtain an answer, he finally shot him. Zudin was tortured by
an officer of the Storm Troopers, who chopped off several of his
fingers, pierced the palm of his right hand, and put out an eye.

By a sudden attack in the N region, the Soviet troops destroyed two battalions of German infantry. Three hundred and
twenty German soldiers and officers were captured. Amongst
the trophies were six antitank guns, four mine throwers, twelve
motorcycles, radio apparatus, and ammunition. In the knapsacks of some of the German soldiers were found gold and silver
objects looted from various captured cities. Corporal Otto Oppel
had on him eight gold and silver watches, twelve wedding rings,
and various ecclesiastical silver articles.

DESERTERS AND PRISONERS OF WAR

The Story of German Soldier Alfred Liskof

I am in Soviet Russia. My mind doesn't immediately grasp
this simple and happy thought.

The desire to run away from the hated world of Hitler horrors was long growing in my mind. But I had to wait for an opportune moment. This opportune moment arrived.

I was serving as a soldier in the small border town of Tiliach not far from the Soviet town of Sokali. Even before the memorable day, June 22, we all felt that something big was being prepared. But what?

Could it be war with the Soviet Union? I asked myself. Is it possible that this crazy Hitler would throw himself into this wild adventure?

I decided to desert to the Soviet Union. I waited until the order for attack was given and at night swam across. On the Soviet bank I immediately fell into the hands of the border guards. There I was well received. I was given clothes, shoes, and food.

All this was unlike the tales of horror the German soldiers were told. Every soldier is told by the Nazi that he must not give himself up, because in Soviet Russia he could expect only torture, horrors, and a frightful death. This is an insolent lie, calculated to scare the German soldier. In Soviet Russia prisoners of war are treated as German Fascists never did and never will treat such prisoners.

And so, I have left behind me a fatherland groaning under the yoke of Fascism, hungry, experiencing the horrors of a war into which the accursed Hitler and his cutthroats plunged it. The people are dejected. They go hungry, but no one dares to complain or to confide his troubles with a neighbor, because the same terror reigns among the civilian people as in the army itself.

In the ranks of the German Army, where I myself was not so long ago, the mood is also one of depression. But everyone is afraid to share his thoughts with others. The soldiers have been taught to distrust each other. No one expresses his thoughts aloud but hides them deep inside himself. A soldier represents a split personality—one that can be seen from the outside, the other that is in everyone's heart. A soldier is afraid to share his secret thoughts because death and the Gestapo await him.

The officer's cane and the threat of court-martial force German soldiers to fight, but they do not want this war; they thirst for peace, as the whole German population thirsts for it.

Now that I am in Soviet Russia I want to say this to my erstwhile comrades:

German soldiers, workers, peasants, men and women! What did Hitler give you? What did Fascism bring you? A life of fear, inhuman deprivation, hunger, poverty, and death. Where is your peaceful work, where are your brothers, husbands, and sons? Bloody Hitler took everything away from you. How long will you stand for that? How long will your immeasurable suffering continue? Hitler dragged you into a new war, against the Soviet Union. In this war Fascism shall find its doom.

Here in the Soviet Union I saw a people of many millions who rose up as one to destroy Fascism.

German soldiers! It is your duty to help destroy Fascism quicker. Turn your bayonets against Hitler and his clique that rule Germany now. This will be a holy task on your part. Peace will come, peace for which the German people thirst, and hated Fascism will be destroyed forever!

Alfred Liskof

> Born in the town of Kolverk, a worker in the furniture factory of Willi Tatzik.

Four German Aviators' Appeal

On June 25 four German airmen came down behind the lines in a dive bomber, Junkers-88. They were: Corporal Hans Her-

Looking over equipment abandoned by Germans on the field of battle

man, born in 1916 in the town of Breslau in Central Silesia; Observer Hans Kratz, born in 1917 at Frankfort-on-the-Main; Senior Corporal Adolf Appel, born in 1918 in Brünn, Moravia; and Radio Operator Wilhelm Schmidt, born in 1917 in the town of Regensburg. This crew was a part of the Second Group of the 54th Escadrille. These fliers landed voluntarily and addressed the following letter to all German airmen and soldiers:

To all German airmen and soldiers:

We German fliers—Commander Hans Herman, Observer Hans Kratz, Gunner Adolf Appel, Radio Operator Wilhelm Schmidt—have flown together for almost a year.

In the past we have flown a Ju-88 to bomb London, Portsmouth, Plymouth, and other cities in England.

Before that we had flown over French cities. Now we were sent to bomb peaceful Russian towns.

We often asked ourselves the question: why is Hitler fighting the whole world? Why does he want to bring death and ruin to all the peoples of the world? Why do the flower of the German people have to die from bullets fired by peoples defending their native land?

No one gave us an answer to this question. We saw each time that the Hitler-started war brought only ill luck and death to all the peoples of Europe, including the German people.

We were often worried by the thought that many innocent women and children perished from our bombs because of this bloody cur, Hitler.

Therefore, this time we dropped our bombs in such a way as to do no harm. We had long harbored the idea of running away from Hitler and of beginning a peaceful life, but we were afraid.

Now that Hitler has declared war on Russia, in which he will doubtless lose his head, we decided to attempt an escape.

On June 25 our group flew to Kiev.

We dropped our bombs in the Dnieper and landed near the city.

We were surprised to be immediately surrounded by armed peasants who took us prisoner.

This again convinced us that the Soviet people are united as one man and that they are prepared for this struggle and will win.

Now we are in Russia. We are well treated here.

Brother airmen and soldiers, follow our example. Leave Hitler the Killer, and come over here to Russia.

Hans Herman

Hans Kratz

Adolf Appel

Wilhelm Schmidt.

Erkki Noontinen and Unto Seppiyalia

Erkki Noontinen and Unto Seppiyalia are workingmen from Helsinki. A little over a month ago they were called to the army along with many other workers who were needed by the White Guard Finns for a new faith-breaking military adventure against the U.S.S.R.

These two workers met in the First Howitzer Battery and decided they had no business fighting for alien interests. Each one vowed to cross over to the Soviet Union as soon as he had an opportunity. A few days after the bandit attack upon the U.S.S.R., Erkki Noontinen and Unto Seppiyalia made their way to the Soviet border. As soon as they crossed the frontier an advance patrol caught them.

These workers dressed in soldiers' uniforms sit down and indignantly tell about life in a land enslaved by German-Finnish Fascism:

"The aims of this war are deeply alien to the people," says Erkki Noontinen. "In Finland all men born between 1921 and 1897 are mobilized. The people do not want this war. Men desert and hide in forests and at their relatives'! At most mobilization points no more than twenty-five per cent appeared. The workers don't need this war. The people of Finland realize it more and more. Peasants and workers are beginning to understand that the war will bring incredible privations.

"It has become particularly difficult to exist lately. There is not enough food, unemployment is increasing, and the cost of living is going up. Now they have brought in the Germans. Our soldiers say about them:

" 'Why did they bring the Germans to us? To eat our bread, and we haven't enough of it ourselves. The Soviet Union will not give us anything now.'

"Food in the army is worse lately. Toward evening the soldiers feel hungry. There is no tobacco at all."

At the end of his story, Erkki Noontinen excitedly declares:

"I didn't want to fight the Soviet Union. And many thousands of our soldiers are like me and my comrade, Unto Seppiyalia."

"Our people have been intimidated and deceived by tales about the Soviet Union for many years now," says Unto Seppiyalia. "The police suppress brutally every attempt of the people to express their true wish—to stop the war and to expel its instigators from our land.

"We know that our example will be willingly followed by many soldiers. They don't want to fight. Wishing to tell the truth about the Soviet Union and about the real culprits of the war, we have written an appeal to soldiers of the Finnish Army. Here it is."

He takes out sheets of paper covered with penciled script. The real thoughts of the Finnish workers are not controlled here by

Fascist dictatorship and terror. Erkki Noontinen and Unto Seppiyalia write:

"Finnish soldiers! We, soldiers of the Finnish Army, Unto
Seppiyalia and Erkki Noontinen, have of our own will deserted
to the side of the Soviet Union. When we crossed the border,
we were met as comrades and were given plenty of good food.

"We didn't want war but the government of Finland sold our
country's independence to the German Fascists and forced us to
go into this insane war against the Soviet Union, which did not
start it.

"You have read and heard of the poverty and suffering the
Germans have brought upon the lands conquered by them pre-
viously. You know in what slavery live the peoples of Norway,
Holland, and Belgium, of Czechoslovakia and other countries.

"The Nazis could not give them anything else but hunger and
barbed-wire blind alleys. They are preparing the same for
Finland.

"We, your comrades, ask you to stop this bloody slaughter
and come over to this side, to the side of the Soviet troops, so
that together with the Soviet Union we can drive the Nazi enemy
out of our land and that traitorous Finnish government too.

"We guarantee that you will be well received here. You will
get plenty of food and will be well treated here.

> "Soldiers of the First Battery, Third Brigade,
> Second Army Corps
> Erkki Noontinen and Unto Seppiyalia."

Rumanian Soldiers Don't Want to Fight

A group of shabby, unshaved, and dirty men has been brought
into the room. These are prisoners of war. Everyone has his
own specialty, his own biography. But irrespective of their age

and trade, their stories agree on one thing: they reveal a picture of Fascist debauch and lawlessness reigning in Rumania, and the overwhelming dissatisfaction of Rumanian workers with the existing regime. Rumanian workers, peasants, and white-collar employees, dressed in soldiers' uniforms, don't want war—they do not want to shed their blood for the sake of the Fascist vultures.

At the table is soldier Toma X. He is twenty-five years old. He has spent one fifth of his life in the army. He is well acquainted with the "charms" of a soldier's life in "Greater Rumania." Hunger, want, no human rights but mockery—the thin, worn-out soldier has had more than enough of all these.

"I don't remember a single instance," says X frankly, "when I had enough to eat in all my time of service in the Rumanian Army. Only now in time of war the Rumanian Army has adopted 'intensified' feeding: every twenty-four hours a soldier gets a loaf of black bread weighing about five hundred to six hundred grams. Dinner consists of pea or potato soup. There is no second course. Meat is given only twice a week, but it is issued in such negligible rations that a soldier hardly recognizes a 'meat day.' For supper, pea or potato soup again.

"After the occupation," says X, "Germany robbed Rumania to the bone. Practically all bread was requisitioned from the peasants. Not so long ago my relatives wrote in a letter that the last of their corn was taken away from them."

Another soldier, Vassili P., told about dissatisfaction with the war started by the Hitlerite clique, of unwillingness to shed their blood for the interests of the wealthy adventurers and Fascist bandits.

"The soldiers were not told the truth," he said. "Even when we were driven by order of Hitler into the war with the Soviet Union, we were deceived basely. Forty of us were rounded up, and the commander of the battalion declared that Soviet Russia

had decided to return Bessarabia to Rumania and that the Red
Army was departing to the old border. 'We,' said the commander of the battalion, 'have been ordered to cross the Prut
in order to verify whether the Red Army departed and to organize a guard against plunder.' Not suspecting anything, we went
into the boats and began to cross the Prut. The commanding
lieutenant remained on our shore. But when we approached the
Soviet shore, a storm of fire descended upon us. We tried to run
back, but when we saw that we were surrounded by Red Armymen, we surrendered."

The Rumanian flier B. declared:

"We were ordered to go out to bomb a Soviet airdrome. But
it did not materialize, as in the first air battle, Soviet interceptors drove us off, and two of our machines, including mine,
fell to the ground.

"About the Soviet fliers," continued B., "I can say this: If
they are all like those we met in the first battle, unlucky is anyone who goes up against them!"

Soldiers Are Driven to Fight for Hated Fascism

A unit of the Red Army took up battle positions on the bank
of the river N. At midday the fighters lying in the trenches noticed that two white handkerchiefs rose behind a hillock.

"Don't take your eyes off them! This is a signal," the commander said to the observers.

The white handkerchiefs slowly approached the line of fighters and in a few seconds men with raised arms quickly ran to
the Soviet trenches.

These were corporals of the Third Battalion, 178th Infantry
Regiment, Berlin Division, Radio Operator Hans Zippel and
Motorcyclist Rut Grosser. They were both born in Berlin. Each

was twenty-seven years old. Three years ago they were drafted into the army and later sent to war by the Nazi cannibals.

At this moment, Zippel and Grosser are sharing their thoughts and reminiscences. They talk angrily about the Hitlerite pack of curs hated by the people.

When the 178th Infantry Regiment was transferred to Rumania, Grosser said to his friend:

"I think that Hitler is starting a new scurvy trick."

The corporal was not mistaken. A day passed—and Hitler's order to march on the Soviet Union was read to the soldiers.

"Our army will perish," Zippel said to his comrade. "Hitler will choke with our blood."

Several days later the soldiers in the Third Battalion, secretly from the officers, passed from hand to hand a leaflet—the call of the four German pilots who flew over to the Soviet Union.

"These are real people, Hans," Grosser meaningfully said. "Be ready!"

The friends understood each other and embraced. The following day the Berlin printer, Rut Grosser, and the postman of the Central German Post Office, Hans Zippel, deserted to the Soviet side.

"The German soldiers keep quiet," say the prisoners. "They are quiet because if any of them should express his thoughts out loud, he would be immediately beheaded or hanged. They all understand that the German army will be smashed. Fascism will be destroyed. The happiness of the people is in the destruction of Fascism. The most horrible thing is in the fact that the Hitlerites send millions of Germans to a sure death, and in the fact that the soldiers have to die for the hated Fascist regime!"

Grosser and Zippel requested the transmission of a letter to their native land in which they say:

"German soldiers and the German people do not want war. They want peaceful work and quiet. German soldiers! Follow our example! Unite and fight Hitler and Fascism, for peace, for progress, for a free Germany."

A Beast in a Cage

He has just been captured. His face is red from the wind and excitement. His small, bleary eyes are bloodshot. His fingers contract spasmodically.

At night his battalion treacherously and thievishly fell upon a border outpost. The battalion of Finnish regular infantry was thrown back by the courageous border guards. The enemy left behind dead and wounded. Lauri Vilgo Yarvilainen together with several other soldiers was captured. He fought with his bayonet, bit, scratched like a wildcat, tried to run away, but nothing helped.

He, Lauri Vilgo Yarvilainen, expected different treatment as a prisoner—mockery and blows, as practiced in Finland. But the decent treatment of the Soviet military doesn't influence his actions or the flow of his thoughts.

He prevaricates, hopelessly prevaricates, evasive like a rabbit throwing his pursuers off his track. From his crafty but stupid lies one thing is irrefutably clear: before us is a finished specimen of a Fascist—most rabid enemy of the Soviet Union. This is not a deceived, frightened Finnish peasant or lumberjack. No. He is, if you please, a master of philosophy, and a teacher of higher mathematics. He is a graduate of the faculty of philosophy in Turku (Åbo). He knows several languages.

It is true that at first he declared that he only spoke Finnish. Then he forgot himself and began to speak German. But about the Germans concentrating their forces in Finland he doesn't know anything, you see. Here the master of philosophy becomes very naïve, like a child.

"Permit us, please; this is a fact known to the whole world."

"I don't read newspapers," says the master, lowering his gaze. "I'm interested only in mathematics. Abstract figures and philosophy."

"Why did you join the Elite Corps if you are not interested in politics?"

"For the sport's sake. I adore skiing."

And to what sort of philosophy does this lover of pure reason adhere?

The same "philosophy" to which highwaymen adhere: rob, burn, and destroy.

At night, Yarvilainen confesses, the Elite Corps men gathered in the woods at the Soviet border, secretive, like robbers setting out on a "job." Here in the woods they were given weapons and uniforms. They were told that it was necessary to attack the Soviet border.

Weapons in their hands, the Elite Guards and soldiers suddenly lunged upon our posts.

The finale of this enterprise took an unexpected and very sad turn for the master. The pockets of this gentleman philosopher are full of red and green banknotes. These are Tsarist and Denikin currencies. Why does he at the front need these museum pieces, "redbacks" and "Ekaterinki" issued by Nicholas II?

Somewhat embarrassed, the Elite Corps trooper confesses that, banking on an easy victory and the restoration of the Tsarist power, he planned to put this money into circulation and bring back from Russia as a trophy a kilogram or two of caviar.

So that is what professors of the Kyander and Ryti gang taught in the Finnish universities to their students—the restoration of capitalism and monarchy.

The enslavement of the Russian people by their own and foreign landowners and industrialists—that's the essence of the "pure philosophy" of the sworn foe of the Soviet land, who attacked peaceful settlements at night.

Thousands of gallows on the highways, hundreds of blown-up bridges, dozens of derailed trains—this is the daydream of this lover of "abstract figures."

Such bloody monsters, such black owls, can be begotten only under the wing of the Fascist night.

When one of the Finnish sergeants major was being questioned, knitting his sandy eyebrows as if his feelings had been hurt, and staring with his light lashless eyes, he replied:

"The major promised us that we would be in Leningrad in two days."

This was perhaps the only promise made by the Finnish bigwigs which was honestly fulfilled. In two days the sergeant major was in Leningrad, disarmed and a prisoner of war.

The Lightning Blow Failed

Eight German soldiers and an officer made their way into the rear of the Soviet troops. They were under orders to scout around and report by radio what they saw. But the Nazi raiders failed in their assignment. Red Armymen noticed them and surrounded them suddenly. The officer ran away, and the soldiers surrendered.

The prisoners were taken to headquarters. They were from different localities. Some were at the front against France. Many had been in Poland in 1939, and then in Greece. For several years they frequently took part in military operations. Each appeared tired, unwilling to fight.

Senior Corporal Willi Baartz is a worker from Westphalia. Mobilized a long time ago, he had been on several fronts.

"Everyone thought," he said, "that the war was coming to an

end, when suddenly war against Russia began. This came like a
bolt from the blue upon our heads. This war is the insanity of
Hitler and his myrmidons."

All these prisoners rate highly the combat capacity of the
Red Army, the daring courage and unity of our fighters.

Friesch is a corporal. In his lapel there is an emblem of the
Iron Cross of the second degree. It has been his lot to encounter
in battle many different troops but nowhere, according to him,
has he seen so much technology and such a powerful army as
the army of Soviet Russia.

"The Red Army is especially strong," said Corporal Baum-
garten. "The Germans didn't anticipate this."

Corporal Etzwailer talks about the war with revulsion:

"The German people are tired of fighting. It is the Nazis who
started the war. This is not the first time they are driving the
soldiers to the front. In the battalion where I was serving many
were sympathetic to the U.S.S.R. Upon hearing of the offensive
against Russia, we dared not violate orders. Our company commander, sensing the soldiers' mood, declared that anyone who
doesn't go into battle will be shot on the spot. The same day our
battalion encountered heavy Soviet tanks and was wiped out."

The discouraged prisoners say, as if summing up:

"The lightning blow has failed—that is one sure thing."

A Conversation with Captured German Airmen

They were being taken past the bright flowers which they were
ready to trample, past the children whom they intended to destroy, past the adults for whom they had made ready their
bombs. They were being taken through a southern Soviet city
which they hadn't succeeded in reaching by plane.

The Nazi airmen—the crew of a Junkers-88 dive bomber—
have been led into a room for questioning. There they stand,

their heads low, fidgety, staring sullenly. There is nothing in the conduct of the Nazi fliers to indicate even distantly some "special qualities" of the Germans. They are disconcerted.

The Nazi airmen's uniforms are made of very poor cloth, dirty gray in color. On the collars of the Hitlerite carrion birds there are yellow buttons, on their shoulders small stripes trimmed with dullish lead piping. The crew of the knocked-down airplane consists of the pilot, Senior Sergeant Major Fitz Hening; the observer, Sergeant Major Heinrich Schmitt; the aviation mechanic, Konrad Beneke; and the gunner-radio operator, Johann Naumann.

The story of the appearance and perdition over the Soviet territory of the Nazi dive bomber Ju-88 is very interesting. It shows convincingly that the mighty blows of the Soviet aircraft are causing irreparable losses to Nazi aviation. The German command on the eighth day of the war was already compelled to transfer hastily solitary planes from the French airdromes, and immediately, without giving them a chance to rest up, threw them into battle.

The crew of this knocked-down airplane had previously operated all the time against England. It was over the British Isles that the crew's mechanic had died. After getting a new mechanic aboard, the Ju-88, which was at a French airdrome near Paris early in the morning of June 30, had been transferred to another base some five kilometers southeast of Kriukov. The bomber arrived there late in the evening. Early in the morning of July 1 the Ju-88 had already been rushed to the front against the Red Army.

The link of the carrion birds took off and flew in "hundkette" formation, which means "a dog link."

The Nazis' very first raid had determined their fate. Over the railroad the plane had been subjected to fire. One of the bullets passed through the entire fuselage. The observer and the pilot both received wounds in their hands from the fragments of shattered glass. After that the Ju-88 was attacked by the Soviet interceptors. The Nazi plane's fuel pump had been pierced. Our pursuit began to approach from below. Trying to save itself from complete destruction, the bomber came down to an altitude of from fifteen to twenty meters and, still chased by our pursuit, began to land.

The Nazi airmen were immediately apprehended by the collective farmers.

What has brought them to the Soviet country? Why have they attacked the working people of this great, peaceful land?

Observer Heinrich Schmitt, born in 1908, formerly a construction technician, takes a long time to think, wrinkles his forehead intensely, and answers in a muffled voice:

"I don't know. Personally, I didn't want anything from you."

"And what does the German people think in connection with your dastardly attack on the Soviet Union?"

"I don't know, we have no bonds with the people."

"And the soldiers?"

"The soldiers are soldiers, they are not thinking. But many say: I wish it would end soon. We are tired of it."

Neither does the plane's commander, Fritz Hening, know why he went to war against the peoples of the U.S.S.R. He shrugs his shoulders and, after a long silence, replies:

"I don't know what we are fighting for. We got our orders."

The commander of the Nazi airplane had no ideas. Like a machine, he began to act when a button had been pressed. However, every one of the Hitlerite highwayman quartet is no worse than the rest. They all convey the impression of people who have long since been trained to live without their own opinion and without their own thoughts. They have memorized the prescribed National Socialist gospel:

"No people in the whole wide world, except for the pure-blooded Germans, are worth thinking about or bothering with."

Observer Schmitt, the most talkative of the lot, speaks of the Italians with contempt. In his view, they are useful to Nazi Germany only as cannon fodder.

"We don't write about this directly," he says, "but it can be seen between the lines. . . ."

Of the French he says:

"When Hitler introduced order in their stomachs, they were still dissatisfied. You see, they claim that they were accustomed to eat more beføre our arrival."

Rumanians, Czechs, Slovaks, and Hungarians are also cannon fodder, in the opinion of Schmitt and other members of his crew. Heinrich Schmitt, as well as Fritz Hening, considers that all the peoples of Europe must be in the service of German Fascism. "Hitler wills so," he says.

"And are the German airmen aware who is prospering and thriving on the lifeblood of the German soldiers and fliers?"

Schmitt and Hening don't understand the question. For they have never before been permitted to think. They are sincerely surprised when they learn of the colossal riches acquired by Hitler and his clique of brigands in the course of the war.

Schmitt's head drops low:

"They don't tell us anything. We are only ordered about."

Their very first raid against the Soviet Union compelled even these mentally castrated individuals to do a little thinking.

"In the war with France," says Schmitt, "we were positive we would win. But in the war with the Russians . . ."

He falters and sighs contritely.

"This is no child's play. This is very difficult. Maybe that's why they transferred us here from France in such haste."

"Why not be more exact? Maybe it was because in the very first days of the war Soviet aviation had destroyed about 1500 Nazi aircraft?"

Schmitt is confused. He remains silent for a long time.

"It must have been a heavy loss for Germany," he remarks at last.

Immediately he becomes scared of the significance of his own words and says rapidly as if reciting a well-learned lesson:

"A soldier must not discuss politics. We have no right . . ."

Radio Operator Johann Naumann unexpectedly supplements that:

"We are afraid of your ground forces. But we are no less afraid of you in the air. Your aviation . . . your fliers . . . we avoid meeting them."

Schmitt rapidly interrupts the radio operator. Recalling how the collective farmers had quickly surrounded and captured the quartet of German airmen, he adds:

"The Russians left a great impression with us. They treat the prisoners well."

"Is that all that made an impression on you?"

"You had everything prepared for the struggle. We have not encountered such preparedness anywhere else."

The others confirm his words by nodding their heads.

They all sit with lowered heads. The Nazi cane always hanging over their heads has been removed. Under the blows of Soviet weapons they are now beginning to understand how inglorious is the criminal war begun by the bloody Hitler against the Soviet people.

WOUNDED FIGHTERS

Aboard an Ambulance Train

The train was coming from the front, carrying wounded fighters, women and children evacuating their small town at the last minute. In the seventh carriage were Sergeant Tupkalo, gravely wounded in the leg, Fighters Shvedoff, Kuzmin, Artamonoff, and several other wounded men from various detachments.

Pale from loss of much blood, the Sergeant was lying down all the time. Kuzmin, wounded in the head by a shell fragment, stayed on his feet and solicitously took care of his comrades together with the nurses and orderlies.

"Comrade Sergeant, perhaps I can make you more comfortable," he inquired and carefully moved Tupkalo over, fearing to disturb the wound.

Quick-tempered, impetuous Artamonoff was nervous:

"Where are they taking me? I want to go back to the front. My wound is trifling."

His wound was not trifling, for a dumdum bullet had hit his hand, but Artamonoff would not yield.

"We are from the Donets Basin, hard as flint."

Yes, and not only Artamonoff, but every one of the wounded men strove to get back to the front again, so great was their hatred for the accursed enemy. From passing trains the wounded received fresh newspapers. When the fighters read about the organization of the People's Army and of the patriotic upsurge of the whole Soviet people, they recalled their own factories and farms.

At way stations, at halts and crossings, the peasants came to the train, bringing milk, sour cream, eggs, and still-warm country cakes for the wounded.

Sometimes German planes circled over the train. Their coming could be guessed by a thin metallic buzz. The planes tried to bomb the roadbed.

At one way station three Nazi bombers raided the train together. Flying low, they let loose with their machine guns, almost in a strafing flight.

The hearts of the wounded fighters burned with anger. A Red Armyman escorting the train entered into combat with the air bandits, answering them with a burst of machine-gun fire. One of the enemy aircraft veered over, a flame darted over its wing, the plane began to fall.

"We fixed that raider!" cried the fighters.

Even the seriously wounded half rose to look at the stricken Nazi plane. It crashed in a field and exploded by the bombs which it did not have time to drop.

Two others hastily fled.

The ambulance train moved on.

Peter Melnikoff

He is twenty-five years old, but appears decidedly younger— no more than twenty. The ruddy color of youth spreads over his cheeks. He smiles provokingly and youthfully. However, for the past five days Senior Political Instructor Peter Melnikoff has seldom been in a good mood. For the most part he gloomily paces up and down the ward, cursing the moment when fate brought him to this "thrice annoying" hospital.

"I wish I could return to my detachment soon," says he. "I have been here five whole days already. My comrades are fighting, but I must suffer on a hospital cot. Devil knows what this is all about!"

Peter Melnikoff belongs to a strong covey of Stalin's falcons who take high-speed pursuits into battle.

If a pursuit pilot notices an enemy plane, he decisively and boldly dashes after it and does not rest until the enemy machine crashes below in columns of smoke and flame.

Naturally, even pursuit pilots sometimes have the experience of an enemy bomber escaping its doom by stumbling into the cover of clouds. The Soviet pursuit pilots consider such days the unhappiest of their lives.

"Didn't work out right, they got away," he says. "Well, never mind, if he got away today, tomorrow he won't."

So it happened to Peter Melnikoff on the first day. The enemy bomber, executing complicated pirouettes in the air, contrived to hide from its pursuer. Melnikoff was most disappointed.

"Just come my way once again," he said. "That will be your end. What a shame that vulture got away."

The next day luck smiled at the airman. The bird of prey appeared again. With great fury Peter Melnikoff and his comrades took off from the airdrome and hurried to meet the enemy. The four-motored German bomber, noticing the pursuits rapidly approaching, fled.

In the sky, bulging clouds floated. A white shroud barred the path of the pursuit pilots. Approximately two kilometers separated the bomber from the nearing pursuits. Several times it dived into the milky mass of clouds and disappeared from the view of its pursuers. At last a skillful maneuver drove it into a clear stretch.

"I gave him the first blow with particular pleasure," Peter Melnikoff relates. "Our pilot Knyazev came to my help. It is hard to say which of us finished the vulture, but I saw that the enemy plane went down precipitately and then crashed heavily on a green wheatfield."

When reporting this episode, Peter Melnikoff smiled a fine, gay, boyish smile. But in a minute he again became preoccupied and gloomy.

"I must manage somehow to be discharged from this hospital sooner. In fact, I am quite well."

"How did you turn up here, in this hated establishment?"

"On the third day of the war, on one of my flights, my engine went dead in the air because of a chance bullet. With the greatest effort I succeeded in landing, but during this landing I banged up my head. That's all. To be sure, I injured my head properly and was even unconscious for some time, but now I feel well, so why do they still keep me here, devil take it! You know, as soon as I hear the sound of an engine in the air, blood rushes to my heart. So that, it seems to me, I must run directly, even in my underwear, pardon me, to join my detachment. For those are my comrades flying, my pursuit pilots. In war every day is precious, and here I lie five whole days already."

Looking at this young airman with his youthful provocative and stern gray eyes, one thinks: how many brave people there are in the U.S.S.R. like him, calm, strong, self-confident, courageous! The Red Army is indeed the flower of a great people, and to defeat this army is impossible—there is no such power in the world.

In the Hospital

"Nurse, please call the doctor. Nurse, I can't stand it. Understand, I can't. My feelings are hurt, nurse. Take off the bandage, I beg you. Call the doctor."

"Calm yourself, my dear, have a little more patience. Understand, we can't let you go before the time. Will you have a cigarette? Here's chocolate. Look, what wonderful lilacs—the Pioneers brought them."

The nurse talks to the wounded pilot as if to a child. But he, a broad-shouldered, tall man, almost cries.

He turns over, facing the wall. He does not want to look at the lilacs, he doesn't want chocolate; the quiet and calm of the hospital oppress him. People with bandaged heads, with legs and arms in plaster casts, demand to be discharged from hospital and hotly assert that "everything's cured."

The old professor, Nikolai Ilyich Gurevich, says, unable to hide his excitement:

"I'm a veteran surgeon. I have been through four wars. But I never saw anything like it. These young men are ready to run away from the operation table, they demand that I should fix them up in twenty-four hours and send them to the front. They swear at me. Over there lies Shura . . . so we all call him. The Nazis have mangled him. We saved his life, but yet he is not content—he wants to go to the front, to the front. This is the first time in my life that I have seen this operation as calmly endured as this. . . ."

The professor plucks his little gray beard.

One thing is heard from every bed: crush the enemy, don't spare your strength. Let's hurry to the front!

"Comrade!" Sapper Semyon Rasin calls to the nurse. "Two of my best friends, Ivanoff and Prokofiev, are at the front. Our trio was inseparable. Write them that I am lonesome here. Let them know, please, be a pal: Sappers, friends in the regiment commanded by Comrade Kruglyakoff! Sappers, friends! The Nazi bullets didn't get Semyon Rasin. Semyon Rasin is alive and well and will see you soon. The Nazis, maybe, miss me too, so let them know that we'll be meeting soon; I'll sock them on the jaw, yet!"

Among the wounded is the very young nurse, Nadya Kunko. The Nazis wounded her in the abdomen. Closely cropped, she resembles a lively roundheaded boy. Her eyes are like cherries washed by the rain.

"I give you my word, my wound is not serious. I should get up soon, I should be getting to my front-line hospital. There, Tatiana and Maruska are sweating without me. What's going on, what's going on—the whole country is on its feet and I am lying here! Tell the girls, convey greetings from Nadya Kunko. . . ."

Here lie wounded fighters—Kirghiz, Uzbeks. . . . They smile at all who approach, wave their hands, and say:

"Thank you!"

Thanks to you, comrades, from all. The whole nation is proud of you!

LETTERS TO THE FRONT

A Letter to Six Sons

Major A. G. Legedzovsky one day received a letter from his parents. We quote this letter:

"My dear children! You, my six sons, are in the valorous Red Army. I give you a behest from your mother and myself: multiply tenfold the mortal blow at the Hitlerite hordes, in comparison with the blow which we, old Russian soldiers, gave the German armies in the First World War.

"Our motherland has equipped you, my dear sons, with a first-class military technique. The Party of Lenin and Stalin has taught and reared you. You have as your leaders the hard-hitting Stalinist hero generals, who are unreservedly devoted to us, workers and peasants. We are all behind you. The whole rear of the country, from young to old, will work, without a letup, in the War for the Fatherland, in the name of victory for the Red Army over the Nazi aggressors.

"Don't worry about us old people. We are working on our native collective farm, like all the rest of the collective farmers, and we will do all right in spite of the departure of the best, most advanced farmers to the War of the Fatherland, for the defense of our country.

"So, my dear oldest son, Anton Gordeyevich, lead your steeled tank detachment for the fatherland, for Stalin, for the Soviet people to a crushing blow on the Nazis!

"You, my dear son, Andrei Gordeyevich, following the example of your older brother, Anton, strike the German Fascists with your unit, as he struck them in 1918, as he struck the White Guard Finns in his time, so you too strike the German monsters a hundred times harder than I struck them in 1916. For freedom, for the honor of the Soviet people, spare neither your strength, nor blood, nor life!

"You, my dear son, Ivan Gordeyevich, Stalinist falcon, naval airman, sink the Fascist enemy's surface vessels and submarines!

"You, my dear son, Grigory Gordeyevich, with rifle and grenade in hand, clear the way on the battlefield of German-Nazi curs.

"You, my little boy, Nikolai Gordeyevich, in your Soviet land plane take vengeance on the Hitlerite carrion birds for their raids on our peaceful Soviet towns; beat them and then still more—on their own soil.

"And you, my dear youngest son, Vitaly, lieutenant of the Tank Corps, lead your menacing machines to storm the brutal enemy, dispatch your shells accurately and well into the maw of the monster; strike at the mad, insolent enemy.

"Our cause is just, we will conquer!

"Your parents,

"Gordey and Sofya Legedzovsky."

Hit the Enemy Harder, Sonny!

When Alexandra Matveyevna returned from the "Dzerzhinsky" textile factory, a letter was waiting for her on the table.

Surely it is my son writing from the border, she thought joyously and hastily opened the envelope. "Mom! I am stationed in camp. I live well. I spend much time in studying. I am preparing to become a lieutenant in the reserves . . ."

"It's always like that: I wish he would write more, what he is doing and how he is. Always no time," the mother grumbled good-naturedly.

On the next day Matveyevna heard alarming news.

War! The faithless enemy had made a highwayman's raid on our land.

Her first thought was of her son. Her thoughts involuntarily turned toward the border.

In the evening a family council was held in the Fadeyevs' household. The second son, Alexey, returned from the Defense Commissariat.

"Mamma! They did not take me yet, until a special order. But many are volunteering. I also wish to leave for the front."

Tender, motherly eyes looked lovingly at her son.

"Decide for yourself, sonny, what's best. I will not hold you back. Don't worry about me; while I have the strength, I shall work. And if need be, the government will help. If I were younger, I would go along with you myself. But now my age won't let me, I'll soon be seventy. But I can be useful here. I'll go to the hospital to take care of the wounded. Mother's heart is big, there's much love in it," said Matveyevna, controlling her excitement.

And afterwards, grasping the pencil firmly in her gnarled fingers, she carefully scrawled:

"Senya! I have received your letter for which I send you a mother's thanks. And I also send you this behest: don't spare the enemy! Defend our sacred land to the last drop of blood. If necessary, give even your life without fear for our just cause."

The same evening another letter was sent to the front.

"Dear little son! I heard today over the radio how the knavish Nazis have made war on us. The bandits wish to deprive us of our happy life. A thief always acts like a thief. Only this time he will not escape with his head. Strike the enemy harder, my little son. Carry out honestly any order of our own Stalin. Don't shame my old age and the honor of the family."

Such a behest Alexandra Ivanovna Arefyeva, an old weaver of the "Dzerzhinsky" factory, gave not only to her Nikolai, formerly a machinist on the water front. Not far from Nikolai's bench stood other machinists' benches, including one of his brother, Georgy. The brothers worked together in the port. Together they had smashed up the Finnish White Guards in the bitterest cold. Now the fatherland called on them for new deeds.

"Don't you get upset, Mother. Brother and I will make it hot for the enemy. And before you know it, Lesha will come to help."

"Absolutely; I will come. Though they did not take me last year, now no one can hold me back. I am already nineteen. They'll find somebody at the Kiroff factory to whom I can turn over my press."

The old weaver stealthily wipes away a tear and talks excitedly:

"Go . . . go, my children, to the just and holy war. My mother's heart feels that you will return with victory."

A Father to His Son

Nikolai Alexandrovich Kamensky, a foreman of the "Krasny Proletary" factory, sent this letter to his son Alexander, who is in the Red Army:

"My dear son Alexander:

"I didn't think that I would be writing on the day after the Hitlerite gang had dared to make an attack on our country. I am certain that as an antiaircraft gunner you have given a good answer to these black curs. You have always dreamed of becoming an artillery man. Well, here you have the chance at last to shoot at a real target; yes, and it seems not only once.

"War! How often we have spoken of its inevitability, and here it is, brought on us by the Fascists. Now every one of us is a soldier: you and I and all our family. This evening as I came from the factory, I didn't even have time to wash my hands, they sat upon me: questions without end. Vanya was especially insistent. As he is near the draft age, he'll soon be in the army. He wishes to go to the military committee in order to be called ahead of time. I tell him: in the military committee there are plenty of people without you—we have innumerable people. And until they call you, you better work at the bench. You are a turner standing at the bench in the repair shop in place of your brother, so your job is to increase production.

"Your grandfather also grumbles. Recently he reached the age of seventy-seven. He says: 'Write to Shurka, to work at his antiaircraft gun without a miss. Write that the whole nation is stirring. We will choke them, but we will not give up our land.'

"You are serving near the city of Leningrad; I do not exactly know what the country is like there. But some of our folk came from near Ramenskoye, from Ostrovtzi; they say that the countryside is blossoming everywhere—in the fields and in the gardens a flourishing harvest is seen. Nowhere else is there such rich soil as our Russian soil, and now the Fascist scum covet it. But it won't turn out their way. Russia has for centuries stood like a wall against anyone who wanted to subjugate it.

"Every day we raise production. In every factory work hustles on a war footing. We grudge neither strength nor time. We will fill the gullet of that greedy snake Hitler with molten metal. Watch out, Alexander, don't disgrace the old Muscovite proletarian name of Kamensky. Don't let the Hitlerites near, stand at your post. Shoot straight, so that none of your shells misses. Mamma has gone away with the children to a resort. Grandfather received a ticket for the rest home. Your wife, Ekaterina Vasilevna, is in full health, as also is your daughter Tamara, who is in the kindergarten; she is improving and growing up in the fresh air.

"Your sister Katya works like a real Stakhanoffite and is strengthening national defense at the factory. Greetings from the neighbors. Well, take care and fulfill your duty. Defend your country and party, and conquer in the name of Stalin. We stay-at-homes will all work for the Red Army and give it whatever it requires. The Soviet land has risen like one man. We'll cut off the head of the bloodthirsty reptile, that's a fact. However hard it may be, we'll cut it off.

"Behind you stands the country—an immense nation, in all its incalculable strength. But if it should be necessary, your grandfather and I and Vanya and Katya, all of us will take up rifles, but we will win.

"Your father,
"N. Kamensky."

BOOK III

CHAPTER IV

A NATION OF GUERRILLAS

In areas occupied by the enemy, guerrilla units, mounted and on foot, must be formed, diversionist groups must be organized to combat enemy troops, to foment guerrilla warfare everywhere, to blow up bridges, roads, damage telephone and telegraph lines, and to set fire to forests, stores, and transports. In occupied regions conditions must be made unbearable for the enemy and all his accomplices. They must be hounded and annihilated at every step and all their measures frustrated.

J. V. STALIN.

The Soviet Information Bureau Reports

NEWS IS BEGINNING TO ARRIVE concerning the operations of guerrilla detachments in the Soviet regions seized by the enemy. Here is one such incident. A train loaded with munitions for the German artillery was making its way along a narrow-gauge railroad branch en route to the front. The convoy of this train observed thick smoke and then flames on both sides of the railroad bed. Desirous of leaping through the danger zone, the engineer greatly accelerated the speed of the train. But the maneuver failed. In the very midst of the forest fire, the track was blocked by burning trees. When the train guards began to take apart the barrier, shots from muskets and a small machine gun sounded. The bold raid by the partisans was crowned with success. The train carrying munitions was blown up. The crews, accompanying the freight cars, were wiped out. The partisans —daring Soviet patriots—managed to disappear in good time.

Retreating to new positions, the Red Army units blew up a bridge over the river. With difficulty the German sappers restored the bridge in two days by installing wooden planks. On the third night the German bridge guards were suddenly subjected to fire from a small near-by island. The Nazi motorboat ordered to the island was damaged by three grenades, and sank. Then a group of soldiers, who were guarding the bridge, opened disorderly fire on the islands where among the reeds three daring partisans hid themselves. Not for nought did the partisans divert the enemy fire toward themselves. At the height of the skirmish suddenly hand grenades began to fly from the shore to the bridge. The surviving German soldiers fled in panic. The partisan group, which staged the daring night raid, sprinkled the bridge with kerosene, set it on fire, then disappeared in a forest bordering the river. The flaming bridge girders collapsed into the river within a few minutes.

Two airmen, Junior Lieutenants Poliakoff and Piskarev, were making their way through the enemy rear. When the officers reached the German-occupied village of "O," instead of streets and homes they found piles of ashes which were still warm. The day before the collective farmers razed everything to the ground, abandoned the village, and joined the partisans. The lieutenants tell of the courage and fearlessness of a commander of a guerrilla detachment, who has been nicknamed "Grandpa." Grandpa's unit terrorizes the Fascists throughout the region. The partisans have destroyed seven German tanks, mutilated telephone and telegraph wires over a great area, tracked down and liquidated a group of enemy motorcyclists.

A partisan detachment composed of collective farmers from the *Put Ilyicha* (The Road of Lenin) and *Krasny Pogranichnik* (The Red Frontier Guard) agricultural associations discovered some twenty large Nazi tanks resting in a dell. Watching the tanks, the partisans noticed that their crews were distributing the fuel from two of the machines into the other eighteen. Realizing that the tanks were forced to pause because of shortage of fuel, the partisans dispatched three scouts to find the regular Red Army units. An ambuscade was set up ten kilometers away from the tanks, along the highway on which they traveled. About six hours later two German trucks appeared laden with fuel for the tanks. The guerrillas felled some trees across the road, forcing the trucks to stop. The drivers and soldiers did not even try to offer resistance. Both trucks were blown up. The following morning Soviet dive bombers called on the enemy tanks and smashed them to smithereens.

A partisan unit made a daring raid on a group of hostile tanks quartered in the settlement of "P" adjoining the front. The partisans attacked the tanks at night while the enemy was on the unfrequented forest road leading to a concentration point. The head tank of the enemy fell into a well-disguised wolf trap. The second tank fell on top of it. The machines which followed swerved to both sides of the road only to fall into deep holes. Within a few minutes five tanks were in the pits dug by the partisans. Shots thundered from the forest. Firing at the forest, the tanks began to back up and stumbled on grenade bunches. Five more machines were crippled.

For five days the scouts of a partisan unit, commanded by the Chairman of the Executive Committee of the T———y Regional Soviet of the Toilers' Deputies, were gathering data on military objectives and numbers of the German troops in the city of N. On July 19 small groups of partisans approached the outskirts of the city, wiped out the enemy patrols, and opened well-co-ordinated machine-gun fire. The Germans raised an alarm and set out in pursuit of the partisans. Firing back, the partisans retreated hastily, luring the foe into the forest fastness. The maneuver succeeded. Directing their main force against the numerically insignificant groups of partisans, the Nazis drew ever farther away from the city. In the meantime, the main striking force of the partisans broke into the city of N from the opposite direction. The partisans annihilated the sentries and with their grenades set on fire the munitions warehouses. Much of the Nazi equipment and foodstuffs was gutted. The partisans killed eighty-five German soldiers and officers, and captured nineteen automobiles, twenty-four machine guns, a battalion headquarters, and sixteen prisoners.

Collective-Farmer Guerrillas

The partisan movement, for the organization of which Stalin has called on the Soviet people, is growing and broadening in the areas temporarily grabbed by the Hitlerite bands. Partisan groups not only destroy isolated Nazi units but also smash entire military detachments. Finding themselves in the Nazi rear, a large part of the population in the Pskov direction joined partisan organizations and are making raids on the German troops, tanks, and train echelons with munitions. Partisans in the vicinity of the village of Ivanovka killed the crews of seven tanks and disabled the machines themselves.

Splendidly acquainted with the locale, hiding in the forests, the guerrillas are elusive. They suddenly appear on the highways, lie in wait for the hostile signal-corps motorcyclists, and destroy them. Partisans strike such terror into the Nazi hearts that the enemy is afraid to bivouac for the night within village limits, spends his nights outside the villages, digs in and puts up elaborate sentry arrangements. Nevertheless, the partisans are mercilessly wreaking destruction. In many places they wreck railroad tracks. Ever-new masses of local populations are flowing into their ranks. The fighters of one of our regiments tell of a meeting with a peasant guerrilla unit in the village of Seleznevo. As soon as the German advance troops passed through the village, fifteen peasants made off for the forest where they organized into a guerrilla detachment. In a few days this in-

creased to forty members who started raiding the hated usurpers. Once they attacked an enemy group which stopped in the
village for the night and consisted of three tanks and a motorcycle unit. The guerrillas set the tanks on fire, exterminated the
entire man power, and captured all weapons.

In many villages local Soviet officials stay behind the enemy
lines to form guerrilla detachments. The populace is certain
that the Red Army will soon deliver a crushing blow to the
Nazis and return. The military correspondent of the newspaper
Krasnaya Zvezda (Red Star) reports the following: All members of the Krasny Luch Collective Farm left their village before the arrival of the Nazis. All their properties had been
removed to our rear in good time. The men who were capable
of bearing arms went into the forest. At night they received
word that two Nazi motorized units were surrounding their village. Armed with a few rifles, four grenades, and bottles of
gasoline, the collective-farm guerrillas, led by a guerrilla veteran of the Civil War, encircled the invaders' camp that night.
After hacking the sentries with their axes, the collective farmers
began to make short shrift of the rest of the Germans. Three
enemy tanks, which attempted to open fire, were showered with
bottles of flaming gasoline and burned down. Forty corpses of
the Nazi motorcyclists and tankists remained on the field of
battle. The Germans who abandoned their machines and fled in
panic were subjected to fire from their own automatic weapons.

How uneasy the Nazis are becoming is indicated by a memo
found on a captured German soldier. In it the German command
cautions its soldiers "not to enter villages trustingly" and is
compelled to admit that "all the time there is taking place rapid
fire by small groups and individuals concealed in the rear."

In the Name of Victory

Slashing cruelly at the German troops, the Soviet units were retreating to new positions. The front moved to the village N. This village had but one collective farm. Almost all night the women farmers heard the artillery cannonade. The enemy was very close.

In spite of the sleepless night, the workday began at dawn. A Komsomol girl, Galya, and a group of other young people had loaded nine trucks with grain from the barn. There were not enough bags; horses were being harnessed to makeshift carts. Every cart, every truck, was being camouflaged with greenery by the youngsters anxious to protect the grain from the Nazi bombers. For the Germans might bombard grain-laden vehicles! Only yesterday morning at about the same time a Hitlerite plane dropped some bombs at such a vehicle. The girl chauffeur had swerved off the highway, zigzagged for a while over the field, and finally entered a small forest, saving herself from the German bombs.

Some forty centners of barley and vetch could not be taken. They were sprayed with kerosene and burned. It was not easy to destroy the property acquired through honest and free labor, through sweat and blood. Two women collective farmers, who together with the rest were dragging the barrels with kerosene, were weeping quietly. Galya was explaining to them:

"We are obliged to do this for the sake of victory."

The people clearly grasped their objective. Not a kilogram of bread, not a liter of fuel, must fall into the enemy hands. They were in a militant mood. They evacuated or destroyed everything of value. This was being done in the name of victory over the loathsome Fascist bloodsuckers.

Milkmaids were driving away the cows. In its accustomed

manner the herd went along the dusty road and at first refused
to turn into the cornfield. But the girls forced the cows onto
the ripening corn and rye. The cattle trampled the crops, the
winter corn, the summer crop, and the sunflowers.

Again, no fewer than eighty girls and women with scythes
and sickles appeared in the fields. They trimmed down the
stalks. Tractor- and horse-drawn rollers mercilessly ruined the
ears, pressing them into the soil. The leader of the tractor brigade, Andrey K., let the plows run over the sugar-beet fields,
perpendicular to the even green rows. All that had grown and
thrived on the 1160 hectares of the collective farm, all was
trampled, replowed, destroyed to the end.

The peasants were saying:

"As a snake can never see the sun, so the Fascist riffraff will
never see our collective-farm harvest."

In the village proper feverish work never ceased for a moment. Fourteen well-fed pigs were slaughtered and presented
to the supply train of one of the retreating Red Army regiments.
The manager of the piggery personally drove the surviving
sows to the regional center, there to load them aboard a freight
train bound for the rear.

"So long as the Fascist swine are coming, we shall drive off
our own, the pure-blooded ones," the manager explained.

"Do you mean that now the German officers will settle down
in your pigsty?"

"Officers, did you say? We built it for the Yorkshire porkers
and not for snakes, the devil take them. Is it possible that the
Germans will make use of our constructions?"

Without another word, the people took apart to the last beam
their piggery, two cow barns, a new stable. The boys drove the
best horses into the forest. They never told anyone why they
were doing that; what for, when everyone knew?

It was even difficult to understand how they could have ac-

complished so much in a single day. They were impelled by
the simple and clear words of Stalin. They were impelled by
a holy abhorrence of the Nazi plunderers. Consequently, they
all acted swiftly, energetically, mercilessly. The locksmith had
smashed with his hammer a cistern of fuel. The blacksmiths
had demolished two combines, sheaf binders, a MO-900 threshing machine. The wrecked machinery and goods were dragged
to the stone quarry and pushed off the edge of the steep preci-
pice.

"Let the Germans try to salvage this!"

The head of the orchard brigade, who had worked as a gar-
dener for eleven years, was saying as he knocked the tiny green
apples off the trees:

"We did not plant for the highwaymen."

The apiary was set on fire. The bees disappeared over the
field in a swarm.

The young people blew up a dam, letting the water out of
the collective-farm pond. A group of the Komsomols left for
the near-by sugar refinery to assist there in the demolition of
equipment.

Some of the merchandise in the village store was unloaded
on carts for removal to the rear, the rest destroyed. Some rolled
out a barrel filled with a cranberry-juice beverage and knocked
out its bottom. The wells were contaminated with rubbish.

Women and men were making for the forest, many with children in their arms.

It is also reported from the Red Army sources that before
leaving Western Ukraine, the workers had set afire the petroleum of Dorogobych and had blown up a factory. At Lwów
warehouses were destroyed.

The enemy reckoned on profiting by the wealth of the Soviet
people. Instead, he is receiving ash-covered earth and bullets

of guerrillas who are helping the Red Army to deliver those smashing blows at the front.

Shoulder to Shoulder with the Army

Their eyes burning with hatred, the collective farmers watched the Nazi airplanes. The predatory birds of the Hitlerite brigands were making their periodic raid on Soviet territory.

Failure greeted the enemy plan. Met by antiaircraft guns and daring "little hawks," the German bombers had not sustained the battle and fled back to their bases. They did not fly back in formation, leaving behind many shot-down aircraft.

"Look, comrades, a Nazi plane is landing!" one collective farmer suddenly cried out.

To be sure, shot down by the Soviet interceptors, the Fascist ship was coming down in quest of a spot for a forced landing. It sat down in a meadow between the settlements.

From the cabin emerged four German airmen. They looked around. No one was in sight. The inviting green wall of a forest beckoned from afar. There was the place to hide in.

Unexpectedly a woman collective farmer appeared on their path. Hearing non-Russian speech, she boldly walked up to the Nazi braves who were armed to the teeth.

"Where do you think you are going?" she asked.

"We are looking for the railroad," one of the plunderers replied in broken Russian. "Where is your railroad?"

The woman pointed out a direction which was the opposite of where they had been walking and directly toward the collective farmers coming on the run. The bandits had hardly made a few steps before they became aware of a large crowd of farmers hurrying toward the place of their forced landing.

The enemies hastily scattered their weapons and notebooks

all over the field. They threw their machine gun into a swamp. They kept only their pistols.

The collective farmers were now standing next to the Germans.

"Lie down!" sounded a threatening voice. The Germans docilely lay down. They were disarmed, searched, and taken to the village. But only some of the farmers were sent to escort the Fascist thieves. The rest remained by their plane. From the forest several kilometers away they dragged trees with which to camouflage the plane that had made the forced landing. A whole grove sprang up in no time.

"A good job, this," commented an elderly collective farmer, wiping his sweating brow. "Now even if Hitler's braves do come raiding, they will find the landing field—like hell, they will."

The captured fliers were turned over to the authorities.

A Village at the Front

The village sprawls at the very highway. Small houses stand on both sides of the road, in the shade of trees.

By one of the little houses stands a stool; on it a pail of spring water and a cup. Many fighters stop, drink a cup of cold water, look about. Two houses away another pail of water and a cup. It is as if the homesteaders are saying:

"Drink, brave warrior, quench your thirst, grow strong, beat the enemy tirelessly."

In a ditch overgrown with thick tall grass the kiddies are at play. The oldest is perhaps ten or eleven years old. On his head is a paper helmet, a homemade sword in his hand. On seeing the approaching people, the boy commands his playmates: "Attention!" and himself peers attentively, waiting for us to come nearer.

"What are you doing?" we ask the boy. "Commanding a unit?"

"No," he answers earnestly. "We are Uncle Semyon's helpers."

An elderly man comes out of the house. He has a stiff and rather strict manner.

"Someone is asking for you, Uncle Semyon," the boy says.

Uncle Semyon lights up a smoke and studies the strangers in silence. Evidently he is in no hurry to open a conversation. His alert suspiciousness is quite understandable. From somewhere in the vicinity come the sounds of artillery fire. The village is in the zone of the front.

After looking over our documents, Uncle Semyon changes his attitude. But seriousness does not leave his face.

"Almost all our folk have left for the army," he explains, "but I have stayed behind. I went over, volunteered, but they won't take me. Too old, they tell me. How am I too old if with one hand I lift five poods?"

He inhales deeply and, slowly emitting the smoke, continues:

"Well, suppose my years are at the sunset, as they say—I'll be sixty soon—yet I do not consider myself an old man."

Semyon Alexeyevich Vershkoff—this is his full name—tells how he and some thirty other men left in the village have organized a self-defense detachment. He is their commander.

"I have the experience. I was a guerrilla in these parts during the years of the Civil War. We will give no quarter to the Fascist scum."

The same little boy comes to him, whispers something to Semyon Alexeyevich, and walks away.

"This laddie's name is Vovka," Semyon Alexeyevich informs us. "A right smart fellow. Yesterday, thanks to him and his friends, we apprehended a diversionist here."

After a pause, he resumes:

"The kids saw a man come out of the woods. They looked him over and saw he was not one of ours. He came over to them and started to talk with them. Then he asked them to bring him some kind of a rag. You see, he had cut his leg. Like a flash, Vovka sprinted for the village and called me out. We came along and nabbed him."

Semyon Alexeyevich is stingy with the details. Later, from our talks with other collective farmers and with the commander of a Red Army unit to whom the apprehended man was turned over, we learned that the story was not at all as simple as he had told it.

When the farmers approached the forest clearing where the stranger was seated surrounded by children, he dashed for the woods whence he opened fire. The farmers' entire armament consisted of one small-caliber rifle. Yet, not one of them wavered or drew away. They scattered, each running into the forest where they surrounded and finally captured the diversionist.

During the cross-examination he turned out to be disgustingly cowardly. The spy confessed at once that two days before he had disembarked from an airplane which landed on our territory. He had been supplied with radio transmitting apparatus and ordered to send information about our army units, train movements, and industry. "Don't kill me!" pleaded the Nazi spy.

"Our nation is not asleep," says Semyon Alexeyevich. "The words of Comrade Stalin live in every heart. We shall be vigilant, decisive, and courageous. There will be no Fascism ruling our land!"

The other day one of three collective farmers working in the field noticed some parachuting diversionists descending some distance away. The farmers had no weapons with them. They grabbed some pickets and rushed to the place where, according to their reckoning, the enemy parachutists must have landed. Without letting them stand up after the landing, the collective farmers belabored the Fascist bandits with their pickets. They struck with all the terrible might of a people's wrath. The fifty-year-old Stepan Grokhotoff, leader of a flax-cultivating group, had killed three diversionists.

"We will smite the Nazis to the last, until we do away with them as we do with weeds," says Stepan Grokhotoff.

Ferocious hatred of the Nazi monsters overflows the hearts of collective farmers. The valiant patriots of their country, they are helping the Red Army to disperse the enemy, and when the need arises, they themselves hit him, without a miss, to the death, on his very head, the venomous snake.

The Partisans

The lieutenant accomplished everything he had been told to do during the reconnaissance. On his way back, two German pursuits lunged at him. The lieutenant accepted battle and with his machine-gun volley shot down one of the planes.

Firing while maneuvering shiftily, the second pursuit pilot had wounded the lieutenant in both legs.

When he regained consciousness in the evening, he found himself in a dell at the bottom of which ran a crystal-clear brook. The lieutenant drank his fill, lowered his wounded legs into the water, slashed the material of his trousers, and bandaged his wounds, rested up, and splashed some bracingly cold water on his face, then began to crawl along the brook downstream.

Several times his consciousness faded. He would drop to the edge of the water, refreshing himself, then crawling again, until his eyes fell upon some small huts smashed by shells, burned down by bombs. There was a smell of smoke, here and there a thin stream of smoke rose upward.

A ramshackle little house at the farthermost end, surrounded by an apple orchard, somehow remained undamaged. The orchard was fenced by fat old lindens. Among the apple trees the lieutenant saw beehives. He crept up to the apiary, was about to shout, when from among the bushes a rosy-cheeked girlish face appeared and disappeared immediately. The lieutenant groaned. His head dropped into the grass. Hearing a rustle, he opened his eyes to see the beekeeper who looked precisely as his kind have been depicted from time immemorial. The beekeeper was sparse, gray-haired, of low stature, and barefooted.

Without saying a word to the lieutenant, he coughed three times and the girlish face showed in the bushes only to disappear again. The grandpa pointed to the lieutenant with his eyes and nodded his head to the right. The girl, obeying the wordless command, went away. The old man took the lieutenant into his arms, like a child, and carried him toward the apiary.

Consciousness deserted the wounded man. And thus, without regaining it, he fell asleep. He came to, when it was already getting dark. There were people among the beehives. The lieutenant heard their voices. They were speaking German, as the lieutenant had soon made out, asking the old man whether he had seen a Russian airman landing in those parts. The old man was apparently deaf. Very loudly he repeated his questions to the soldiers who in turn roared at the top of their voices the German and Russian words. But the grandpa kept saying in Russian and in German:

"I don't understand. I don't understand. I say: I can't hear. I have become hard of hearing, that's what it is."

One of the soldiers yelled to him:

"How come the old dog knows our language?"

In the same querulous tone the old man answered to the effect that in 1915 he had fallen into captivity, spent three years in Bavaria, and picked up his knowledge there.

The soldiers demanded honey. The old man replied that honey would be ready later, in August, and if they did not believe him, let them go ahead, break into the beehives, and take whatever they could find.

"You old hound," one of the Germans said, "maybe you hid the Russian flier there too, where there is a lot of bees?"

The old man mumbled something in reply. The soldiers began to yell again, but the grandfather stood his ground.

"You slap this hound, Willi, and let's go."

Willi slapped the old man, and the lieutenant could hear a short moan. Then everything became still, the people went away, the old man was quiet.

"Grandfather, what do you say, Grandfather?" the lieutenant called in a muffled voice. "What's the matter with you, Grandpa?"

"Nothing, the sons of bitches almost broke my jaw," the old man answered as he came over to the lieutenant. "You remain lying for a while."

"I can't loll about. I have an urgent report. Do you understand? I must be taken somehow to our people."

The grandfather was silent, keeping his ear cocked for the evening sounds. The girl emerged from the twilight.

"They've gone off along the Crooked Lane," she said.

"Whom have we got there?"

"Sysoy is sitting there."

"Tell him in the cuckoo language that two are coming; they have no machine gun."

The girl left.

In a few minutes a cuckoo sounded very quickly in the distance. It stopped and after a short interval cuckooed two more times. The grandfather listened, his entire body tense. Another ten minutes passed and far away in the forest two shots were fired. The grandfather said:

"He's lame, they rejected him for the army, but he is some marksman. And all the time he is paying court to my Aniutka. Did you hear those two reports from the forest? That's his work. Are you comfortable, lying there?"

"I am all right."

"Aniutka bandaged you up. She studied that. Toward night, we'll move you to another spot. That will be the real stuff for you, no worse than in a hospital."

"I must be moved to my headquarters, not to a hospital!" the lieutenant was angry. "I tell you—I have an urgent report."

"You don't have to yell, just tell me your story, mayhap I'll be able to help."

The lieutenant told the beekeeper about his important mission. The command must be informed of the movement of an enemy transport train and must send sappers to the bridge to blow it up and troops to prevent the enemy from crossing the river with those supplies.

The beekeeper listened to the lieutenant absent-mindedly and the more excited the latter grew the more indifferent the grandfather seemed to be toward his story.

It was in a different place that the lieutenant woke up—a cave breached in the loamy mass of a hill. A fire was burning in the cave. Around it sat people with rifles. There were six of them, old and young. The girl whom the lieutenant had seen at the beehive was stirring with a spoon in the kettle suspended over the fire. In the corner the lieutenant saw the white figure of the beekeeper. A stocky fellow walked into the cave. He limped noticeably.

Aha, that's Sysoy, thought the lieutenant.

"Well, how many is it today?" asked a bearded man who was apathetically staring into the fire.

"Five," Sysoy replied vaguely.

He sat down by the fire, virtually next to the lieutenant, took a knife out of his pocket, and made five notches on the butt of his rifle.

"How about the stone pit?" Sysoy queried after a while. "Have the scouts gone?"

"Lavrushka has escaped," Anna said. "Sit down, the food is ready." She removed the kettle from the fire. "Grandpa, shall I wake up the flier or should we let him sleep?"

"I am not sleeping," the lieutenant responded.

"Have some macaroni with us," Anna invited and a sunny smile again lighted her face. "I have cooked some macaroni in milk. The women are taking care of the cows in a forest, quite far, but they bring the milk to us. Wait, don't you move, I'll pour it in the saucer for you."

A shadow flashed in a reflection of the fire and the lieutenant saw a thin little boy with enormous eyes shining rapturously. He sat on his haunches next to the beekeeper and whispered something. The old man dropped his spoon and arose.

"Enough!" he commanded. "We'll finish eating later. You dress, Sysoy! Let's see, this one is a little wider, that's for you. And I'll wear this one. Matvey, you call together your fellows in the quarry. Lavrushka, you run over to the Ivanovo folk, let them pass the word over the grapevine that we concentrate at the bridge when the cocks crow the second time."

All who were in the cave left, except Sysoy, Anna, and the grandfather.

"It's like this, comrade officer," the beekeeper said, sitting down next to the lieutenant. "This is the disposition I make of it," he put in the fancy military word. "Not far from here is a quarry. We have been breaking rock for the highway, and we have enough dynamite left for three bridges yet. Everything would go smoothly, but lately some Germans have appeared in the quarry itself. Some kind of headquarters. Automobiles are standing there. Soldiers walk around. Now, here's the idea. Sysoy and I will do away with the sentries. I can chatter in German I still remember from the last war when I was prisoner. In the meantime, our chaps will come along with Matvey. So, we will rescue the dynamite, and kill off the Germans, and take an automobile so that by sunrise Sysoy can bring you to our lines."

"I will not let the flier go," Anna blurted out. "How can he go? He'll bleed to death, that's all. He is staying here."

"She inherited her character from me," the bookkeeper said merrily. "A hard-boiled young lady. It looks as though Sysoy will have to ride alone. He knows all the roads. You just write to your people what to do, and he'll deliver it."

"Let me have the bag, please," the lieutenant requested. He started writing his report.

At dawn a strong crash awakened the lieutenant. Clay, sand, and rocks were falling down from the roof of the cave.

Anna was standing at the entrance to the cave.

In a minute another explosion resounded. The lieutenant laughed. The girl turned to him and put a finger to her lips. It was perfectly quiet in the forest. The lieutenant wondered at the girl's order. But now his ear caught a distant roar of aircraft.

A few more minutes passed and from the same direction whence the first explosion sounded came a terrific din.

"They are bombing!" the lieutenant shouted. "Listen, Aniutka, our planes have come!"

"That means Sysoy got through," the girl said and sighed with relief.

CHAPTER V

A PEOPLE IN ARMS

Side by side with the Red Army and Navy thousands of workers, collective farmers, and intellectuals are rising to fight the enemy aggressor. Masses of our people will rise up in their millions. The working people of Moscow and Leningrad already have commenced to form vast popular levies in support of the Red Army. Such popular levies must be raised in every city which is in danger of an enemy invasion, all working people must be roused to defend our freedom, our honor, our country—in our patriotic war against German Fascism.

J. V. STALIN.

The People of One District

STALIN'S APPEAL found an ardent response in the hearts of the workers of Moscow's Kiroff District, as it did throughout the country. Old and young rallied round the militant red banners, ready for the holy War for the Fatherland.

Immediately after the leader's appeal, thousands of workers, engineers, technicians, office employees, gathered at meetings and demanded that they be enrolled in the People's Army and sent to the Red Army at the front.

Lemesh, not a party member, a lathe operator of the Stankonormal Factory, addressed the meeting:

"I ask to be enrolled as a volunteer in the People's Army. I am ready to go to the front to defend my fatherland. We will beat the enemy as our people beat Napoleon in 1812 and as they beat the Germans during the Civil War."

Syroezhkin, a Communist from the same plant, who fought against the White Guard Finns, submitted an application requesting that he be sent to the front.

During those days hundreds of thousands of workers of the Kiroff District turned in such requests.

From the Paris Commune Factory alone, hundreds of fighters joined the People's Army; scores joined from the Krasnokholmsky Factory. Among them were Rukosuev, a veteran dyer, and Peter Dmitrievich Kazakoff, sixty-three-year-old night watchman and participant in the Civil War. How persistently Kazakoff demanded that he be enrolled in the People's Army! He was told at the factory that he was too old. But he went to the district recruiting station and made his demands there.

Alexey Gorkoff, from the Tekhfilts Factory, asked to be taken into the Red Army. He showed the enemy the strength of Soviet weapons during the war against the White Guard Finns.

Fifty-one-year-old Nikolai Pavlovich Savin, from the same factory, joined up. During the Civil War he fought heroically for the happiness and freedom of the Soviet people. And now again his machine gun will mercilessly cut down the Fascist monsters.

Many of the volunteers from the Kiroff District were relatives of those very Red Army men and commanders who were already valiantly fighting the insolent enemy. An apprentice at the First Cotton-Weaving Mill, seventeen-year-old Bankoff, whose three brothers were already at the front, gave no one any rest with his pleas to be sent to the front. Now he has been accepted into the ranks of the Moscow People's Army.

Entire families took up arms. The Bolotin family work at the same mill, from which hundreds of men joined the Red Army and People's Army. Ivan Ivanovich, the father, was foreman of the steam room and had worked in the mill for thirty-five years. It was his home. And when his country was threatened, he gave himself up entirely to the defense of his fatherland. He was enrolled as the first volunteer. Now he has been appointed political leader of a unit.

His son Evgeny, apprentice in the machine shop, will be in the same unit. Vladimir, another son, also enlisted.

Maria, his daughter, was an accountant in the same mill. She asked to be sent to the front to care for the wounded. The wife of this outstanding man, the mother of these splendid children, came to ask for work in the mill—through her work, to the best of her abilities, she wanted to help the Red Army crush the Fascist jackals.

These are the mighty reserves of the Red Army.

To Arms!

A peaceful schoolhouse has undergone transformation. It can't be helped—there's war! The desks have been removed and army cots installed. Over the door of the teacher's office hangs a new sign: REGIMENTAL HEADQUARTERS. The physics laboratory quarters the 1st Platoon of the 2nd Company. Machine gunners occupy the classroom where but a month ago children were studying geography.

The map of Europe still hangs on the wall. Bright patches of color indicate countries; and heavy black lines, their frontiers. Holland, Belgium, France, Norway, Denmark, Yugoslavia, Greece. All are now stamped by the spiderlike cross of the swastika, drowned in blood, painted the ominous color of the brown plague.

Members of the People's Army stand before the map. There are three of them—a tall, slim man with silver-streaked temples, a downy-cheeked youth, and a man in a Russian shirt open at the neck. The latter is a baker; he works at the hot ovens watching the fluffy, tasty loaves. As soon as his shift was over he ran here, worried, hardly taking time to remove his apron.

"My name is Vladimir Mikhailovich Opochenkoff," he quickly told the regimental commander. "The boys left without telling me anything about it. I beg you to let me join the platoon."

His request granted, Vladimir Mikhailovich now comfortably settled down in the classroom and appeared as much at home there as he did in his bakery. He began a conversation replete with the terms of his trade.

"Well, boys, let's bend them into a pretzel; and we'll make them pay for it, too." Glancing at the map, the gagster added: "Don't you think that's too big a loaf for him, and on an empty stomach? His eyes are bigger than his mouth; he'll choke."

People's Army volunteers! Comrades and friends; today they also become front-line companions. Can anything else bind people closer than this lofty feeling?

"We are a peaceful people, but our armored train stands ready on a siding . . ." they used to sing at their parties and outings in quieter times.

The armored trains have now been switched to the main tracks. Peaceful people have become stern fighters, courageous warriors. The Zotoff brothers, both tailors, are accustomed to operate needles and scissors, but if need be . . .

"Comrade Commander, you've got to sign me up," said the elder brother to the battalion commander. "My brother signed up on the quiet, he got here ahead of me. But he can't fool me. I'm also fit for the People's Army. We'll beat the Germans together."

Zotoff tosses his documents on the table, slaps them with his hand: "Everything's here! You have no right to turn me down. I've plenty of energy, you can rely on me; I won't fail."

With a smile, the commander sends him to his brother's platoon. And the people continue to pour in!

Here are the innumerable reserves of the fatherland! They rise as one, and each stands with the rest in a single file! They all come—veterans of the war of 1914 and Civil War guerrillas —and they will fight as of old.

And still they pour in. The Moscow Film Studios company marches in smart military formation, keeping in step. They have different trades now—they are mine throwers, scouts, machine

gunners, snipers. Gevorgian, assistant director of the studio, is
now assistant political commissar of the company. Dmitry Vassiliev, codirector of *Alexander Nevsky*, is in the ranks. Berezko,
who together with Dzigan just completed the film about the First
Cavalry Army; Simkoff, who assisted Romm in filming the epics
about Lenin—they, too, have joined up. An entire platoon of
mine throwers is composed of cameramen. They are headed by
Lieutenant Nikolayev who, after the war against the White
Guard Finns, completed the film *The Artamonoff Case*. His col-
league Smirnoff brought his automobile to the regimental headquarters.

"Please," he addressed the commander, "accept my car for
the use of the regiment."

Nina Mikhailovna, his wife, came with him:

"I am ready for any work. I can be a nurse, cook, laundry-
woman. I have a college education. I can be of use to the regiment."

"With such people I'll go into battle with confidence. Excellent people! After brief training they'll become experienced
fighters." Thus speaks the gray-haired veteran battalion commander. In the last war against Germany he was in the famous
Brusiloff break-through in the Carpathians; he was in numberless battles, was wounded, was decorated three times with the
Cross of St. George.

"I'll show the bandits again that we still have plenty of gunpowder, and it's dry," he says with a fiery twinkle in his amaz-
ingly youthful eyes.

A Hero's Great-Grandson

Among the tens of thousands of Moscow patriots who joined
the People's Army was Artemoff, great-grandson of the famous

leader of a guerrilla detachment during the patriotic war against Napoleon, a peasant then known as Artem Sherstianoy. Of his great-grandfather and himself, Artemoff related:

Ninety kilometers from Moscow in the Ugodsko-Zavodsk Region lies the village of Bukhlovka. This village was very tiny in 1812. Virgin forests flanked it on either side. Bukhlovka was alarmed by the news of the approach of Napoleon. The peasants put their heads together, figuring their next move. Artem Sherstianoy stood up, a powerful man despite his sixty years. By word of mouth, Bukhlovka quotes his speech to this day.

"Well, my little muzhiks, what shall we do?" Artem asked. "Wait for the enemy with our hands folded? Give him our grain, our hay, our cows, horses? Never!"

And Artem suggested a plan of action, the usual plan of Russian people when a brazen enemy violates their borders. They decided to meet the French in a body. The women and children with their belongings and cattle were sent far into the forests. The roosters were all slaughtered so that their desperate crowing at dawn would not betray to the enemy the location of the defenseless women and children. Stacks of hay and grain were burned. Leave nothing to the enemy! The muzhiks armed themselves with pitchforks and axes, organized into a guerrilla party, and, led by Artem, began to wipe out small French units ruthlessly, mercilessly. Soon the Bukhlovka detachment was joined by the peasants from neighboring villages Chubarovo, Serezhino, and Kruglino. The enlarged guerrilla detachment attacked the French units ever more frequently, and great were the enemy losses. But Artem's detachment didn't limit itself to guerrilla warfare; many times they joined the regular Russian Army, participating in its battles. The guerrillas took part in the battle of Tarutino where fifteen peasant guerrillas died the death of the brave.

Artem's great-grandson is now sixty years old, the age of his great-grandfather when he became a partisan.

Despite his age, Artemoff is in perfect health and is successfully mastering sharpshooting and machine gunning. He signed up with the machine gunners.

"I couldn't," says Artemoff, "stand on the sidelines during this gravest moment for my country. My limbs are still strong; I'm fit for long marches, and I'll beat the hated, accursed enemy. Just as my great-grandfather beat the French, so will I, with the Moscow People's Army, mercilessly crush Hitler's Nazi hordes."

Artists Who Fight

Lobby of the Moscow Art Theater. The traditional semicircle of chairs, the customary form for all the meetings of this remarkable Russian theater.

Precisely at the appointed time, in walk the actors, director, stagehands, make-up men. Their bearing is military, for they are a detachment of the People's Army. To the leader's appeal to rise in defense of the fatherland and to crush the enemy, the theater responded with a unanimous decision:

"With arms in hand and to the last drop of our blood we will defend our beloved fatherland from the bloodthirsty Fascists."

Veterans of the theater—those decorated for their artistry with government orders, Communists, Komsomols—make up the front ranks. Among them is F. N. Mikhalsky. Chief administrator, decorated by the government, he has worked in the theater for twenty-three years. Mikhalsky and Dmitri Shverubovich, chief of the production department, were the first volunteers from the Moscow Art Theater. Shverubovich grew up with the theater, traveled throughout the Soviet Union, Europe, and

America with it. Joseph Rayevsky, actor, director, and teacher in the theater, twice decorated by the government, was also in the ranks. Others included Vasily Novikoff, Communist, Honored Artist of the Republic, participant in the Civil War. Here too are Ivan Morozoff, a member of the theater for fifteen years; Leonid Popoff, assistant stage mechanic; Pavel Semyonoff and Stepanoff, all stagehands, the last-named a Merited Master of Sports, and many others.

Beside the theater's veterans stand the youngsters, so well known to our audiences: Bataloff, Konsky, Ryzhoff, Kirilin, Ludvigoff, Kisliakoff, Akimoff, Nikolayev, and others.

Keeping in step smartly, the detachment is off on its first march, led by S. Uspensky, assistant director, who fought in the World and Civil Wars.

On that same day detachments from the Bolshoy Theater and the Nemirovich-Danchenko Theater also departed in the ranks of the People's Army.

Together with all the people, representatives of the world's most advanced Soviet art arose to destroy the enemy and secure victory.

D. D. Shostakovich, the composer, sent the following letter to the newspapers:

"The Soviet intellectuals, together with the entire people, rise to defend the beloved fatherland from German Fascism. Many authors, composers, and artists are already at the front; many are joining the ranks of the People's Army. I have also volunteered.

"I've devoted my life to music, to the creation of new musical works. This art is as dear to me as all achievements of mankind in the realm of culture. German Fascism has stretched its bloody paw toward the Soviet Union. German Fascism wants to revert mankind to primitive barbarism. Hitler's boot is suffocating the best sons of Germany. French, Polish, Czech, Serbian, Greek, Norwegian, Rumanian, and other European peoples are enslaved. Hitler's ally, Mussolini, is strangling the Italian people. Nearly all of Europe is caught in the nightmarish vise of Hitler's regime of hunger, concentration camps, and death.

"I've joined the People's Army to fight for my fatherland. I am a Soviet intellectual and I have joined the fight against the enemy of all progressive mankind, against the enemy of culture and civilization, and I appeal to all who hold dear the fate of peoples, the fate of culture and human advancement, to do likewise.

"Composer D. Shostakovich."

The Fighters of the People

They were motivated by two feelings when they joined the People's Army: love for their country and hatred for the Fascists.

Here they are, the representatives of the great army of the people. An old professor and a young worker, a composer and a collective farmer—Russian, Uzbek, Jew, Tartar—all to whom is dear the country that has nurtured them.

People of various professions and ages were gathered in Colonel Potapoff's unit. Sogomonian, a graduate student of the School of Chemistry of Moscow State University, is a subunit commander. Diankin, a geology student of the 5th Term, is his assistant. Professors, associate professors, laborers, and collective farmers are the fighters.

There is, for example, Mikhail Petrovich Titoff. At the end of 1916 he was a soldier in the 729th Ufimsk Regiment and fought the Germans on the Western Dvina River.

"You read the papers nowadays, and it's just the same. They

were so smashed up at the crossings that the river was choked with their corpses. Still they came on. But they were scared of the Russian bayonet; they were also afraid of the cavalry. As soon as they saw the cavalrymen they would shout, panic-stricken, 'Cossacks!' To them, every cavalryman was a Cossack."

Eighteen-year-old Anton Gukoff seizes every opportunity to pour out his complaint:

"I volunteered and demanded that I be sent immediately to the front. What's there to wait for? The Fascist reptile should be crushed immediately! It shouldn't be given even one extra minute! And they enroll me in the People's Army; they're going to teach me. Why teach?"

He recounts everything he can do. He's an athlete, he has terrific endurance, he has sturdy fists, can shoot a rifle. What else does a fighter need?

Anton Gukoff was not alone imbued with such burning desire to meet and knock out the enemy. All Soviet youth is seething with a desire to rush forth and meet the Nazi bandits.

The more sober "old men" try to cool their ardor.

"Save the powder. Don't waste it in words. Training is necessary. The Soviet fighter must not only be brave and willing, he must be a skilled warrior. Study, study, and study! We must master the science of battle and only then get into it to come out victorious. Isn't that right?"

"Of course!" the young agree. "But we are anxious to come to grips with them."

They are studying. In a near-by stadium they learn the art of bayonet charge, grenade throwing, and the overcoming of obstacles. The scorching sun beats down upon them, parches their throats, makes breathing difficult. But no one pays attention to the sun—there's a war!

Constant, intense, hard-hitting training continues.

One thing is striking. People of utterly different characters, different interests, different cultural levels, have come together. Let's say, for instance, Alampiev, associate professor of geography from Odessa, and Sergeyenko, a Ukrainian worker. Before the war they had not suspected each other's existence.

But the time of trial has come; their fatherland has called: "To arms!"

And here they are—in an unbroken file of Soviet patriots ready to defend the country where both of them were born, where they studied and worked. The feeling of kinship characteristic of all Soviet people is even more accentuated in them, as it is throughout the nation.

Geographer Alampiev has brought maps from home. Reading the reports of the Soviet Information Bureau, he explains the military operations on the map. And each member of the People's Army sees clearly the gigantic line of the front where the valorous Red Armymen are fighting the frenzied enemy.

The reading of newspapers in Sogomonian's unit has become exceedingly interesting. Member of the People's Army, Professor of Economics Milashevich, a veteran of the Civil War, has been interpreting the news so interestingly that the reading has turned into absorbing lectures. Young fighters listen to him with immense interest.

Because of their health, Professors Milashevich and Grigoriantz received their discharge papers a few days ago. It was sad news for everyone, especially for the professors themselves.

"I can't reconcile myself to it," said Professor Milashevich quite upset.

He went to the commanding staff.

"I," he said, "volunteered for the People's Army as I once did for the Red Army during the Civil War. Now, when my country is in danger, I can't stand aside, away from the struggle. I will find no rest on the sidelines."

"My dear professor, you have a weak heart."

"Heart? Oh, yes, yes! I have a heart! We all have Soviet hearts! And when our country calls its people to arms, the heart will not forgive him who does not take up his rifle."

They tried to convince him that a fighter must be strong and healthy. They argued with him. He listened attentively, nodded his head as if in affirmation, but wouldn't agree with the commander's arguments.

"What shall I do? There is nobody to lecture to and I don't want to bury myself in papers. At least make me an orderly; I won't leave!"

This veteran fighter with a great ardent heart was asked a simple question.

"And what about discipline? Is that the way to take it? 'At least make me an orderly; I won't leave'? If the order to discharge you has been signed, you must obey. Discipline comes first of all."

And Professor Milashevich, who only a few minutes ago argued excitedly and refused to leave the barracks, drew himself up in military fashion and said quietly:

"Forgive me. You are right. Discipline is discipline."

Back in his subunit he took leave of his young friends. It was a warm, extensive parting. He told them that if needed, he'd return at once. He'd come as a fighter and a Communist, and side by side with them, the young fighters of the People's Army, he'd fight to the last drop of blood, defending his native land from the enemy's encroachment.

The world knows no more menacing call than the call of the motherland:

"To arms!"

The People's Army Takes the Oath

The brothers stand in line. The evening air rustles the shaggy branches of the forest.

Vasily looks sidewise and, affectionately, at his brother. He still thinks of Mikhail as a little boy who needs tender care. There is a difference of ten years in their ages.

The Rozhkoff brothers were sent to the same detachment of the People's Army. They stand shoulder to shoulder, in the file with the other fighters. They experience the same lofty feeling of people who are about to take a solemn oath.

Today these powerful and sacred words sound as never before; deeper and stronger they penetrate the hearts:

"I am always ready, upon the order of the Workers' and Peasants' Government, to defend my native country—the Union of Soviet Socialist Republics."

Mikhail Lukanoff, from their company, having stepped in front of the file, is taking the oath.

His hand is firm on his rifle. It fits his grip well although until now he has never handled a gun. He is more familiar with the drawing pen of a construction engineer. But the need arose, and Lukanoff, with the greatest diligence, undertook to master the arms.

. . . "I swear to study conscientiously military science . . ."

They fortify their solemn oath with their everyday deeds. The camp awakens at five in the morning. It grows quiet in complete darkness, after the last news broadcast has been heard and the radio quietly plays the solemn music of the *Internationale*. The long summer day is completely occupied with intense military training.

People of peaceful professions consciously and persistently are remaking themselves into able warriors. Everything else has been pushed into the background. The fatherland is in danger; all thoughts, all desires are concentrated upon a single goal— to master "the A B C's of battle" in the shortest possible time, in order to speak to the enemy "in the language of artillery."

"All my boys are in a confident and militant mood. They are all impatient to come to grips with the damned Fascists. With such fighters I am afraid of no test. Don't worry about me, my dear ones, everything will be fine."

These lines were scribbled and mailed home hurriedly on a postal card by Konstantine Zaitsev. He sent it just before the oath was taken. Before the war he was a journalist. His correspondence from ports and docks appeared in the newspaper *River Transport*. On the first day of the war, he felt again that he was Senior Lieutenant, an officer in the Red Army; this was not the time to remain in the reserves.

The Senior Lieutenant rates his fighters highly. In the few days they have spent together, the commander noticed remarkable persistence and will power in many of them. Next to Lukanoff, who has returned to the file, stands Nikolai Bugachev, a turner from the same plant. He has proved himself a clever scout and was made commander of a section.

A trifle farther away stands a platoon composed entirely of students of the Auto Mechanics Institute. The other day, at tactical games, they were the "enemy" parachutists who landed in one of the forest clearings. Three other platoons were ordered to locate and destroy the "enemy." The student mechanics were so skillful in covering up their trail and they camouflaged so cleverly that it took enormous ingenuity and effort to locate them. But despite all their artfulness they couldn't outwit Pavlichuk, a fighter of the 2nd Platoon. He tracked them down and together with the section commander, Diadichkin, had so quietly and suddenly brought up his fighters and surrounded the "en-

Old foundry workers signing up for the People's Army
(the "Serp i Molot" iron and steel works, Moscow)

emy" so completely that there was no escape. He'll make a magnificent scout.

And Glopyrev? Isn't he great? Almost forty, he has plenty of experience. He knows the habits of the beasts of the forest. He knows the cries of birds. You can't fool him by hiding in the tree foliage. Without seeing a man, he can determine his whereabouts. Valentine Grigorievich Glopyrev joined the People's Army and brought along his four-footed friend, the shepherd dog Dingo.

"A complete scouting crew," someone joked.

Georgy Schmidt brought two motorcycles to the camp—his own and his brother's, who was in the Red Army. Kapitonoff, an elderly locksmith, brought his own tools. He has set up a traveling shop under the pine trees, and his skilled hands are doing much useful work. Alexander Genritzi, chairman of the Red Star Sports Society, contributes not only his excellent bicycle but also many years of experience as a racer.

Konstantine Zaitsev looks over the people before him. They are all welded together in a great friendship reinforced by iron military discipline.

Now it is Mikhail Rozhkoff's turn. He steps forward. His young voice is clear and resonant:

"I, a citizen of the Union of Soviet Socialist Republics, joining the ranks of the Workers' and Peasants' Red Army, take this oath and solemnly swear to be an honest, brave, disciplined, vigilant fighter. . . ."

His brother looks at him affectionately and his heart beats in unison with these clear-cut words of the sacred oath. The People's Army is taking an oath for the fatherland:

"To defend it gallantly, skillfully, with dignity and honor, not sparing my blood or life itself in attaining complete victory over the enemy."

A Hot Day

For many days now the regiment commanded by Colonel Kutepoff has been defending the approaches to the city of D.

"We have enough shells and bullets and in any event we do not intend to retreat," says Kutepoff.

When you come within the disposition of the regiment, it is evident at a glance that his fighters would sooner die than retreat. There is strict discipline in the city. Communications work without a hitch. Persons are checked with calm vigilance. Positions are thoroughly fortified. The regiment has dug in. All attempts of the German air force, artillery, and tanks to uproot them have failed. Deep trenches braced with timber are well covered and expertly camouflaged.

The observation posts are reliably equipped. Many kilometers of interlinking trenches guarantee unfailing communication. The regiment has beaten off one German attack after another with great losses to the enemy.

At night a scouting party reported that enemy tanks had concentrated in the forest, ready to launch an attack. Colonel Mazaloff, in charge of artillery, ordered fire directed at those points. Three howitzer batteries struck simultaneously. The shells exploded in the forest clearings where the enemy tanks were assembled. The explosions came one after another and merged into a terrific din. After fifteen minutes all was quiet again. Scouts reported that eight tanks had been destroyed and that the rest hastily moved away, advancing toward the fringe of the forest. At dawn, seventy German tanks came out of the forest and opened a hurricane of fire from cannons and machine guns. The Soviet antitank guns remained silent as yet, their location thus remaining undisclosed. But artillery of support went into action.

After losing a few more tanks, the Germans were forced to launch an attack before they had prepared for it with a barrage. They deployed and, while advancing, continued to fire without aiming. An antitank ditch lay in their way. Sidestepping it, a group of machines in close formation came upon a mine field. In a few seconds seven tanks were blown up. From the trenches you could clearly see how the German tank crews leaped through the hatches to be mowed down instantly by our machine-gun fire. The remaining tanks outflanked the ditch on two sides and emerged before the forward edge of our defense. Simultaneously, a German headquarters machine and trucks with infantry leaped to the highway from the forest, apparently considering the victory assured. The left-flank company was ordered by its commander, Lieutenant Khoroshev, to open machine-gun cross-fire. In one and a half minutes the bodies of German soldiers littered the entire fringe of the forest. Those in the headquarters car were killed on the spot. A similar fate overtook the German infantry consisting of two companies, which marched out in close formation to the opening, evidently intending to carry out a psychological attack. Only the proximity of the forest enabled some of them to escape, but most of them were cut down by machine-gun fire. In the meantime, tanks continued to advance. Some were already on the highway. Lieutenant Khoroshev noticed them and gave orders to sappers, through Field-Telephone Operator Gromoff, to destroy the bridge which had been previously mined. The first heavy tank had already crossed the bridge. A few seconds more and . . . but it was precisely those few seconds that the Soviet sappers didn't give the Germans. Letting the first tank pass, they blew up the bridge under the very noses of the others.

Lieutenant Vozgrin's battery, posted at the highway, opened point-blank fire at the tanks which stopped. Three tanks were very soon destroyed. Allowing a heavy tank which broke through to approach closely, the guns damaged its caterpillar track with a shell. The tank stopped but continued to fire. Sergeant Tarasevich then crawled up to it and threw a bottle of gasoline at the red-hot exhaust manifold. The tank caught fire. Its crew jumped out. Tarasevich with a revolver shot laid low one of the Nazis, and wiped out the rest with a hand grenade.

Upon seeing their tanks on fire, the German infantrymen, who were ready to march out of the forest, now lay prone on the edge of the forest. In the meantime, the tanks in the center were still advancing, coming within three or four hundred meters of our infantry. The tanks were drawing armored platforms with infantrymen. Some of the infantrymen were seated on the aft parts of the tanks themselves, shielded by their armor. Our antitank guns opened fire only when the tanks came very close. One tank was struck, then another, third, fourth. The howitzers lifted their fire from the machines and directed it at the forest fringe, thus severing infantry from the tanks. The German reserves couldn't get through. The remaining task was to destroy the tanks and infantry that broke through.

The antitank guns shot about ten tanks, but they in turn were put out of action for the most part. The surviving tanks were already crossing the front line of trenches. It was now up to the infantry. Fearlessly leaping out of the trenches, the fighters showered gasoline bottles at the tanks that broke through. One bottle, barely missing its target, glanced off. A German officer opened the upper hatch, looked at it scornfully, and twirled his mustaches.

His rifle in his lap, Lieutenant Khoroshev saw clearly this gesture from his commanding post. A shot rang out. The German had no time to close the hatch; his body slumped over. The turret gunner got up to pull his officer in, but he, too, was shot by sniper Serbienko. The number of tanks was rapidly diminishing. Those left were all within the Soviet positions. The infantrymen were jumping off the armored platforms and tanks and showered our trenches with grenades. Captain Gavriushin, battalion commander, deciding that the time was ripe for action, ordered his antitank guns and machine guns, which were situated in the depth of defense, to open fire. Simultaneously, infantrymen lunged into counterattack. Unable to withstand this fire and afraid to accept the bayonet charge, the Germans began a disorderly retreat. Three more tanks were on fire. The remaining tanks also retreated, trying to cover up their fleeing infantry with their fire. The Germans ran into the tall rye, abandoning their arms and tearing off their insignia of rank. At the approaches to the forest they were met and accompanied by the fire of our howitzers. Only one tank still remained within our positions. Its caterpillar track smashed, the tank stood within forty meters of the commanding post and fired at the blindage behind which sat Lieutenant Khoroshev and Captain Gavriushin. But the shells couldn't penetrate the two-meter embankment. An antitank gun was moved up to closer range and its first three shells destroyed the tank. The fourteen-hour battle was now subsiding. But our howitzers were still shelling the forest, where the retreating Germans must pass.

The battlefield was clearly visible from the regimental observation point. In the trampled rye lay groups of dead German soldiers. Battered tanks were everywhere. Red Armymen brought in Iron Crosses and medals thrown away by the Germans in the rye. Scouts rolled German bicycles and motorcycles up to the headquarters. The pile of trophies grew. Colonel Kutepoff, Battalion Commissar Zobkin, and Chief of Staff Captain Plotnikoff summed up the day's work: thirty-nine enemy tanks destroyed, two companies of enemy infantry annihilated, a headquarters car and trucks taken. It was a hot day, but the results of the battle were excellent.

DOSAEV	VOLKONSKY
Boris Alexandrovich	Grigory Nikolaevich
18	50
Toolmaker	Actor of Theater of One-Act Plays
I joined the People's Army in order to show, in battles against the enemy of mankind, what a Soviet patriot is capable of performing.	The task is clear—to defend our fatherland from the evil enemy. The country which raised such military leaders as Suvoroff and Kutuzoff is invincible. (I played the lead in the film *Suvoroff*.)
Comrade Kaminsky, an old mechanic, told me when I was leaving, "Go ahead, Boris. Be confident. I'll replace you."	Our country has neither mediocre nor irreplaceable people. Before our eyes people grow, mature, and expertly master new tasks.
Practiced army drills. After dinner got acquainted with Red Army regulations and then our commissar gave us a talk.	It was with joy that I joined the ranks of the People's Army. The high spirits which reign here have strengthened even further my confidence in victory over the enemy.

ABALYMOFF	KHARITONOFF	FILIPPOFF	BORISOFF
Nikolai Alexandrovich	Mikhail Vasilyevich	Nikolai Ivanovich	Ivan Vasilyevich
34	48	20	26
Engineer-geologist	Pensioner	Restaurant chef	Office worker
Unfortunately I have no military profession. But I ardently love my wonderful country and am ready to fulfill any assignment.	My son Nikolai, a Komsomol, is in the army now. After hearing the speech of our leader, I decided to help my son destroy the enemy.	My father said, "Since you are the oldest of my children, it's your privilege to rise in defense of our fatherland." I was happy to join the ranks of the People's Army.	Some years ago I commanded a battery. I was decorated with the Order of the Red Banner. Now, in the ranks of the People's Army, I am commander of a unit.
I was working on an interesting scientific problem lately. It will be completed by my colleague, Engineer Khalif.		Two waitresses were studying to become cooks. They will be glad to replace me and will do the work well.	I was replaced by Trusoff, secretary of the Komsomol Committee. If he is called, there will be other skilled hands to replace him.
During the first days I experienced how military training gives one confidence and instills discipline.	After only two days with the People's Army I felt reborn. I felt grand, even acquired military snap.	I made friends with Komsomols Aleksin and Dosaev. We are in the same unit. We promised one another to be first in study and in battle.	From the very first day, without losing any time, I started practical work: formed my unit, got acquainted with the fighters, and began training.

SURNAME	KOZLOFF	TYAN-DUK-CHUN	RUBINSTEIN
NAME, PATRONYMIC	Frol Frolovich		Lev Efimovich
AGE	20	47	34
OCCUPATION	Truck loader	Salesman	Writer
What is your specialty in the unit?	I am a sniper. That's my military profession. I shall strike the Nazis without a miss.	I am a Korean by nationality but my country is the U.S.S.R. I'll fight for it to the last drop of blood.	While still a boy, was volunteer in 1919. Was scout on numerous occasions at Chernigov. I think my experience will be helpful.
Who replaced you in the shop?	When I left for the recruiting station, a boy came to the garage to replace me. He's a Komsomol, which means he'll manage the job.	I changed shifts with Comrade Yudkevich. He promised me he would work two shifts. I'm sure he'll keep his promise.	Here, too, I'll find time to write. Have plans for a book on a fighter in the People's Army. I have already given much thought to this theme. As for characters, they are all around me
Your first days in the People's Army.	I am happy and proud of the confidence placed in me. The first days will always live in my memory.	It is not my privilege to serve in the army, but I try not to fall behind the others, and I think I shall not fall behind.	First days in the People's Army is prologue to action against the frenzied enemies of mankind.

CHAPTER VI

FIGHTERS BEHIND THE LINES

We must strengthen the Red Army's rear, subordinating all our work to this cause; all our industries must be put to work with greater intensity to produce more rifles, machine guns, artillery, bullets, shells, airplanes; we must organize the guarding of factories, power stations, telephonic and telegraphic communications, and arrange effective air-raid protection in all localities.

J. V. STALIN.

Younger Sisters

EVERYONE IN THE SOVIET UNION who has any strength can be useful at this time.

After a day's work in the factory, a worker goes on duty in his apartment courtyard. After feeding her children, a woman joins others in drilling for defense. A young woman, a factory worker, rushes to the Blood Transfusion Institute, to offer her blood for the wounded. All, no matter how great or small their work, are moved by the same feeling—to do something more than their immediate jobs or duties.

When you enter a recruiting station, you wonder what all those girls are doing there. You meet them in almost every room. College students, high-school girls; serious, slim, with fluffy hair, at first they look strange in this tensely busy office where men report to be sent to the front the same day.

But at once you see that none of the girls is idle. They all occupy definite posts; each has her own duties. All threads come together where the commissar of the station is at work.

Some work in the dining room where departing fighters dine. Others help to put out the wall newspaper; any is ready to help the fighters secure some information or other to assist them in filling out their applications. Alert, efficient, they do everything quickly and willingly. They evince personal interest in each and every man; their attitude reveals that warmth and real concern which mean so much in these times.

245

A fighter leaving for the front is sitting on a bench with one of the girls; he speaks shyly but trustfully.

"Look, I'm a little upset. I'm leaving a boy here; but he'll be O.K. without me. It's my little girl I'm worried about." He fumbles and looks questioningly at her. "I'm ashamed to talk about it, but with you, it's like talking to a sister. I spoiled my girl. She won't even go to sleep without me. I know it's wrong; but that's how it is. Please visit them; help my wife. I ask you as a brother."

The girl nods. Her lips are tightly pressed.

"I'll do everything, I promise you. I'll do everything I can," she says.

Indeed, the men treat them like their younger sisters; and the girls understand it. They are requested to place a child in a nursery, to visit a wife, to carry a message to a mother, to wind up some business the man had no time to attend to before leaving. They are always here, ready to help, to listen, to carry an errand. A man leaving his wife behind asks:

"Visit her. Tell her something, like a girl friend; you can find the words."

The girl nods. "I'll drop in on her."

And in each kind, sympathetic heart there ever grows a single, irresistible, overpowering thought, so that gnashing her teeth, she wants to shout:

"Avenge!"

Take revenge upon the murderers who have neither honor nor country, who dared to raise their bloody hand over the land of peaceful labor.

Avenge! Wipe them off the face of the earth! That is the cry of their hearts.

At the Lathe

"Yesterday during my entire shift I made only eight. But today, in an hour and a half, I produced ten."

She sounds quite proud. You can't blame her. For only yesterday Nina Uryvaeva took her place at the lathe of the Textile Machine-Building Plant. You see, she hasn't wasted any time; her progress is evident. A true Soviet patriot, she tried to master her work in the shortest possible time.

Time is too precious now; every hour counts. The young woman concentrates all her attention and will on one thing: she must carefully grind the ends of that piece of steel. Her hands are not used to the work; the lathe doesn't respond fully; it's with much tension that she makes it obey her. She knows all the theory of operation but her movements are uncertain yet.

Nina is completely absorbed in her work, her mind closed to all other thoughts. It is only during lunch hour that her concern for her husband returns. He is there, somewhere on one of the countless sectors of the enormous front, fearlessly fighting the evil-bringing Hitlerites. She becomes more reticent, more reserved. She can't wait for the end of the lunch hour; she hurries back to the shop to start up the lathe entrusted to her.

She is now taking her husband's place, and this realization brings her comfort. The disquieting thought that she is idle while he risks his life no longer torments her. Through her work, with every completed tool, she is helping him and his comrades.

Thousands of Soviet women feel the same way today. Sisters, mothers, wives of brave fighters, all women patriots, share this feeling. With complete self-denial, they are helping the Red Army defeat a terrible and treacherous enemy.

Asya Bolshakoff's brother is at the front and soon her husband will leave. The country needs skilled hands in various fields, and this fragile woman already stands at her big lathe. She seems to have inexhaustible energy, so fully is she engrossed in her work which improves by the hour.

Zoya Ivanovna Kirsanova, an engineer, works at the next lathe. The work is easier for her; she is splendidly versed in theory. She reads a complicated blueprint with the same ease that a musician reads a most involved score. All she requires is practice; a great deal of practice and in a month or so she'll be able to replace the foreman. Everything for the front! If this is what is wanted, Kirsanova, without false pride, is ready to take any work in which she'll be most useful.

Every Soviet woman now reasons the same way. Wives of mobilized men come asking to be taught trades quickly. They want to replace their husbands in industry. The employees of factory administrations come; they think it is more important now to be right in the shops than in offices. No, they are not planning to leave their old jobs; things will be done as usual. But after their day is over, they want to devote three hours to learning the trade.

Short-term courses have already sprung up at the factory. In two months, Erglis, a typist, will become a turner; Kazlova, head of the distribution department, will operate an automatic machine all by herself; Shulenina, an accountant, will become a lathe operator. Forty-two more girls will become valuable workers in the shop, replacing men leaving for the front.

Zhigin, Selivanoff, Glebkin—the best-skilled workers—are instructing the girls at the bench. Engineers Druzhinin and Peskova give them theoretical foundation.

Needless to say, it's hard at times! After a day's work, women tackle new, unfamiliar problems. But who is stopped by difficulties these days? Who lacks strength? Who can rest until everything possible is accomplished, until everything expected is done?

"I saw my son off to the front," says Zoya Alexandrovna Kozlova. "I know the enemy doesn't ask him whether he is tired. Those at the front give all their physical and moral strength. Can we, then, act differently? Our conscience, our honor, our duty as human beings and as citizens will not permit us to act differently."

These words of a mother are understandable to millions of people. Millions of hearts of working sisters-in-arms, heroines of labor, respond to them by giving themselves entirely to the sacred cause of the defense of the fatherland.

Moscow College Girls

Massive stone walls, familiar courtyard, arches, and columns —the University of Moscow. Here everything breathes memories of the great Russian patriots who ardently loved their people and had a burning hatred for its enemies. Belinsky, Ogarev, Lermontoff, Mendeleyev, Chekhoff, Timiriazev—what a galaxy of names. The pride of the nation, they all came out of these auditoriums.

The citadel of Russian culture and education! It won't suffer the fate of the Paris Sorbonne, of Warsaw and Brussels institutions of higher learning.

No! Never!

Look at these young men and women—students of the university. Look at this youth, the direct descendants of those who wiped out the White Guard hordes and armies of interventionists, who chased the German Army of occupation out of the sunny Ukraine in 1918.

Katya Kulikova's friends know that no matter what happens, you can't get a whimper out of her, let alone tears. But now her eyes are moist. She stands before the desk of the selective board, her face red with excitement, for her feelings have been hurt.

"It's not fair; it's unjust," she chokes, biting her lips to control the treacherous tears which tickle her throat.

She wants to be enrolled in the courses for nurses who are to be sent to the front. She has already applied. She has a GSO Badge (a badge awarded those who have taken courses and passed examinations in first aid—the letters stand for Ready for Sanitary Defense). She feels she has the right to be at the front. She thinks members of the board are "heartless people." They don't want to accept her because the board's physician has found that she is susceptible to tonsillitis. She has enlarged glands.

"But it's really nonsense," the girl says with deep conviction. "It isn't at all important. I haven't been sick in three years. I'm an athlete. You can see that I'm strong and I have a great deal of endurance.

"All right, then," the persistent girl announces. "If that's the case, I'm going to the doctor immediately to have my tonsils removed. Just try to turn me down after that!"

What a girl! She leaves the room rejoicing because she has achieved what she wanted. The members of the board follow her with admiring glances.

In the next room she is surrounded by girl friends. They are all awaiting their turn. They don't want to leave until they have received their assignment.

One after another they come into the recruiting room. Students of history, physics, mathematics, biology. They represent all the semesters from the first to the fifth. Composed and determined, they get excited only if rejected.

"Listen, Comrade Zaykova," says the chairman of the board softly, trying not to offend. "We understand your feelings. But you mustn't forget that you have a child."

"That is irrelevant," replies the young woman, attempting to appear gruff in order to hide her emotions.

"But who will take care of him?"

"His grandmother. We discussed everything at home before I came here."

"Do you realize all the hardships?"

"Very well. I'm a fourth-year student of history, I know what war means."

"Well, what shall we decide? You won't regret it later?"

A frown appears on her beautiful face; her eyes look reproachfully; she is evidently insulted by the question.

"I'm not a little girl who acts thoughtlessly."

What can you do with someone like that? Is it possible to reject her? Her decision had been nurtured in her heart with every atom of her being. A quiet, simple, artless love for the native land. The woman leaves her child to help defeat the enemy—the enemy that has no mercy on children and women, the enemy who has broken into our peaceful homeland.

She acts on the spontaneous impulse of her heart, but sound, sober consideration only reaffirms the correctness of her action. Hers is a simple thesis:

"I'll be defending my child at the front. That is the only way to prove my devotion for him."

You look at this young woman, at her friends, at the young faces of the students radiant with the noble inner excitement, and you think: how immeasurably rich is my country! Rich in strong characters and stout hearts. No, such can't be broken, they can't be bent!

This is the same Russian woman who "will stop a galloping horse, will enter a burning house."

Machine gunner, parachutist, air-raid and chemical-defense instructor—yes, she has long been preparing for the trying hour of war. Elena Rokobolskaya, a physics student, may consider herself ready to defend her country.

"But they don't take women into the combat units where you fight with weapons in hand," she regrets. "Well, I'll be a nurse. Maybe I'll get the chance to handle a machine gun. Anything can happen at the front."

Simple girls, intelligent, nice, gay. The richness of their character reveals itself even more in the face of this emergency. There are not one, or two or ten, but an endless multitude of these ardent patriots of the Soviet country.

Selection is strict, extremely strict. The smallest defect is sufficient for rejection. Nevertheless, everything is filled, there are no openings. It is necessary to organize new courses, start new groups.

And those rejected for the front-line duty have taken up a new idea; they are going to state farms, into the fields to help gather the abundant crop. There, college girls will replace the men who have left for the front, thus contributing their share to the national effort to crush the enemy.

The university is seething with life. Some are leaving for the X-ray courses which were established on the students' initiative by the People's Commissariat of Health. Some go to work in the Moscow factories, others to help build fortifications.

Downstairs in the university polyclinic there is an unusually large crowd of patients. The waiting room is packed. Is it possible that so many are sick? No! The girls have come here to give their blood which will help many a wounded soldier at the front to get back to his feet.

Sisters-in-arms worthy of the men who have joined the Peo-

The "Soviet Village" Collective Farm (Awarded the Order of Lenin),

ple's Army, these young women patriots are rising to defend their country.

In these menacing days the Russian women, the Soviet women without big-sounding words, without needless tears, but with their work and heroic deeds, are showing what they are capable of in their burning hatred of the enemy, in their fiery love for their country.

YOUTHFUL PATRIOTS

In Step with Grownups

Two little girls with green kits slung from their shoulders stand at the gates of the house No. 22 Bolshaya Yakimanka, Moscow. Leaning against the wall, they watch attentively everything happening in the courtyard and in the street.

A woman, carrying a large can, comes out of the house.

"Look, there she goes again," whisper the girls, exchanging glances. They run into the yard and call quietly:

"Tanya! Tanya!"

A redheaded girl, about eleven, quickly appears from nowhere, like a little mouse.

"Listen, Tanya. Run over to the kerosene store, and if you see that woman there, explain that at times like these she shouldn't keep more kerosene at home than is required for one or two days."

The girl, looking very stern, hurries away.

In a minute or two the woman appears from around the corner. She looks quite guilty and is explaining something to the little Pioneer girl who walks alongside. In an even more severe voice, the girl repeats:

"See that it doesn't happen again."

Three tiny lads, their knees soiled with earth and chalk, stop in front of a house. An elderly woman answers the bell and looks at them in bewilderment.

"What do you want?" she inquires, lifting her brows.

"We want to know," the kiddies blurt out, "why you have no water in your barrels? And why your house is not provided with sand? You ought to know why sand is needed now," the oldest of them says significantly.

"Yes, of course I know," she replies. "But we have no one to do it. The janitor can't do everything alone."

The boys begin to knock on the doors of other apartments and leave only when the tenants have armed themselves with shovels and pails.

While fathers and mothers work in the factories and mills, Pioneers and other school children see to it that everything is in order in the houses.

With a feeling of great responsibility, the little citizens fulfill the orders of the air-defense headquarters. Like industrious ants, they labor in the yards, helping the house committees and janitors.

A group of school children is cleaning up the rubbish in the yard of No. 14 Malaya Yakimanka. The girls take a note somewhere to return with blue rolls. Now every apartment in the house will have lightproof shades.

At No. 26, little boys stuff bags with sand, while the girls play with babies. With the outbreak of the war, many women left their homes to work in the factories and didn't have time to put their children into nurseries and kindergartens. The Girl Pioneers took it upon themselves to care for them in the meantime.

The Pioneers have found a good deal of important and necessary work for themselves and other children living in the same apartment, house, or street.

Every day there are new tasks to be done.

A crowd of people, young and old, have gathered in a small garden in front of a house. Red Army recruits watch little girls in Ukrainian costumes perform their national dance; they listen to a children's chorus from a neighboring school.

Somewhat aside, two adolescents—a boy and girl—sit at a table marked with a sign, SERVICE BUREAU.

"What kind of a bureau is this?" asks a recruit.

"If you've received your notice while at work and had no time to let your family know, write them a letter now and we'll deliver it in no time," explains the boy.

"You don't say! That's downright handy!" The recruit is touched by the children's concern and happy to be able to send his wife a letter. He shakes the kids' hands heartily.

In helping the families of mobilized men, the Pioneers and school children display sympathy and understanding. It will suffice to cite this example:

It happened that in one of the apartment houses on Sofiysk Embankment, four children and an old woman were left temporarily alone in the family of a mobilized man. As soon as the Girl Pioneers heard about it, they came over and offered their help. They cleaned the place, did the laundry, shopped, cooked dinner, and played with the children.

And they did this daily until the draftee's wife returned from the maternity hospital. She didn't know how to thank the Pioneers.

There are many such occurrences. They bespeak the mighty unity of the Soviet people.

Schoolboy Radio Operators, Chauffeurs, Firemen

Outwardly things look just about the same here as before the war. Flowers planted by young botanists blossom in their beds in the wide yard. The grass of the spacious court is green and fresh.

But closer examination reveals many changes in the Moscow House of Pioneers. Here are a group of boys with gas masks—they are on patrol duty. A Girl Pioneer passes; she wears the arm band of a first-aid unit. Some are practicing the Morse code. Along an asphalt walk others are pushing wheelbarrows full of sand which is later poured into bags sewed by the children themselves. In one of the rooms some children are attending a lecture on what to do during an air raid.

Three young girls—Mila Valdner, Lena Kisarova, and Katya Rosovskaya—have come to see the director of the House.

"Give us something to do; we too want to help. All the kids are already working," they say bitterly.

The girls are members of a dramatic circle. They understand that now their place is not on the stage of the House of Pioneers but wherever they can be most useful. That's why they have come to the director.

"Do you want to go to the telephone exchange?" Akhapkin asks. "It's interesting work."

The trio exchange glances, and in a chorus answer:

"We'll go."

A few minutes later they leave the House with a message to the telephone exchange. In the hall, they call out happily to the old watchman:

"Good-by, Grandpa. We're telephone operators now."

The Moscow House of Pioneers became the staff headquarters for directing children's activities in helping the front and the rear. Young patriots, who only yesterday were busy in the various circles, studios, and laboratories of the House, today all, as one, are working for defense.

Tamara Alexandriti, one of the best radio amateurs of the House, expressed a desire to work at any radio station where technicians left for the front. She knows the field well. She has designed and constructed a radio set which received an award at the All-Union Radio Exhibition. She's an expert Morse operator. Transmission of forty signals a minute is considered "good," but Tamara can handle seventy or eighty.

A few days ago Tamara passed a brush-up test at the Radio Committee with the mark of "Excellent." Now she is engaged by one of the radio stations.

Thirty-nine other radio amateurs of the House of Pioneers have begun work in various radio institutions. They at once display examples of self-sacrificing work. Victor Rodionoff, with his assistants, Boris Kirnenko, Alexander Shipershtein, and Boris Khrisanfoff, did an exemplary job with their radio station. They repaired all the transmitting apparatus and even made contact with several points which theretofore had been silent for months.

Work goes on from morning until night in the automobile shops. Young mechanics and drivers are doing an urgent job; the engine workers have been ordered to fix two cars for the Red Army. These boys who constructed the "motoroler," famous among Moscow's school children, are working well. One of the cars is ready to start on its way.

A group of young drivers, very recent recipients of licenses, are working in various Moscow garages. Misha Zyrianoff, a Pioneer, for several days now has been at work in the garage near his school. Yura Alexeyev received such sound training in the House automobile shops that when he reported to the garage he was made a Mechanic of the Fourth Class.

The day is drawing to a close. But the director's office is still a hubbub of children's voices. Chiefs of detachments, brigade leaders, and heads of various groups report on the day's progress and receive assignments for the next day.

All have left. Only three boys remain—Misha Finkelshtein, Ilya Brusin, and Gleb Komarovsky.

"What shall we do?" they inquired of the director.

"There's work for you too, fellows," he replies. "Three of our firemen have left for the front. You are strong, healthy lads. You be the firemen."

"I'm willing," Gleb Komarovsky responds first.

"I am too," says Misha Finkelshtein. "But what kind of firemen will we make?" he smiles apologetically.

"It's all right, we'll teach you," explains the director. "Is it settled, then?"

The kids nod emphatically. They are happy and proud; they, too, will help defend the fatherland.

The Village During the War for the Fatherland

Peter Lizunoff, the blacksmith of a collective farm, was leaving for the front. Other mobilized members of the farm were seeing him off.

The blacksmith said:

"We will crush the Fascists; yank them out by the roots like weeds."

He was thoughtful momentarily, then added as if talking to himself:

"It's a pity I haven't trained someone to take my place. The administration will have to find someone. This is a busy time—harvesting, haying."

But the administration didn't have to search for or train anyone to replace the blacksmith. That same night came Sergey Baykoff, Yegor Makaroff, Ivan Sinelshchikoff, and Boris Morozoff, Komsomols and students of the local high school.

"We came to have a word with you," they addressed the chairman of the collective farm. "Our blacksmith, Uncle Peter, has gone to the front. He was very worried about how the farm will get along without a blacksmith . . ."

"I," Sergey Baykoff interrupted his comrades, "can repair any lock. You can be sure I can handle a piece of iron.

"We'll fix the threshers first," he continued. "One of them has a broken blade. We will weld it. You just entrust us with the keys to the smithy."

The chairman looked at the unruly mops of their hair, their rolled-up sleeves, their eyes which had suddenly acquired a mature expression. His fingers tapped on the desk as he thought it over. After a moment's thought, he said:

"I'll trust you with the keys, but we have no coal with which to start up the forges."

The kids soon found a solution to this problem. They remembered Erofey Petrovich, an old charcoal maker who was also an expert at producing tar and turpentine. He lived on the outskirts of the village. The boys came and asked his help.

"Yes, fellows, I can start immediately," said Erofey Petrovich when he heard their story. "We'll have the pit dug in no time. We'll collect the logs from among the villagers. We'll have coal; we'll have everything. Our very stubbornness will knock out those Germans."

In two days the forge had coal. For two days and two nights Erofey Petrovich was at the coal pit cleaning out the openings through which gray clouds of smoke emerged. Then, black with coal, smoked through, he appeared at the office of the collective farm and declared:

"The coal's ready. Let the boys start forging whatever is needed."

The boys went to work. They fixed the thresher, the hay mower, two wagons, welded on the heads of three scythes.

New jobs came along. The farm needed a shelter against air raids. The boys began to build it.

The girls didn't lag behind, either. They also organized to help the farm. They planted cabbage, weeded cucumber and turnip beds twice, harrowed the potato field, watered the vegetable gardens.

Valya Khlopotova, Lyuba Nikultseva, Anya Kharitonova, and Zina Puzyreva pledged to grow a crop three times greater than last year's.

Vasily Akimovich, brigade leader, was skeptical.

"Weigh your words well before you say them," he said to the girls. "This is no time to throw words around."

The girls spent the night figuring out, drawing up plans.

In the morning they brought their plans to the chairman.

"Sure thing," he said.

During these great days of the War for the Fatherland, everyone in the Soviet village, from seven-year-old children to to seventy-year-old men, works from dawn to dawn on the collective-farm fields, in the dairies, orchards, works in order to give the Red Army and Navy—to all the Soviet people—more bread, more vegetables, more milk and meat.

After the air-raid shelter was built, the boys began to repair the barns. Kolya Lizunoff turned out to be a crack carpenter. He built fine troughs for the cattle.

"Just look what talents were hidden," said the farm's warehouseman. "Who ever suspected that Kolya Lizunoff was a carpenter? He always had a hankering for science, was preparing to enter a technical institute."

"Every one of us will discover his talent if he is a true son of his homeland. Is not our homeland our own mother?" answered the chairman.

As if to confirm his words, Dusya Komarova unexpectedly to all turned out to be a tractor driver. Everyone knew that she had never even been near a tractor. And all of a sudden collective farmers meet her driving a tractor. What do you think of that?

It seems that two years ago her girl friend taught her a bit, but it was done "on the sly"; nobody knew. When the war started, she went at once to the machine-and-tractor stations and asked to be given a test. The results weren't too good. But that didn't discourage her. She asked permission to work with an experienced tractor driver and within a few days she learned the basic rules of operation.

"Now I'll have to learn the finer points of repair and then everything will be in order," she says. "The drivers who transferred from tractors to tanks are smashing the enemy at the front; we girls who have taken up the steering wheels of the tractors say to them: 'Smash the snakes with all your might. Don't worry about the jobs you have left. We, who replace you, will manage them.' "

Posters hang on the walls of the Savin Collective Farm office. They say: EVERYTHING FOR THE FRONT! EVERYTHING FOR VICTORY! OUR CAUSE IS JUST—THE ENEMY WILL BE DESTROYED—VICTORY WILL BE OURS!

Leonid Kutakoff, a schoolboy, has two brothers, Pavel and Alexander, at the front. Pavel leads a tank against the enemy, Alexander is a cavalryman.

Leonid would have liked to follow in the steps of his brothers. But he is only fifteen. He understands, and he tries to do his utmost, working in the rear. He didn't know how to mow; he learned. Leonid never thought he would have to do carpentry; the need arose and he learned how to handle an axe and a plane.

The young people on the farm started to collect scrap iron.

"The more iron and metal, the easier our victory," they say. "We searched the entire village, beginning in the streets and yards and ending in the attics. And we turned in thirty wagon-loads of scrap iron."

There is pride in their words, pride in their simple deed, because from those thirty loads, according to their calculation, if not a heavy tank, then surely a whippet tank can be built.

The sun is setting behind the green ridge of forests. Its last rays stretch like red stripes over the green fields. A group of children, scythes resting on their shoulders, are returning from the fields. In their midst walks Mikhail Gavrilovich Kharitonoff, an old man.

"Now you, here, lad," he says, turning to the eleven-year-old Yegorushka Makaroff. "You like to shave the tops off. Bring your scythe down lower, don't swing it too much; you can cut your foot that way. Don't rush; walk evenly. Don't try to catch up with the others. You have neither the strength nor experience. When you get the right swing, forge right ahead; I won't say a word."

"All right, Uncle Misha," says Yegorushka. "I'll remember."

Then the old man tells the boys how he beat the Germans in 1916.

The children listen eagerly. The field is so quiet that one can hear the buzzing of the gnats swarming around a poplar and from afar the bleating of a lost lamb.

Blue mist of twilight envelopes the village. The green expanse is disappearing under the foggy vapor. Not a light is visible. Complete quiet . . . Such calm that it seems everything is asleep, the sky, the field, the darkened forest. Big July stars twinkle through the slowly drifting clouds. But this quiet is deceiving. If you listen closely, you hear the measured tread of the village sentries. They are on duty, guarding bridges, the office, the village Soviet, the club, and the school.

The dark silhouettes of horses disappear into the night—a

group of Komsomols on night duty going to guard the collective-farm fields. Always on the alert, listening closely to the rustle of the wheat, the noise of the wind, chirping of insects, they vigilantly guard the collective-farm property.

The village adolescents daily, hourly, grow stronger in body and spirit. Their hands become more skillful, their eyes sharper. Daily, hourly, they develop the qualities of stern fighters, defenders of their great motherland.

BRIEF ANSWERS

What Have You Done for the Front Today?

The newspaper *Komsomolskaya Pravda* addressed this question to its readers—rank-and-file Soviet citizens.

GILEV
Foundry worker,
Frunze Plant,
Moscow

Comrade Stalin appealed to the people to produce more weapons for the Red Army. On my shift I produce four times my quota.

LUPANOFF
Student of Technical
School No. 1,
Leningrad

I am a student but I have already undertaken highly skilled work. My job was to assemble a unit for a certain factory. It was completed two hours ahead of schedule.

KUZNETSOVA
A woman railway
dispatcher, Chita

I dispatch trains on schedule. Don't detain them even for a minute.

PODSHIVALOVA
SOFRONOVA
*Women brigade
leaders at Krasny
Perekop Factory,
Yaroslavl*

We fulfilled our seven months'
plan ahead of schedule and gave
the country 751 kilograms of
yarn above our assignment.

TEPIN
*Turner at a railway
depot, Tumen*

I produce four times my norm on
my shift. I have already fulfilled
my fifteen-month plan.

KONDRASHOFF
*Pattern maker,
Stalin Auto Plant,
Moscow*

I was given an important assignment. Worked seven shifts in succession and fulfilled it one day
ahead of schedule. My work was
appraised as excellent.

YAKOVCHUK
*Locomotive engineer,
Kiev*

Our train was suddenly surrounded by Nazi cutthroats who
wanted to get our valuable
freight. I gave it full speed and
the train rushed past the enemy
like a cyclone. They only managed to shoot through our com-
pressed-air hose, but the train
crew repaired it on the run.

SOBOLEVA
*A woman worker at
Electrosila Plant,
Leningrad*

Our sheet-metal cutter left for the
front. His work was considered
unsuitable for women. I have
taken his place and will work as
well as this comrade who went to
the front to crush the Fascists.

GUSEV
Worker at
Electropribor Plant,
Leningrad

I suggested a new method of hollowing out a cone. When applied, it greatly increased the productivity of labor.

ZAKHAROFF
A turner at the
Bicycle Plant,
Moscow

I was assigned to rush production of thirty-two wheel naves and I accomplished my task twelve hours ahead of schedule. The results were perfect.

VASSILIEV
PROSTOFF
Workers of a bicycle
factory, Moscow

The two of us are doing the work of four. Two others have left for the front. Our comrades won't lack "gifts" for the cannibals!

What Have You Done for Victory Over the Enemy?

The newspaper *Komsomolskaya Pravda* addressed this question to its readers. The laconic answers vividly tell how hundreds of thousands of young patriots working in the rear, together with the gallant fighters at the front, are forging victory over the enemy.

KIRILL CHIRKOFF
A steelworker

Steel is the bread of war. Our enemy will be fed his fill. I doubled my output. I smelt high-grade steel.

EVGENIA RUDNEVA
A girl student

I am a blood donor. I give my blood for those who are ready to give theirs to the last drop. I am leaving to work on the farm to help in the harvest. I know that my blood and my work will help to bring about the victory.

ALEXANDRA RUMINA
A woman worker

I operate eight machines. Constantly overfulfill my assignment. I head a first-aid detachment. Through my work and military preparedness I am helping to crush the enemy.

VICTOR SHORIN
A student

In the house where I live I organized a self-defense group. I am political instructor there. Every house must become a fortress inaccessible to the enemy. This will secure our victory.

ANNA PETRIKOVSKAYA
A singer

My voice is my weapon. I sing for the men going to the front. With a brigade organized by the Moscow State Conservatory I am going to tour the posts of the front-line army. I have also become a nurse and I will study more in order to master this profession.

VICTOR LURIYE
An engineer

I have completed the research for the preparation of two-layer stainless steel. Its rapid introduction will save the country tens of thousands of tons of precious metal. I also have replaced my friend, who left for the front, in supervising the mechanical tests of the quality of the output. I work in such a manner as to make the trademark "Hammer and Sickle" an unquestioned guarantee of the plant's products.

ALEXEY ROMANOFF
A fireman

A fireman is a fighter at the rear. Our duty these days is to guard the safety of the city. I was an ordinary fireman: now in the war I have become chief of a fire-engine unit. My unit is always in a state of military preparedness. I also supervise the work of volunteer firemen, instruct them in camouflage and fire prevention. I am certain that the enemy's fire will be extinguished. Vigilance will ensure our victory.

ELIZAVETA VORONINA
A housewife

I was on duty in the street until dawn. Detained a stranger who had no documents, took him to headquarters. After that I looked around the yard; checked to see whether there was water in the barrels. I know every single window in our house. Then I got Tamara Raskazova out of bed— it was her turn to go on duty. I remember how sixteen years ago her mother returned from the maternity home and showed us her baby girl and said, "Here's my Tamara. She will have a happy life. Not the life I had." Now time has come for Tamara to defend this life. She's a nice girl, excellent student, a Komsomol. We carry sand, clear out attics, paste paper strips on windowpanes. Our work is small but it, too, is important for defense. To my mind if the country is a fortress, then every city, every house must be a fortress. Thus we will achieve victory.

MARGARITA KULAGINA
A teacher

At night I am on duty in school. Mornings I lecture to the pupils in the higher grades. I am political instructor of the school self-defense unit. I will spend my evenings instructing housewives. I know well how to do it because I have four defense badges (sharpshooter, etc.). In an air-raid alarm I'll do what I did at the time of the first test alarm: I go down to the children's shelter, have a talk with them, tell them stories, play with them. These are my insignificant deeds. Every minute of my life I am thinking of those at the front defending our happy life. As I write this, I look at the telegram before me; it's from a friend at the front.

"Be confident. We will be victorious."

We, here in the rear, will help in their victory.

BORIS BASHMAKOFF
Secretary of a
Komsomol Committee

All members of our organization are mobilized for defense needs. They make up six detachments. I found out how many know how to handle a gun; for those who don't, I set up a circle. All the girls study first aid. I work like a teacher. Visit dormitories daily, explain the rules of conduct in wartime.

LUKA DANILOFF
A mechanic

Without quitting my work, I am learning to fly. Soon I hope to be piloting military planes.

IVAN SASS
Locomotive engineer

I drive trains which overfulfill their norms by 600 to 700 tons.

V. I. LEBEDEV-KUMACH
Famous poet decorated
by the government

Peaceful Soviet people used to sing: "The song helps us to build and to live." Now, at this time of the great War for the Fatherland, the song will help our courageous people to defend their sacred land and to destroy the sworn enemy of mankind.

All Soviet poets and composers are filled with a single desire: to help their country and their people through their creative work.

Since the outbreak of the war I have written a number of military marches: "Fight unto Victory," "Onward, at the Enemy," "Forward, for the Fatherland," "The Holy War," "Crush the Enemy without Mercy"; a song about the naval Captain Svetoff, another "For the Honor and Glory of Our Fleet"; army chants: "We Are Very Cordial People." I have written new words to the song "If War Comes Tomorrow." Almost daily I write poems for the leading Red Army and Navy newspapers.

THE FACTORY—A STRONGHOLD OF DEFENSE

In the Shops of the Stalin Auto Works

Nothing, seemingly, has changed in the Stalin Auto Works. Exactly on the appointed hour, the cars roll off the assembly line. The rhythm of work in the shops hasn't been broken once. On the board showing norms of production new figures of higher productivity are marked after the shift is over. A Socialist competition to fulfill the six months' plan ahead of schedule is under way among brigades of turners, mechanics, foundry workers, blacksmiths, patternmakers, electricians, and others.

There are no outward changes in the life of the plant. But every day, every hour, brings more news of unprecedented labor enthusiasm, of the great patriotic upsurge which possesses the hearts of the people.

More cars than scheduled are rolling off the assembly line. Timoshkin, Zakharoff, Klichenko, Gerassimoff—Stakhanoffite workers of the plant—fulfill their quota from 160 to 170 per cent per shift. News of ever-rising productivity comes from all departments. The task of uninterrupted, timely supply of the assembly line with all necessary details in order to hasten production is being successfully accomplished by all shops of the plant.

A group of women from the foundry—Popova, an accountant, Marieva and Kucherova, from the dispatching department, Pushkina, a file clerk—asked the head of the foundry to teach them industrial trades. They said:

"We must be prepared at any moment to replace skilled workers who leave for the front."

Kurbakoff, Zhukoff, Lomovtsev, Maloletnev—foremen of the Fourth Assembly Department—appealed to all the other foremen to organize courses for new women workers. These experienced foremen wrote in their appeal to their comrades:

"Soviet patriots, masters of high productivity, are now exchanging their working benches, their tools, for the weapons of the fighters of the Red Army. They are going to the front. Soviet women, deeply devoted to their native land, come to replace the heroic sons of the Soviet people. Housewives, old and young, girls who never worked in shops—they all come. Our duty, the duty of every foreman, is to do everything to help the new workers to master industrial trades. We, the foremen of the Fourth Assembly Department, pledge to teach the new workers their trades in the shortest possible time, to transmit to them all our knowledge and experience. Soviet women, patriots of our country, will replace every lathe operator, turner, mechanic, toolmaker who leaves for the front. We appeal to all foremen not to spare either time or effort in helping these women to become skilled workers. Comrades foremen, time does not stand still. Let's get down to business!"

Indeed, no time was wasted. Immediately several groups of women started studying under the foremen's supervision. The news that a group of new women turners, students under foreman Ganchuk, had turned in their first work traveled all over the plant.

"All parts are well done; no defects," was the official appraisal of the work.

The same thing can be observed throughout these days. After the end of the shift, men and women workers don't hurry home but surround planning officials, controllers, and foremen and bombard them with questions: "How was our brigade's work today? How did the shop do?"

The sense of duty to the fatherland in these decisive days makes both foremen and workers stay around to make sure that everyone on the next shift reports for work, so that not a single machine will stand idle.

In some departments you see a communiqué from the front and a shop-production bulletin hanging side by side. Two bulletins, from the front and from behind the lines. Both here and there people concentrate all their strength, all their talents and abilities, to achieve one thing—victory. Their deeds fortify their aspirations.

Zilberg, a woman stockroom employee, was on vacation when the war broke out. She went to the nearest Red Cross office.

"I was a blood donor before. The front needs blood for transfusion to the wounded. Take my share."

A group of girls who gave their blood during the war with the White Guard Finns appealed to all women to have blood tests so they would become donors whenever the necessity arose and thus save the lives of wounded fighters.

Inventors and industrial efficiency experts consider it their sacred duty to speed up the application of new inventions, devices, and methods of work. New inventions must be promptly applied in production. Everything that helps to economize on precious metals or high-grade steel, everything that helps to bring about a higher productivity of labor and improve quality of goods, must be applied at once.

Tromova, a housewife, came to the Fourth Assembly Department. Her husband was called into the Red Army.

"I worked once as a turner," she said. "Now my hands can be useful for my country. I can replace my husband."

She took his place at the lathe.

The working rhythm of this giant auto works is constant. Many thousands of workers in the plant work with redoubled energy, permeated with a feeling of responsibility for securing the victory in the War for the Fatherland.

At the Moscow "Cautchouc" Plant

The radio appeal of J. V. Stalin, Chairman of the National Defense Committee, which appeared in the newspapers, was read to the workers of Shop N-4, Moscow Cautchouc Plant by Engineer Goreloff during the lunch hour.

Stalin's words were the militant call to action. They went directly to the hearts and minds of all at the meeting and found the most ardent response in everyone's heart. That could be read on all serious attentive faces, in their eager eyes fixed on the speaker, in the new vigilance that reigned in the shop.

Stalin's concluding words, "Forward to our victory!" were drowned in a thunder of applause.

Goreloff called on the workers to increase their productivity, to work as befits Soviet patriots.

The speech of Controller Novikoff was full of wrath and hatred for the enemy.

"The enemy is attacking our fatherland. He wants to take away our free life," he said. "Let us crush him! Let us smash the Nazi cannibals anywhere and everywhere! I have submitted a request to be taken into the ranks of the defenders of our fatherland. I am certain that many will follow my example."

All who spoke at the meeting were imbued with patriotism, firmness, readiness for sacrifices, and boundless devotion for Stalin.

Engineer Bukhalenkoff, Worker Churkin, and Chief of Shop No. 2 Kovalev spoke of the unity of front and rear, the unity against which the hordes of Nazi monsters will crack their heads.

"Today," said Kovalev, "our rear is a part of the same front. Here we are ensuring the Red Army's victory. In the rear we must work with the same tenacity and self-denial with which our gallant Red Army fights. Let us multiply tenfold our present output. Let us give the Red Army substantially more and better production! The rear together with the front must form a single powerful fist which will deliver a deadly blow to Fascism."

Malakhovsky, a gray-haired worker in overalls, mounts the platform. His posture is youthful, his head high.

"My son," begins this veteran of labor, "is at the front. I received a good letter from him: 'We will smash the contemptible Fascists wherever they show their repulsive snouts.' This letter gave me a great deal of new strength. In response to Comrade Stalin's appeal, I pledge to raise my productivity so that I'll be doing the work of my friends who are leaving to defend our fatherland."

There are many women in the shop. Seredinskaya makes a spirited speech on their behalf.

"Our husbands are leaving for the front. There is now much work to be done at the rear. We shall replace the men. And if need be, we will go along with them, weapons in hand, to defend our free life!" she exclaims.

Panfilova, a girl Komsomol, announces that several girls have asked to be sent to the front, where they can be of service, and that the rest of the Komsomols are ready to follow them.

In tense silence, a draft of the resolution is read by the shift foreman, Voskresensky.

"In the great patriotic war of liberation we will defend our land to the last drop of blood. We will destroy the Fascist barbarians and their accomplices. . . . Our best people will join the People's Army. We will double and treble our output. We will make an inaccessible stronghold of defense out of our plant."

The resolution is adopted unanimously. The shop resumes its usual life. But each worker is still thinking of the meeting, with a new realization of his own place in the great patriotic movement of the entire Soviet people.

The Solemn Pledge of a Factory

The night shift was over when the radio loud-speaker announced that J. V. Stalin, Chairman of the National Defense Committee, was to speak.

Wherever the loud-speakers carried the familiar voice of the leader, crowds of workingmen and -women gathered. They drank in every word of the speech, their faces tense and determined.

The people didn't leave until long after the speech was over, until long after they heard Stalin's call, "Forward to our victory!" They felt the need of sharing their feelings and thoughts, of proclaiming for all to hear their readiness to fulfill their sacred duty to the fatherland.

This is the spontaneous way in which the meeting started at the Hammer-and-Sickle Plant. The speakers used as their platform rolls of metal cable or poles of iron bars.

Their speeches were passionate, excited, and courageous. They were brief, like military reports, for everyone in the factory felt he was a soldier of the Revolution.

"Comrades," began Kirill Chirkoff, a steel smelter. His eyes took in the crowd. He removed his working cap, discolored from the flames and with blue goggles on the visor, and continued: "In a single shift our brigade has doubled their output of steel. This is the way we are going to work further."

Doubled their output in a single shift! The significance of these words was clear to everyone present. Behind this modest statement was a heroic deed, self-sacrificing labor of patriots who, in the rear, never forget the front.

The steel smelters of the Hammer-and-Sickle Plant keep the stream of hot steel flowing constantly from the open hearths.

Workers of the Hammer-and-Sickle Plant know full well the value of each ton of metal. They know that it means more shells to annihilate the Fascist hordes. Each drop of steel is a deadly bullet into the hearts of the enemy wolves.

Operators of the rolling mill of the Hammer-and-Sickle Plant can work full speed; there is plenty of metal and no shortage is expected. There is a ceaseless cascade of metal.

At meetings in the rolling-mill departments the same spirit is evident in the speeches. Each ingot, each sheet of rolled metal, means new machine guns, shells, rifles.

The Stakhanoffite workers, taking the floor one after another, promise to keep the Red Army amply supplied with death-dealing steel to stuff the Fascists with.

At these meetings they spoke not only of heroic labor. In the face of the great danger hovering over the fatherland, when it is a matter of life and death to the Soviet state, each worker of the Hammer-and-Sickle Plant remembered his other, his military profession.

"Comrades coworkers," said Varfolomeyev, head foreman of the foundry. "During the Civil War I drove an armored car. Now I have joined the People's Army."

And while the meeting was still on, Foreman Filin began making a list of volunteers for the People's Army.

"Put my name down," rushed Chegarkoff, foundry helper. "I'm a machine gunner. In 1919 I sewed them up with a 'Maxim.' Now I want to try my hand at a Degtiarev machine gun."

Among the enlistees were sappers, medical orderlies, signal-corps men, artillerymen, couriers.

Such lists of volunteers were being drawn up in all the other shops. In the rolling-mill department Engineer Parnev, once a member of the Red Guard, made up a list of his former comrades-in-arms who were now employed in the same shop.

"On November 7, 1917," said Alexey Andreyevich Ukhoff, "gun in hand, I fought for the establishment of Soviet power. I now beg to be taken into the People's Army in order to crush the reptile crawling at our land."

By its work and people the Moscow Hammer-and-Sickle Plant has blood bonds with the front. Now, as in the years of the Civil War, the plant is sending hundreds of its nurslings to the front.

Among them are persons of every service—pilots, tank drivers, antiaircraft gunners, infantrymen.

Their vast reserves are in training in the ranks of the People's Army. The rolling-mill operators, smelters, cranemen, puddlers, with Stalinist fearlessness and tenacity, will fight for every inch of the Soviet soil and will repel the Hitlerite brutes and cannibals.

The workers of the rolling-mill department adopted the following resolution:

"The crack Nazi divisions and escadrilles have already found their graves on the battlefields. Our fields will become the graveyard of all Fascist hordes."

Speeches of workers, resolutions adopted at meetings sound like solemn oaths taken before the fatherland, like a military vow to the beloved Stalin.

Donets Basin in These Days

On the very first day of the War for the Fatherland, the workers of the Donbas (Donets Basin) worked in their workshops, at the blast furnaces, at the rattling rolling machines, and in mines with tenfold energy, iron concentration, determination, and unprecedented *élan*.

From every mine and plant—from Chistyakov and Dzerjinsk, Gorlovka and Kramatorsk, from Makeyevka and Krasnoarmeysk—came in news about the labor exploits of the heroes of the industrial rear of the fatherland.

At the Mariupol plant "Azovstal" the milling-machine operator, Kobetz, started to work on four machines. On each of these milling machines he fulfills one and one-half quotas a day.

The miner, Ivan Golubtzoff, of the Gorlovka Mine No. 19/20, working with his friend, Timberman Nikolai Butenko, fulfilled his shift-quota 2000 per cent. That day these two men did the work of twenty miners.

The Lutugin Mine in Chistyakov region was behind the plan. Now the workers of this mine have greatly increased the output. The foreman of the coal heavers, Omelchenko, told his friends: "Let us show, boys, what the Donbas miners really are." Now his brigade overfulfills the quota day after day.

Hundreds of tons of coal are now being produced above the plan in this powerful 320-meter-long coal rake.

In the Coal Mine No. 3-BIS of the same region, on the twelfth eastern coal road, three men usually worked at handling and trausporting the conveyor. Prokofy Besedin, a young carrier, decided to replace those men when they left for the front. Working with unusual speed, not wasting a minute, he carried fifty-five sections of the shaking-coal conveyor and two drivers. Having completed this work one hour before the end of his shift, Besedin took a shovel and helped the coal heavers shovel the coal on the conveyor.

Borer Peter Malinovsky, competing with the well-known borer Alexey Semivolos, replaced three men on June 28. He moved from place to place, thus boring in three coal roads, and fulfilled the quota 380 per cent.

Coal heavers Gurenko, Kovalev, and Boichenko of the Evdokiyevka Mine No. 16/17 of the Budennovugol Trust consistently fulfill their work from two to three times above the established quota. The coal heavers of Baranoff's brigade in one shift have fulfilled the day's plan of the output of coal of the whole coal road.

The woman coal-car operator, Khizenko, fulfills her quota from 300 to 320 per cent. The women operators of the electric coal carriers, Ivashina, Verblyudova, and Baydina, are overfulfilling the established quotas by 200 per cent. The operator of the milling machine, Semenkevich, of the Kramatorsk Ordjonikidze Plant, from the very first day of the war has been fulfilling from three to four quotas a shift.

The coal hewer, of the Gorlovka Dzerjinsky Mine, Ezersky, fulfilled more than a two-month quota in coal output during the month of June.

The mobilization in Donbas region is being carried out with great efficiency. Thousands of men flock to the Stalinsk City Military Commissariat, and to the assembly points. Nearly every young man called for military service has a military specialty. One is a tank driver, the other an artillery marksman. And there stands a young man with dark eyes. He is a parachutist, sharpshooter, and machine gunner.

As in the days of the Civil War, when all the population of the Donbas, young and old, arose to fight the German invaders and White Guards, so it is now. The labor of Donbas arose, menacing in its wrath.

Mothers and wives, seeing their sons and husbands off to the front, wished them to destroy the enemy.

"Look, son!" said an old woman to her son, coal hewer at Mine No. 30 Stalinugol. "Shoot them straight through their dogs' hearts! I rely on you, my son!"

In these days, women replace their husbands who leave for the fronts to fight for the fatherland. They replace them at the machines and in mines.

In the Proletarskaya Mine of the Makeyevsk region, the housewives Kirushina, Gorshkova, Pavlenkova, and others have already started to work in the coal mine. Scores of women these days operate the electric coal carriers and motors of the powerful conveyors.

Front and rear are an inseparable whole.

Each ton of coal, each ton of steel, helps the fatherland in its sacred war against the dark forces of Fascism. The Donets miners, metallurgists, machine builders, chemists are fully aware of that. Donbas is forging powerful armaments of victory.

ON THE HARVEST FRONTS

In a United Upsurge

The wide fields of the Vyselki Collective Farm named after Stalin lie amid the quiet Vozh and Mech rivers of the Ryazan Province. In the evening mist they seem calm and deserted. But as soon as one reaches Vyselki Village realization comes that the calmness is deceiving. Along the railway, around the fields, and in the village walk vigilant sentries.

Vyselki Village wakes up when the heavy dew on the grass and on ripe wheat begins to sparkle under the first rays of the sun. The hay mowers are the first off to work. Hurrying, they exchange jokes:

"They say, 'Mow the grass while it is moist.' Would I like to mow down that snake Hitler, instead of the grass!"

"Wait, we'll mow him down with the roots."

After the mowers come women with rakes resting on their shoulders, young women, children. All—beginning with eight-year-olds to ancient men—work in the fields. The girls of the field brigade hurry to work, their bare feet treading the wet grass. They look preoccupied and serious. There is much work ahead. The men went to the front, time is short. The crop is abundant; it seems that the very earth wants to take revenge on the enemy by giving all her fruits to her defenders. The cabbage leaves are curling up and one can already see the contours of immense heads. Ripening tomatoes, bright red-and-green beds of carrots and onions. Vyselki Collective Farm must harvest 284 hectares of grain and vegetables and seventy-eight hectares of hay in the shortest time. The task is not just to harvest but to attain the best results ever achieved.

The earth steams. Pink clouds loom on the horizon. The sun, as though trying to make up for the cold spring, beats down on the tanned backs of the girls. Bending over the carrot beds, they weed conscientiously and quickly.

Their finger tips are callused from the work. Their hands move expertly and freely. The faces of these fifteen- and sixteen-year-old girls are preoccupied. Tanya Shishkova looks at those ahead of her and says in a hurt voice:

"They are ahead of me again. No matter how I work they are always at least a half meter ahead of me."

Anna Pavlovna Isayeva, the village teacher, is among the weeders. On the very first day of the war, she went with the others out into the fields and now she works like an experienced Stakhanoffite.

Kolya Froloff, the blacksmith, walks across the field toward the hay mowers. He is laden with carrots, cabbage, beets, tomatoes, and scallions.

The mowers work self-confidently; a swing of the arm, a turn of the body, and the thin silvery blade disappears into the grass with a faint ring. There is the rustle of the falling grass, a juicy crunch, and a pile of new-mown hay, almost half a meter high, appears.

"They will fulfill at least a quota and a half," muses Kolya Froloff. "Yesterday old man Ivan Filippovich Anikin got mad at us. Because of his age, we made him a watchman. So yesterday we came to borrow his scythe. He has a very good one. He was furious. 'I'm not any weaker than the others,' he said. We didn't get the scythe. When he's off duty, he himself mows."

Along with the adults work barefooted youngsters, weeding rows of wheat and oats.

The school children have shown very good results in their

work. More than once they overfulfilled adult quotas by 150 per cent. It is a truly heroic country where even adolescents in the trying hour of war perform such great labor deeds, proving their overwhelming valor and love for their native land.

After a hasty lunch, the people hurry to the fields. Kolya Froloff is finishing the repairs on the last thresher. The first and second brigades weed and harrow the cucumber beds. The men plow around the vegetables. Mowers work without straightening their backs. Their faces are bathed in sweat. They swing their scythes with a powerful sweep and pause for an instant only to wipe off the perspiration. In the distance there is a herd of horses. The collective farmers look around the field and momentarily their faces lose their preoccupation.

"What a crop!" they say.

Their scythes begin to sing louder in the grass full of sweet aroma of honey and the buzzing of bees.

At night the brigade leaders reckon the results of the workday. The women's field brigade has overfulfilled their weeding quota many times over.

"Let this poisonous viper, Hitler, choke with anger," says one woman. "Let him know that the Ryazan countrywomen can take in the harvest without the muzhiks. Yes, we'll complete the harvest! Tomorrow we'll work even better. Not a grain, not a cabbage head, will we leave in the field."

Oblique shadows stretch across the village, from huts and apple trees in the farm orchard. The farm youth are off to build a bomb shelter. A son of a local farmer, Sergey Isayev, son of a local peasant and second-year student in the Electro-Technical Institute, conducts classes in anti-air-raid defense.

At eleven o'clock the village is deserted except for the sentries. Anna Osipova and Tanya Shishkova guard the newly reconditioned cars. Sergey Solomonoff peers attentively into the darkness as he rides his horse. He is guarding the railway tracks while two old collective farmers guard the bridge.

The sentries are posted at the pigsties, cattle barns, stables, granaries.

This constant military preparedness is reflected in everything, in the behavior and activities of the people.

"He thinks he'll grab our crop," says the old farmer Ivan Filippovich Anikin, on fire-prevention duty. "He thinks it will be simple, but . . ."

Ivan Filippovich thumbs his nose:

"That's all he'll get from us."

He adds with conviction:

"Napoleon was a mountain of a man; but still we smashed him. And this bastard will get such a smack in the teeth that his nose will bleed. Our army is powerful, our rear is sturdy, and as for the crop, since my childhood I haven't seen a better one. We will harvest it, harvest everything to the very last blade of grass. So we can go on fighting until the complete destruction of this reptile. No, Hitler will never see our bread. He might as well stop trying to jump higher than his omphalos. The only place he will finally get for himself will be a hole in a stinking swamp, six feet long and eighteen feet deep, so his carcass will not reek in that grave."

The moon shines over the Stalin farm. The village is in deep short sleep. Only at intervals one hears the crow of a cock or the careful tread of the patrol. And so, until morning, filled with work, more news from the front, and new victories.

The Crops

The farmers of Stavropol villages are experienced folk— they have seen a lot. Their attitude toward the war is professional, calm, and businesslike. The word "front" is the most ordinary one and no one is put out by its sound. The local people often use military terms to indicate certain localities: "The best winter crop is beyond the Kugutyansky trenches"; "Wheatfield along the Kevsalinsky front"; "Our pastures stretch from the old trenches to the dairy farms." Every village, every street, was once a front sector.

Junior Commander Ivan Maltsev, a former frontier guard, sent his father a letter from the Bessarabian front.

"My dear Dad, Fedot Sergeyevich: We are quite busy here. When we bested the White Guard Finns, you said they weren't such a strong enemy as the Germans you beat and smashed in the Ukraine. Well, you were right, but I'm beating them up properly. We have killed so many of them that when I look at them lying there it seems there are more of them than melons on our fields. We have been wiping them off for five solid hours, without a breathing spell, and when our units came up, even they were surprised."

Fedot Sergeyevich rereads this letter to a circle of villagers and certifies:

"Now I myself admit that Ivan has turned out to be as good a machine gunner as I used to be. We used to . . ."

But there is no time to hear what used to be; lunch hours are too short for that. Life is too tense and swift. The grain is harvested. Those who left for the front gave strict behest to harvest with military dispatch. Before leaving for the front, the agronomist Ivan Ivanovich Khvatkoff had overnight revamped the harvest plans in such a manner that the shortage caused by men leaving for the front would be unnoticed if all the rest pitched in. The best brigade leader, Ivan Ivanovich Kuzminoff, before departing for the front, took his successor, Vasily Maiboroda, to the field and asked:

"Tell me, Mai, just looking it over, how much will you get out of this field?"

Maiboroda estimated that he should harvest about 180 poods per hectare.

"Right! Then write to me and tell me that you got 30 centners. And if you get less, it means you're no good as a brigade leader."

At the meeting, the chairman of the collective farm pledged that not a single grain would be lost this fall.

Darya Antonovna Ziberova, chairman of the executive committee of the village Soviet, spoke as she struck her shoulders with her palms several times:

"You know that during the Civil War, the Whites slashed me on the back with their rifle ramrods. They beat my father to death. My husband died in battle. My first-born child was shot. But you also know how we can repay for our blood. My oldest son, Alexander, is in the Red Navy already fighting the Fascist scum. We all, our families, have had to do some fighting. We all know how to handle arms. We are familiar with the smell of gunpowder. They can't scare us with war. Tomorrow at dawn we shall all go to harvest."

They made great pledges. The "For the Five-Year Plan" Collective Farm in Kuguty Village, Petrovsky Region, is not one of the largest, as farms go here. It has only 1000 hectares of wheat. They pledged to achieve an average crop of 100 poods per hectare. One hundred thousand poods, 100 carloads, is a great task for such a small collective farm.

Three combines arrived to work in the fields on as many sectors of the field. Combine No. 16 drove up to Maiboroda; it was operated by Grigory Duppa, one of the oldest combine operators of the region. He drove over to the brigade which had 380 hectares of wheat, oats, and barley. Duppa said he would manage all by himself.

Maiboroda walked among the wheat. Only his head was visible above the grain. He grabbed a handful of wheat and twisted it.

"It's too early for you to start working, Comrade Duppa. Look at the chaff, it will get stuck in the machine. You'll have to wait. We will let the teams work in the meantime."

Four mowing teams came out, three drawn by horses and one by oxen. After the very first round the mowers were soaked in perspiration; the grain was heavy. The sheaves fell nearly one upon the other. Now they had to be stacked. Ten women follow each mower, stacking the grain.

In Stavropol Region they don't like to tie the grain; there is too much of it and under one pretext or another, the women tried to get out of this work every year. Many didn't know how to do it at all.

Now old women who knew well how to do it came into the fields to instruct the young. By the end of the day girls in bright kerchiefs, so wet that you could wring them out, worked as well as their instructors, Pelageya Sarayeva and Pelageya Tarasova, whose names were both on the Red Board of Honor.

Darya Antonovna Ziberova's daughter and son-in-law came from the city to visit her. They met in the field and there they remained, tying the grain, loading it and carting it away, until the end of the harvest. Taras Vorobyev's son, Mikhail, a teacher, came to visit his father during his vacation. Today he is a Stakhanoffite of the harvest. The local teachers, Elizaveta Mikhailovna Leontovich, Klavdia Lukyanovna Sarayeva, Paulina Danilovna Yegorova, together with groups of school children, came down to help; they did not return to the village until the work was finished, becoming excellent farmers.

Alexey Lagutin, assistant bookkeeper, was sent into the fields from the office. Mikhail Shepetev, the shepherd, came from the far-off pastures, leaving the herd with his helpers. Mariya Voropayeva, wife of a railroad man, came from the station. Many new people joined the brigade. But it is impossible to tell these newcomers among the others; they have learned the work and they won't leave until the 100,000 poods of grain are poured into the collective farm's granaries and elevators.

When the war first broke out some were secretly worried that there would be a shortage of hands.

There was no shortage. Even the farm's brick factory didn't stop, but is about to bake 70,000 bricks for the new House of Culture.

Only no hands were assigned to finish paving the main street of the Kuguty Village. The hired skilled pavers wanted to go home when Ulyana Nikanorovna Belykh came to them.

"Don't go yet. I have written to my son in the Red Navy that our village has become like a city. It seems that I wrote prematurely. Don't go. We will get a brigade to assist you."

She visited the cottages and gardens and brought into the street her friends Nadezhda Filipovna Siusiukina, Agafya Sergeyevna Belykh, and five more elderly women. They armed themselves with shovels, hods, and rollers. Now the construction of the pavement is only a little behind schedule. Today the chairman of the collective farm brought from the regional center a supply of textiles worth 30,000 rubles.

"This is the bonus for overfulfilling the farm's wool-delivery plan."

Who would refuse to dig through such colorful cottons, percales, and silks? Yet, nobody came! The people in the brigades said, "Too busy . . . Later . . ."

"The people have become like iron," asserted Maiboroda.

The silent tenacity reflects the people's burning wrath and hatred for the Fascist jackals who dared set their boots over the boundaries of the great Soviet country.

"Beat them and beat them and beat them again until there

will be nothing left but a wet spot as from a squashed toad," replied collective farmer Fedot Maltsev to his son. "The crop is good, as usual. An average of 100 poods, as it was when you were here. We've been harvesting the same amount for the past five years. The hay was good, both the uncultivated and the clover. We have stored enough for a year and a half, and if you use the cruder one, you can stretch it for two years. We harvest at a military pace and the grain is good although in places a little overripe. But it can't be avoided."

Work hums calmly in these villages where the people know the meaning of war, where everyone knows how to fight to the last breath, how to fight and conquer.

On Collective-Farm Fields

The road winds through the forest into the field. The rye rustles, tall as a man, strong and heavy. The collective-farm fields of Moscow Province look like a sea rolling in the wind. Each ear of rye is five inches long and contains at least seventy grains; the stalks are strong, straight.

Harvest! It's the subject of talk everywhere, in fields, in dairies, in farm offices. Everybody talks about it, women, old men, school children. They talk about it because the richest crop is ripening before their very eyes; because everything— rye, oats, wheat, potatoes, cabbages, vegetables with edible roots —promises an increase of seventy or perhaps all of 100 per cent over last year.

The mowers start for the field with the rising sun. There are young girls among them.

Ten days ago Anna Yegorova, secretary of the youth committee, summoned them and said:

"Listen, girls! We must learn how to mow. You will practice on weeds, and in a week you'll be able to mow clover."

There were ten of them. Scythes over their shoulders, with Yegorova they went beyond the vegetable gardens for their practice. At night their backs ached so, it seemed they would not be able to get up the next morning. But on the next day the girls mowed twice as much. The swing of their scythes became even; they cut the weeds at the very roots, but without striking the ground.

One thing the girls couldn't learn yet, to sharpen the scythes. But the men helped them out. They worked in groups—two men and four girls on each sector.

"Don't fall behind, girls," called out the mowers.

"Don't rush," others instructed. "And don't swing the scythes for nothing. Try to cover at least three arshins."

The harvesters! There'll be plenty of them. All the women, all the high-school children who can handle a sickle will come out to harvest the grain as soon as it is ready. And it will be threshed immediately by hand, by threshers and combines. And then at once winnowed, loaded upon wagons, off for the railways and grain elevators.

This was the decision of all the men and women collective farmers, of all the boy and girl Pioneers and school children. There could be no other decision, for there was a war on. They all know that they must work with military efficiency, as if at the front. They heard the radio appeal of Comrade Stalin, Chairman of the National Defense Committee, and they fully understood the profound threat to their homeland.

Anna Yegorova together with Sergey Alexandrovich Leonoff, the farm's chairman and accountant, called in the school children.

"Look here, kids," said the chairman. "It's time to end idleness."

"Wait a minute, Comrade Leonoff," Alexander Taratynoff, the accountant, spoke up in defense of the children. "Some of them carry water; some weed and water the vegetables."

"That's not enough," Leonoff continued. "Not for you. You should be given a real assignment. Line up like fighters and march out to collect leaves and stalks for fodder. The quota will depend on your age. You'll be paid for your workdays. Is the assignment clear, comrades?"

The children understood perfectly. They understood that in three days they were to collect forty tons of coarse fodder. They understood that during the harvest they would be following the combines to gather the lost grain, that they would be driving wagons loaded with supplies. Their understanding made them happy for it meant that they, children, were considered a great force entrusted with a matter of state importance.

The farm has another age group—fifty years and up. It is clear that they cannot help with weeding, haying, or collecting coarse fodder. They are rather too old. But they, too, want to work and help their collective farm.

"Let's organize them into a guard unit," someone suggested.

It was a correct and timely suggestion. During the harvest the farm needed many watchmen to guard the fields, the threshing grounds, the barns. The crop must be safe! The farm property must be guarded from the enemy, against any "accident."

You should see how joyful it made the old men to be given this job. They spent the entire morning cleaning their old rifles, sharpening pitchforks and axes. At night, accompanied by their dogs, they set out each his own way for the fields, dairies, and barns. The lights from their lanterns covered with dark kerchiefs burned dimly.

The people vigilantly guard the fruits of their labor.

CHAPTER VII

THE GREAT FRIENDSHIP OF THE PEOPLES OF THE U.S.S.R.

The enemy . . . is out to seize our lands watered with our sweat, to seize our grain and petroleum secured by our toil. He is out to restore the rule of estate lords, to restore Tsarism, to destroy the national culture and national statehood of Russians, Ukrainians, Byelorussians, Lithuanians, Letts, Estonians, Uzbeks, Tartars, Moldavians, Georgians, Armenians, Azerbaijanians, and the other free peoples of the Soviet Union. . . .

. . . The peoples of the Soviet Union must rise against the enemy and defend their rights and their land.

J. V. STALIN.

The Newspaper Pravda *Writes*

THE UNION OF SOVIET SOCIALIST REPUBLICS is a great multinational state. Race prejudices are buried in the irrevocable past. In the U.S.S.R. there are no divisions into "great" and "small" peoples. All citizens of the great Soviet country, regardless of nationality, enjoy equal rights. In this progressive and humanitarian principle lies the strength of the Soviet state, its moral superiority over Fascism which seeks to push mankind back into a barbaric era.

The friendship of the peoples of the Soviet land finds especially vivid manifestation in these history-making days. All peoples, nationalities, and tribes which inhabit the territory "from Finland's chilly cliffs to fiery Colchis," from the Baltic shores to the Pacific Ocean, have risen like a formidable wall against the Fascist robbers.

Ukrainians, Byelorussians, Uzbeks, Kirghizs, Kazaks, Tajiks, Armenians, Moldavians, Letts, Georgians, Tartars, Azerbaijanians, and Karelo-Finns, millions of Soviet patriots of a multinational land, imbued with one desire, to win the war, are competing on the fields of battle in courage and valor, as they are heroically smashing the enemy. Among those decorated by the Presidium of the Supreme Soviet of the U.S.S.R. are the names of Hero of the Soviet Union Junior Lieutenant Stepan Zdorovtsev, Hero of the Soviet Union Captain Alexey Anton-

enko, Captain Alexander Tsurtsumia, Senior Lieutenant Vodrik
Gazazian, Lieutenant Khasan Ibatulin, Lieutenant Joseph Krol,
and many other representatives of all the nationalities of the
Soviet Union who are defending their fatherland. Each Union
and Autonomous Republic is performing stupendous deeds of
labor heroism; the people know that the clash with Fascism is
a battle in a life-or-death struggle, a battle for freedom, for
honor, for the fatherland.

Grand and mighty are the nation's patriotism and the labor
heroism in the danger-fraught days of the War for the Fatherland. The finest traits of the Soviet people, their will, character,
intrepidity, moral strength, love for their land, come to the fore
in their heroic exploits against the hated enemy. The Soviet people are united as never before!

At a meeting of the "Volna" Collective Farm in Karelo-Finnish Soviet Republic, the fishermen said:

"The freedom-loving people are suffering unheard-of op-
pression and humiliation at the hands of the frenzied Hitlerite
bands. The hour of reckoning with the Fascist marauders is
near. Fascism will be wiped off the face of the earth."

Khalimakhon Suleymanova, a woman brigade leader, speaking at a meeting of Tajik farmers, voiced the feelings of all of
them:

"We must mobilize even more of our energy for the front.
Give our entire strength to our fatherland."

These are the thoughts of the entire Soviet people.

Friendship of the Peoples—a Great Force

In an interval between battles, Red Armyman Kocherga
jotted down:

"Shapoval from Poltava, Sidoroff from Moscow, Litvinoff

from Byelorussia, and the Ryazan collective farmer, Zelenin, heroically resisted a superior enemy force in defense of their fatherland. We acted in close co-operation with our infantry, which also displayed examples of bravery. Our infantry several times wanted to force the Fascist scoundrels to accept their attack, but the knightly curs were scared stiff of the bayonet charge. The Russian bayonet is well known to them."

This fragmentary note clearly reflects the whole gigantic power of the unity of the peoples of the Soviet Union.

All the peoples of the multinational country have risen like a stormy sea of wheat on their collective-farm lands to defend their great and just cause against the attack of the bestial Fascist barbarians.

The fraternal ties binding the peoples of the Ukraine, Russia, Byelorussia, Georgia sprang up in a distant past. They have grown strong and proved an overpowering force against all enemies. In the seventeenth century, in the struggle against the Polish gentry and the regiments of the mercenary German robbers, the Ukrainian people destroyed the enemy and drowned them in the Dnieper. In the Swedish invasion, Russian, Ukrainian, and Byelorussian people defeated the enemy in the Battle of Poltava. The Ukrainian people did not follow the traitor Mazeppa, and Cossack regiments gallantly fought for their beloved Ukraine. It was so, too, during the Napoleonic incursion.

Throughout the entire history of the Russian, Ukrainian, and Byelorussian peoples, in times of great trials, they always united into a single mighty force, always striking hard at the enemy, always attaining victory.

Peoples of the Soviet Union, bound by unshakable ties of friendship, are ready for any sacrifice to save their beloved country from Hitler's aggression, to finish the war with complete rout and annihilation of Fascism.

When a Friend Is Wounded

They made another attempt to force a strategic position.

The Germans resumed their attack for the third time. A handful of Red Armymen, headed by Machine Gunner Semyon Barkoff, withstood the pressure of an entire company. Barkoff maintained incessant fire. He did not leave his machine gun for a second. His equanimity and coolheadedness never deserted him. He would let the Nazis approach very near, then shoot them with point-blank fire. Only at times would he turn to his assistant, a Ukrainian named Peter Shevchenko:

"More bullets, quick!"

"Yes!" Shevchenko would answer, bringing more from the trench.

But once, when he returned with fresh cartridge ribbons, he saw that his front-line friend was wounded. Barkoff's head fell on his breast, but his hand remained on the machine gun. Even when wounded, he continued to mow down the enemy. Blood flowed down his face. The Nazis came very close. It seemed as though they would surround him at any moment.

Shevchenko unhesitatingly ran up to the machine gunner.

"Semyon, try to hold out a bit longer," he said to his friend. "Press the wound with your hand."

He carefully laid him on the grass and took over the machine gun.

Under his hail of lead, the Fascist company retreated.

Barkoff's eyes were closed. Silently he bore the tormenting pain. Shevchenko bandaged his wound and put his flask of water to his lips.

An order came to move to a more favorable position while awaiting reinforcements.

"Leave me here. . . . Don't lose time over me," whispered the wounded man.

But how could Peter Shevchenko abandon his friend on the field of battle?

No! He will rescue his friend even if it means death for himself. He lifted the gunner on his shoulders and carried him with great care.

The wounded man had to be brought to the field hospital quickly. The road led through a swamp. Shevchenko walked knee-deep in water. It was hard going. In the heat of battle he hadn't noticed that he himself had been shot through the shoulder. Now the wound made itself felt. It began to burn. Almost dropping from exhaustion and pain, he continued to walk.

Finally he reached the field hospital. After tenderly putting down the wounded, Shevchenko fainted.

They lay side by side in the same ward. When Barkoff, all swathed in bandages, regained consciousness, he looked at his neighbor affectionately:

"Thanks, friend," he said.

Red Armyman Leonid Grishanin tells simply and grudgingly of his heroic deed:

"We were launching an attack on the Nazis. Senior Lieutenant Vlasoff led us. We would follow him through fire and water. How he fought, our commander! Bullets and shrapnel rained and whistled all around him. The commander crawled ahead; we followed. Then rising to his full height, the Senior Lieutenant took us into the attack.

" 'Forward, for our fatherland!'

"We went into a bayonet charge. The Germans caught plenty; many of them fell, never to rise again.

"I turned around and saw our commander fall, wounded by an enemy bullet. I picked him up and carried him into the dug-out which I made earlier. But I had scarcely time to dress his wound, when I saw three Nazis creeping into the trench. I jumped out like an arrow, gored two with my bayonet and knocked down the third one with the butt of my gun. We carried the commander away from the field. Now he is recovering in the hospital. We are waiting for him!"

The remarkable friendship of the Soviet warriors matured and was tempered in the fierce battles against the enemy—strong, powerful, pure, and unbreakable friendship!

It inspires people to exploits. It helps them mercilessly to destroy the enemy on all fronts of the War for the Fatherland, on land and in the air, wherever the Fascists appear.

Russian and Ukrainian, Turkmen and Byelorussian, Tartar and Georgian, are united on the field of battle by inviolable ties of friendship.

If a friend is wounded in cruel battle, his comrade carries him from the field. When a friend is wounded, his comrade takes his place and fights on until his last breath.

A Friendship in Combat

The Nazi soldier and officer represent two different worlds which have nothing in common, except fear of each other and mutual hatred. Before going into action, the Fascist officer dopes his soldier with liquor; while in action, he spurs him on with a gun.

In the Soviet Army, the fighter and commander are brothers in spirit, in ideology, in love for their great land of freedom, brothers in their hatred for Fascism.

Lieutenant Krysoff received three serious wounds in battle. He was losing blood rapidly but continued to command his

In intervals between battles the men publish their "Boyevoy Listok"
("Fighting Sheet")

fighters. The enemies noticed that the Soviet commander was dying and decided to finish him. Shells and mines exploded around Krysoff and he was almost buried under the flying earth. The lieutenant would have perished if it were not for the great friendship and valor of the Soviet fighters.

Red Armyman Tomiloff, facing a hurricane of artillery and machine-gun fire, crawled up to the Lieutenant, bandaged his wounds, and carried him away, out of the battle zone, on his shoulders. A day later, that same Tomiloff saved the life of Junior Lieutenant Drobin and carried Fighter Masloff from under fire.

There is a law in the Red Army: every fighter must co-operate and always help his comrade with fire, bayonet, grenade, shovel, or personal attention.

Senior Lieutenant Budaragin, fulfilling this law, performed heroically when the plane piloted by Major Ovcharenko was forced down behind the enemy lines and both the Major and his radio operator, Kosyrev, were badly wounded. Lieutenant Budaragin dragged the wounded men on his shoulders for twenty-two kilometers. He would carry the Major for two or three kilometers, as far as his strength held out. Then he would return to pick up the radio operator. Thus he staggered on, bloody sweat running all over him, his legs almost giving out under the burden; hungry, his lips parched, he had given his entire supply of water to his wounded comrades.

The great fraternal feeling which welds the peoples of the Soviet Union has become a source of noble deeds that will fill the annals of the War for the Fatherland.

A group of doctors were evacuating a hospital. For two hours the Germans had been pouring lead and destructive bombs on it. Doctors and orderlies carried out the wounded and placed them on a ship. When the people and hospital equipment were all removed, it became clear that the boat was overloaded. The doctors selected from among themselves the oldest and most experienced of the medical personnel and ordered them to accompany the echelon. Those selected understood that their comrades were remaining behind to meet their death. They refused to board the ship; they wanted to share the common fate. They had to be placed aboard by force; those on shore cut the mooring ropes and the ship sailed away. A handful of the brave was left on the dock. They started to make their way to their own army. They proceeded under fire, this group of some two hundred people. Only two of them failed to reach the army and died in their comrades' arms. The others reached their units, many of them carrying upon their backs the wounded, sick, and exhausted comrades.

Here is another of the numerous examples. A regiment was moving to a new position, while in action. The enemy tried to wipe out the Soviet officers, to force them out of action. Company Commander Abakoff was badly wounded. If it hadn't been for the prompt action of his courier, Kvashnin, Abakoff would never have seen his comrades again. Kvashnin ripped off his shirt, put on just before the battle, and bandaged the commander's wounds. Then he carried him to the rear.

When the commander and the fighter were taking leave of each other (Kvashnin was impatient to return to the battlefield), the commander gave him his automatic rifle.

"Take it," he said. "I trust you with my rifle; shoot the Nazis with it for me."

Thus they became brothers in blood and in arms—the Soviet commander and his courier, whose brave heart never skipped a beat until he took the rifle from his commander's hand.

Seeing tears in the courier's eyes, the commander said:

"Don't mourn me. I'll be back to use my rifle."

Unwritten laws of Soviet friendship are vividly illustrated in the bloody battles against Fascism. A Red Armyman raises his rifle just in time to shoot a Nazi officer about to kill his platoon commander; another fighter drops behind his unit in order to carry a peasant, wounded by the Fascist robbers, many kilometers to the rear; a peasant hides a wounded lieutenant in an apiary—all these examples, recorded and preserved for posterity, are but a tiny fraction of what is happening every day on the battlefields.

Georgian Fighter Saves Russian Commander's Life

Bochorishvili, a Red Army fighter, was in hand-to-hand encounters three times, exterminating the enemy with bullets, bayonet, and rifle butt.

In one of those actions Bochorishvili and his section commander were surrounded. Without losing a second they dug in and opened well-aimed fire. Each shot fired by the coolheaded snipers brought down one of the bandits. Afraid to risk closer approach, the Fascists opened machine-gun fire. Both Bochorishvili and his section commander were wounded.

The heroic Red Armyman decided to break out of the enemy's encirclement and save his commander's life at any cost. He put the heavily wounded commander on his back and crawled on all fours, hiding behind hillocks and seeking out hollows.

Exerting his last strength and ignoring his pain, Red Armyman Bochorishvili reached his unit and thus saved the life of his commander.

A Warrior of Soviet Bashkiria

Senior Sergeant Bagautdinoff, a twenty-two-year-old Bashkirian collective farmer, was in action for the first time. The orders were to reconnoiter a farmstead. Bagautdinoff led his section through the forest toward an elevation.

Camouflaged, the section reached the farmstead and took cover behind a grilled fence. There was a house in the rear of the fenced-off yard. Bagautdinoff noticed that the enemy occupied dugouts on the right side of the house. Three of our scouts from another section approached the opposite end of the yard.

Upon seeing the scouts, the enemy soldiers—there were several dozen of them—jumped out of their trenches with triumphant cries, to attack the heroic trio. They were approaching the place where Bagautdinoff's camouflaged section had taken cover.

"I'll open fire," whispered the machine gunner.

"No," replied Bagautdinoff, "wait until they run right past us."

When the enemy was about forty meters away Bagautdinoff ordered:

"Fire!"

The sub machine gun fired for all it was worth, point-blank. The Nazi soldiers did not understand where the fire came from; they fell on one another.

It was sure death to run back to the trenches across the open lawn and the enemy took shelter behind the house. The Soviet machine gun immediately ceased fire. In the ensuing silence, Soviet men began to count the enemy killed and wounded lying within their range of vision. There were forty-nine.

How long did the silence last? An hour? Half an hour? Ten minutes? Hard to say. . . . Under such circumstances a minute might seem like an hour.

Deceived by the silence, the Nazi soldiers came out from behind the house and, unprotected, stood talking in the open. A fat man in black leather coat and leather breeches was gesticulating with his hands. He was their commander. Bagautdinoff took over the machine gun and, with a spurt of fire, laid down the commander and six more soldiers.

The reconnoitering assignment was carried out and Bagautdinoff took his section out of the battle.

The section of Bashkirian Sergeant Bagautdinoff wiped out fifty-six Germans in killed and wounded, without a single casualty to itself.

Finns of the Red Army

In the ranks of the Red Army there are Finns who gallantly fight against Hitler, the enemy of all mankind.

Captain Galonpoiku, a Finn, is commander of a battalion. The Finns, Junior Lieutenants Hiprelainen and Kempi, of the same battalion, proved themselves courageous fighters. Machine Gunner Sylander was wounded in action.

Junior Sergeant Matti Pertunen, who joined the Red Army as a volunteer, was born in the district where the immortal epic of the Karelo-Finnish people, the *Kalevala*, had been recorded.

Once Pertunen's section, on reconnaissance, approached a house on Finnish territory. At that moment, Finnish soldiers ran out of the house and made for their trenches in an attempt to escape the well-aimed fire of Soviet artillery. Pertunen's section opened fire. About fifteen soldiers rushed at Pertunen. The section greeted them with more fire.

"Surrender, Russians!" shouted the Finnish officer, who ordered his soldiers to outflank the section on the left.

"I understand Finnish very well," recounts Pertunen, "and I ordered my men to retreat in the opposite direction."

In this encounter the section destroyed nineteen enemy soldiers and lost only one man of its own.

The next day the unit was again in action.

"We read Comrade Stalin's radio speech," said Pertunen,

his blue eyes shining in his sunburned face. "We swore to defend every inch of Soviet soil with the last drop of our blood.
After that, our entire section resumed reconnoitering.

"There are five Finns in my unit, the rest are Russians. We
were passing through a sticky swamp, jumping from one stump
to another, preparing to wait in ambush. We covered quite a
distance. Suddenly I saw four enemy soldiers at our rear. At
once I threw a grenade and fired four shots in rapid succession.
That group was wiped out. We advanced again.

"We did not walk far when we encountered machine-gun fire
and a mortar shell fell near by. I ordered:

" 'Forward, attack!'

"The section rushed ahead and the enemy soldiers fled. We
continued on our way, when I saw a soldier hiding behind a
stump and aiming at us. I fired at him and followed it up with
a grenade. After this 'treat' he could not even say 'thank you.'
But at that moment the enemy opened automatic-rifle fire on our
flank. I took my unit out of the battle.

"In that encounter we destroyed five Fascist soldiers without
sustaining any losses ourselves."

In a subsequent action Pertunen's section again distinguished
itself. They shot a "cuckoo" out of a tree and flooded some
enemy trenches with hand grenades. For that battle special
credit is due to Rifleman Muller, also a Finn.

"The next time I reconnoiter, I shall absolutely capture and
bring back a 'mouthpiece,' " says Pertunen.

You can rely on the word of this fearless Soviet patriot.

The Patriots of Free Estonia

The mighty ranks of the People's Army are growing each
day. Estonian workers, peasants, and intellectuals are ready to

defend their country with their lives and to smash the Nazi raiders.

At the Tallinn recruiting station a lively registration of volunteers goes apace. Here can be seen factory, construction and office workers, as well as peasants from distant villages. Within two hours hundreds have applied for the People's Army.

Kuldmaa, head of a ship-repair yard, approaches the desk. He is forty-six, participant in the World and Civil Wars. Now he wants to take up arms again to defend his native land from the Nazi barbarians. His request is short and snappy:

"Send me to the front!"

Shoemaker Arvo Eerme is also among the volunteers:

"In 1905 and in 1917 my father fought for the workers' cause; now it is my turn. I want to fight the Fascist curs to the very end. Send me into battle as soon as possible! I'm ready!"

A member of the board asks Edward Lekhter, a carpenter:

"You have a large family; have you thought of them?"

"Yes, very much," he replies. "But I can secure the safety of my family only through the destruction of the Fascist marauders. I have firmly decided to join the Red Army in order to defend our fathers, our mothers, our children, our labor, our freedom, our great fatherland!"

Artemenok, a worker of the Baltic Manufactory, came to the recruiting station with his wife. They both wanted to fight for their country. Aza Sergeyeva, a woman worker of the "Leek" Tobacco Plant, wrote in her application: "Send me to the front as a nurse. Teach me how to handle arms. I want to care for the wounded and, if need be, I'll strike the enemy with gun in hand."

The Voice of Free Germans

Peasants of Shved Village, in Krasnoyarsk District of the Volga-German Republic, addressed the following letter to German peasants:

"We German peasants of the Volga-German Republic have created for ourselves a happy, prosperous life. We don't know the yoke of Fascist taxation; our property is not auctioned off for nonpayment of debts; we don't experience hunger, poverty, or landlessness. The Soviet state has given to the peasants of Shved—one of many hundreds of villages in the Volga-German Republic—6123 hectares of land, to be used free of charge and in perpetuity.

"The brigand war, incited by Hitler, has already killed hundreds of thousands of German peasants. Frenzied Fascism is now sending new millions of German peasants to war against the Soviet Union. We, the Germans of the Volga, together with all the peoples of the Soviet Union, have risen to defend our homeland, our honor, our freedom. We are responding to the appeal of Comrade Stalin by smashing the enemy not only at the front but, through our self-sacrificing labor, in the rear.

"German peasants, we call upon you to help in the destruction of Fascism, the worst enemy of advanced mankind. Hitler has forced you to take up arms; turn them against the Nazi ravishers who have enslaved Germany and who are sending you to meet a certain death. Come over to the side of the Soviet troops, as the best of you have done already. Overthrow Fascism! Win for yourselves a free and happy life! Death to Hitler and his hangers-on!"

The appeal was signed by Fritz Hoppe, Heinrich Horr, Heinrich Hardt, Hedwig Welmer, Dorothea Degraf, Helena Baumgartner, Sofia Zwinger, Hatherinan Horre, Christina Hubert,

Alexander Guenther, Sofia Degraf, Johannas Airich, and many others.

Baba Kafar Muradoff

The excellent Surakhan oil lies in great deposits that extend for many kilometers. Geologists carefully probe the earth, following every turn and twist of these deposits. Sometimes the trail is lost and the next well is dry. Does it mean that all their efforts have been wasted? Of course not! In locating oil and marking its deposits on the map you can't avoid dry wells. They help to define more precisely its flow and there is more certainty that the next boring will result in a gusher.

We will give the Red Army as much petroleum as it demands! This is the war slogan of the Baku Bolsheviks. Prospecting does not slacken even for a day.

Baba Kafar Muradoff is one of the best-skilled workers who conduct the highly responsible boring tests.

Who in the Baku oil fields does not know his tall figure, his creased brow, his alert, merry, sparkling eyes, his impetuous movements, his excited, throaty voice which resounded at meetings at the outbreak of the War for the Fatherland?

Forty-year-old Baba Kafar symbolized the liberated Azerbaijan people. He respects work and knows how to work. It was no accident that he was entrusted with the high honor of election as a Deputy to the Supreme Soviet of Azerbaijan.

Baba Kafar was drilling a well when the war broke out. If up to June 22 his brigade exceeded all the speed quotas for boring, then now you can't describe their work except in Baba Kafar's own words:

"They rush to meet the oil with the same fervor with which our Red Army rushes into battle."

At the height of boring, a member of the brigade, Kazi Babayev, was called up for the army. He was immediately replaced by a girl named Nadya Pulianova.

Baba Kafar Muradoff's brigade consists of strikingly different people, beginning with nineteen-year-old Nina Pyatakova and up to seventy-year-old Gamza Mirzoyev. The brigade is famous for its perfect co-ordination precisely because old Gamza works with youthful speed while the assistant foreman, young Nina Pyatakova, startles one with a maturity characteristic only of most seasoned oil prospectors. Garan Djamaz and Roman Panteleyev, drillers of two different shifts, compete with each other with equal success. This friendly, enthusiastic brigade constantly sees and feels the guiding presence of their chief, Baba Kafar, who works both shifts.

"When does your shift end?" they ask him jokingly.

"I started my shift on June 22, and I'll go off only when the last track of the last Fascist cur is wiped off our soil."

Constantine Isianoff, who drilled fifteen wells in half a year, Zakirya Isianoff, Shishkanoff, and many others of the best masters followed the example of Baba Kafar by going on permanent duty.

Baba Kafar knows with what longing the petroleum-hungry Hitlerite bands lust after the gem of the Soviet oil fields. He, himself, his whole brigade, the housewives, and school children guard the Soviet wells. Day or night, a stranger cannot appear in the oil fields without being halted by a guard.

Baba Kafar cannot find adequate words to express his admiration for the courage of Soviet warriors. The name of Kemal Kasumoff, the celebrated daring commissar from Baku, is always on his lips.

The oil center of Baku honors Baba Kafar Muradoff, hero of the labor front, who on his sector has displayed courage and readiness for self-sacrifice such as are displayed by all true sons of the great family of Soviet peoples.

STALIN SPEAKS AGAIN

The following report was made by Joseph Stalin, as Chairman of the State Defense Committee, at a meeting of the Moscow Soviet and representatives of other organizations, November 6th, 1941, on the eve of the Twenty-Fourth Anniversary of the Great October Socialist Revolution:

TWENTY-FOUR YEARS HAVE PASSED since the victory of the October Socialist Revolution and the establishment of the Soviet system in our country. We are now on the threshold of another year—the 25th of the existence of the Soviet system.

Usually at meetings celebrating the October Revolution we have devoted ourselves to summing up our successes in the sphere of peaceful construction in the year just past, and indeed we are still in a position to sum up these results. Our successes in peaceful construction are increasing not only from year to year but from month to month. What these successes are and how great they are is known to all our friends as well as to our enemies.

But the past year was not only a year of peaceful construction. It was also a year of war against the German invaders, who treacherously attacked our peace-loving country. Only during the first six months of the past year were we able to continue our peaceful construction. In the second half of the year over four months have been spent in fierce war against the German imperialists.

The war has thus become a turning point in the development of our country for the past year. The war has considerably curtailed and in some branches completely stopped our peaceful construction. It has compelled us to reorganize all our work,

313

placing it on a war footing. It has transformed our country into a single all-embracing rear—serving our Red Army and Navy. The period of peaceful construction has come to an end. The period of war for liberation against the German invaders has begun.

It is quite in place, therefore, to raise the question of the results of the war for the second half of the past year, to be precise, for more than four months of the second half of the year, and the task we are setting ourselves in this liberation war.

I have already stated in one of my speeches in the beginning of the war that the war had created a serious danger for our country, that a serious danger was facing our country, that it was necessary to understand and realize this danger and reorganize our whole work on a war footing.

Today, as a result of four months of war, I must emphasize that this danger—far from diminishing—has on the contrary increased. The enemy has captured the greater part of the Ukraine, Byelo-Russia, Moldavia and Estonia, and a number of other regions, has penetrated the Donbas, is looming like a black cloud over Leningrad, and is menacing our glorious capital, Moscow.

The German Fascist invaders are plundering our country, destroying the cities and villages built by the labor of the workers, peasants and intelligentsia. The Hitler hordes are killing and violating the peaceful inhabitants of our country without sparing women, children or the aged.

Our brothers in the regions of our country captured by the Germans are groaning under the yoke of the German oppressors.

Defending the honor and freedom of the country, courageously repelling the attacks of the brutal enemy, setting examples of valor and heroism, the fighters of our army and navy compelled the enemy to shed streams of blood.

But the enemy does not stop before sacrifices; he has not

even an iota of regard for the blood of his soldiers, he is hurling ever new detachments on to the front to replace the disabled
troops and is straining all his strength to capture Leningrad
and Moscow before the winter sets in, for he knows that the winter holds nothing good in store for him.

In the four months of the war our losses in killed are 350,-
000; missing 378,000; and our wounded number 1,020,000
men. In the same period the enemy has lost in killed, wounded
and prisoners more than 4,500,000 men. There can be no doubt
that as a result of four months of war, Germany, whose reserves
of manpower are already giving out, has been weakened to a
considerably greater degree than has the Soviet Union—the
full volume of whose reserves is only now coming into play.

COLLAPSE OF THE "BLITZKRIEG"

In undertaking an attack on our country the German Fascist
invaders calculated that they would certainly be able to finish
with the Soviet Union in a month and a half or two months—and
reach the Urals within a short time.

It is necessary to add that the Germans did not conceal this
plan for a "Blitz" victory. On the contrary they advertised it in
every way. Facts, however, have revealed all the shallowness
and groundlessness of the "Blitz" plan. Now this crazy plan
must be considered a complete failure.

How is one to explain that the "Blitzkrieg," which succeeded
in western Europe, was not successful and collapsed in the east?
What did the German Fascist strategists count on when they
asserted that within two months they would finish with the Soviet Union and in this brief period reach the Urals?

Their calculations were based, in the first place, on their
earnest hope of creating a general coalition against the U.S.S.R.,

of drawing Great Britain and the U.S.A. into this coalition by intimidating the ruling circles in these countries beforehand with the specter of revolution, and in this way completely isolating our country from the other powers.

GERMAN POLICY FAILS

The Germans knew that their policy of playing upon the contradictions between the classes in separate States, and the contradictions between these States and the Soviet Union, had already produced results in France, the rulers of which had allowed themselves to be intimidated by the specter of revolution—had refused to resist, and terror stricken had placed their native land under the heel of Hitler. The Nazi strategists thought the same thing would occur with Great Britain and the United States of America.

The notorious Hess was sent to Britain by the Nazis for this very purpose in order to persuade the British politicians to join the general campaign against the U.S.S.R. But the Germans miscalculated. Despite Hess's efforts, Great Britain and the United States, far from joining the campaign of the Nazi aggressors against the U.S.S.R., proved to be in the same camp with the U.S.S.R. against Hitlerite Germany. Far from being isolated, the U.S.S.R. on the contrary found new allies in Great Britain, the United States and the countries occupied by the Germans.

It turned out that the German policy of playing on contradictions and intimidating with the specter of revolution had exhausted its possibilities and was no longer suited to the new situation. And not only is it no longer suited—it is fraught with great dangers for the German invaders, since in the new conditions of war it leads to directly opposite results.

Secondly, the Germans counted on the instability of the Soviet system, on the instability of the Soviet rear, believing that, after the first serious blow and after the first reverses suffered by the Red Army, conflicts would take place between the workers and peasants—that strife would begin between the peoples of the U.S.S.R.; that uprisings would take place; that the country would fall apart; and that this would facilitate the advance of the German aggressors clear to the Urals. But here also the Germans badly miscalculated. The reverses of the Red Army did not weaken, but on the contrary strengthened the alliance of workers and peasants as well as the friendship of the peoples of the U.S.S.R. More than that—they converted the family of peoples of the U.S.S.R. into a single indestructible camp —selflessly supporting their Red Army and their Red Navy.

SOVIET SYSTEM PROVED STRONG

Never before has the Soviet rear been as stable as it is now. It is quite likely that any other state having sustained such territorial losses as we have now, would not stand the test and would suffer a decline. If the Soviet system has so easily withstood the test and has consolidated its rear still more, it means that the Soviet system is now the most stable system.

Finally they believed the German Army and the German Navy would be able by their very first blow to overwhelm and disperse our army and our navy—clearing the way for an unhindered advance to the interior of our country. Again the Germans miscalculated—overestimating their own forces and underestimating our army and navy.

Of course our army and navy are still young. They have been fighting for only four months. They have not yet had time to become a professional army and navy—yet they are confronted by the professional navy and army of Germans, who have been waging war for two years. But, in the first place, the morale of our army is higher than that of the German Army, for it is defending its native land from foreign invaders and believes in the justice of its cause. The German Army is waging an annexationist war and plundering a foreign country, without any chance of believing even for a single moment in the justice of its base cause.

A WAR OF DEFENSE

There can be no doubt that the idea of defense of one's native land—the very idea for which our people are fighting—must breed and actually does breed heroes in our army, who cement the Red Army. But the idea of seizure and plunder of a foreign country, for which properly speaking the Germans are waging war, must and actually does breed in the German Army professional plunderers, devoid of any moral backbone, who corrupt the German Army.

Secondly, while advancing into the interior of our country the German Army increases the distance separating it from the German rear. It is compelled to operate in hostile surroundings. It is compelled to create a new rear in a foreign country—a rear which, moreover, is disrupted by guerrillas. The guerrillas fundamentally disorganize the supply of the German Army. They make it afraid of its rear and kill its faith in the stability of its position. But our Army operates among its own people, enjoying the steady support of its rear. It has an assured supply of manpower, munitions and food and a firm faith in its rear. That is why our Army has proved to be stronger than the Germans expected and the German Army weaker than might have been expected, judging from the boastful declamations of the German invaders.

The defense of Leningrad and Moscow, where our divisions recently dsetroyed some thirty regular German divisions, shows that in the fire of war for our native land there are forged and have already been forged new Soviet fighters and commanders, pilots, artillerymen, trench-mortar operators, tank crews, infantrymen and seamen, who tomorrow will become the terror of the German Army.

There is no doubt that all these circumstances taken together predetermined the inevitable collapse of the "Blitzkrieg" in the East.

THE CAUSES OF THE TEMPORARY REVERSES OF OUR ARMY

All this is true, of course. But it is also true that, along with the favorable conditions, there are also a number of conditions unfavorable for the Red Army, as a consequence of which our Army has suffered temporary reverses, has been compelled to withdraw, and compelled to give up to the enemy a number of regions of our country. What are these unfavorable conditions? What are the causes of the temporary military reverses of the Red Army?

One of the causes of the reverses is the absence of a second front in Europe against the German Fascist armies. The fact is that at the present time there are on the continent of Europe no armies of Great Britain or of the United States which could wage war against the German Nazi troops. Therefore, the Germans do not have to split their forces and wage war on two fronts—in the west and in the east.

This situation means that the Germans, considering their rear in the west secure, are free to move all their troops and the troops of their European allies against our country. The situation is now such that our country is waging the war of liberation alone, without anybody's military assistance, against the combined forces of the Germans, Finns, Rumanians, Italians and Hungarians.

The Germans boast of their temporary successes, and laud their army to the heavens, asserting that—army for army—they can always defeat the Red Army in battle. But these German assertions are empty boasting. If this were true it would be incomprehensible why the Germans resort to the help of Finns, Rumanians, Italians and Hungarians against the Red Army, which is fighting exclusively with its own forces, without any military assistance from the outside.

ABSENCE OF A SECOND FRONT AIDS GERMANY

There is no doubt that the absence of a second front in Europe against the Germans considerably relieves the position of the German Army. Nor can there be any doubt that the appearance of a second front on the continent of Europe—and undoubtedly this must appear in the near future—would essentially improve the position of our army to the detriment of the German Army.

Another cause for the temporary reverses of our Army is the shortage of tanks and partially of aircraft. In modern war it is very difficult for infantry to fight without tanks and without sufficient aircraft cover in the air. Qualitatively our aviation is superior to that of the Germans and our glorious airmen have won fame as fearless fighters. But as yet we have less airplanes than the Germans.

The quality of our tanks is superior to that of the German tanks and our glorious tank crews and artillerymen have more than once put to flight the much lauded German troops with their large number of tanks, but still we have several times fewer tanks than the Germans. Herein lies the secret of the temporary successes of the German Army.

One cannot say that our tank industry is working badly and gives our front few tanks. No, our tank industry is working very well, and is producing no small number of excellent tanks. But the Germans are producing many more tanks, for they now have at their disposal not only their own tank industry but the industries of Czechoslovakia, Belgium, Holland and France. Were it not for this circumstance the Red Army would long ago have routed the German Army which never goes into battle without tanks and which cannot withstand the blows of our units if it has not got superiority in tanks.

There is only one means to reduce to zero the German superiority in tanks, and in this way radically to improve the position of our army. This means consists not only in increasing several times the output of tanks in our country, but also in sharply increasing the output of anti-tank aircraft, anti-tank rifles and artillery, anti-tank grenades and trench mortars, in building more anti-tank ditches and all other kinds of anti-tank obstacles. This is our task now. We can fulfill this task and we must fulfill it at any cost.

THE "NATIONAL SOCIALIST" PARTY

Who are the "National Socialists"—this enemy in our country? The German invaders—that is, the Hitlerites—are usually called Nazis. The Hitlerites, it seems, consider this to be incorrect and stubbornly continue to call themselves "National Socialists." Thus the Germans want to make us believe that the Hitlerite party—the party of the German aggressors who are plundering Europe and have organized the outrageous attack on our Socialist State—is a Socialist party.

Is this possible? Can there be anything in common between Socialism and the brutal Hitlerite invaders who are plundering and oppressing the nations of Europe? Is it possible to regard the Hitlerites as nationalists? No, this is impossible.

Actually the Hitlerites are not nationalists, but imperialists. When the Hitlerites engaged in gathering German lands and in reuniting the Rhineland, Austria, etc., there existed certain grounds for considering them nationalists. But after they seized foreign territories and enslaved European nations—the Czechs, Slovaks, Poles, Norwegians, Danes, Dutch, Belgians, French, Serbs, Greeks, Ukrainians, Byelorussians, the Baltic peoples, etc.—and began to strike for world domination, the Hitlerite Party ceased to be a nationalist party. It became an imperialist party—a party of plunderers and oppressors. The Hitlerite Party is a party of imperialists and, at that, of the most rapacious and predatory imperialists among all the imperialists of the world.

Can the Hitlerites be regarded as Socialists? No, this is impossible. Actually the Hitlerites are the sworn enemies of Socialism—out and out reactionaries and Black Hundreds [prerevolutionary Tsarist terrorist groups] who have deprived the working class and the peoples of Europe of elementary democratic liberties.

To cover up their reactionary, Black Hundred nature, the Hitlerites denounce the Anglo-American internal regime as plutocratic. But England and the United States of America possess elementary democratic liberties. There exist trade unions for workers and employees. There are workers' parties and there is a parliament, whereas in Germany under the Hitler regime all these institutions have been destroyed. One has only to compare these two sets of facts to understand the reactionary nature of the Hitlerite regime and all the utter falseness of the

German Fascists' harangue about the Anglo-American pluto-cratic regime.

HITLERISM COUNTERPART OF TSARISM

As a matter of fact, the Hitlerite regime is a replica of the reactionary regime which existed in Russia under Tsarism. It is known that the Hitlerites trample upon the rights of workers, the rights of intellectuals and the rights of nations just as will-ingly as the Tsarist regime used to do. It is known that they also organize medieval Jewish pogroms just as willingly as the Tsarist regime used to organize them. The Hitlerite Party is a party of the enemies of democratic liberties, a party of medieval reaction, of Black Hundred pogroms.

If the frenzied imperialists and outstanding reactionaries still continue to don the mask of "Nationalists" and "Social-ists," they do so to deceive nations, fool simpletons, and cover with the flag of "Nationalism" and "Socialism" their rapacious, imperialist nature.

Crows in peacock feathers . . . But no matter how the crows plume themselves, they remain crows.

"Every means must be used," says Hitler, "to ensure the Ger-man conquest of the world. If we want to create our great Ger-man Empire, we must first of all drive out and destroy the Slavonic peoples, the Russians, Poles, Czechs, Slovaks, Bul-garians, Ukrainians and Byelorussians. There is no reason why we should not do so."

MEN INTO BEASTS

"Man," says Hitler, "is sinful from birth. He can be ruled only with the help of force. In handling him, any means are permissible. When policy demands it, one should lie, betray and even kill."

"Kill," says Goering, "everybody who is against us; kill, kill. Not you are responsible for this, but I. Therefore, kill!"

"I deliver man," says Hitler, "from the humiliating chimera which is called conscience. Conscience, like education, cripples man. I have this advantage, that I am not deterred by any theoretical or moral considerations."

In one of the orders of the German command to the 489th Infantry Regiment dated September 25th and found on a dead German non-commissioned officer, it is stated: "I order you to open fire against every Russian the moment he appears, at a distance of 600 meters. The Russian must understand that he has against him a resolute enemy from whom he cannot expect any leniency."

In one of the addresses of the German command to the soldiers, found on the body of Lieutenant Gustav Zigel, a native of Frankfurt-am-Main, it is stated: "In war, you have neither heart nor nerves. These are unnecessary. Suppress your feelings of mercy and pity—kill every Russian, every Soviet person—do not stop even if before you there is an aged man or woman, boy or girl. Kill. In this way you will save yourself from destruction. You will secure the future of your family and you will become famous forever."

Here you have the program and the instructions of the leaders of the Hitlerite party and the Hitlerite command—a program and instructions of a people who have lost all semblance to humanity and who have sunk to the level of wild beasts.

These people, devoid of conscience and honor, people with the morale of beasts, have the impudence to call for the destruction of the great Russian nation, the nation of Plekhanoff and Lenin, of Belinsky and Chernyshevsky, Pushkin and Tolstoi,

Glinka and Tchaikovsky, Gorky and Chekhoff, Sechenoff and Pavloff, Repin and Surikoff, Suvoroff and Kutuzoff.

A WAR OF EXTERMINATION

The German invaders wish to have a war of extermination against the peoples of the U.S.S.R. Well then, if the Germans wish to have a war of extermination, they will get it. From now on our task, the task of the fighters, commanders and political instructors of our army and our navy will consist in the extermination to the last man of all Germans who have penetrated the territory of our native land as invaders. No mercy to the German invaders! Death to the German invaders!

The routing of the German imperialists and their armies is inevitable. The fact alone that in their moral degradation the German invaders, having lost all human semblance long ago, sank to the level of wild beasts—this alone goes to prove that they have doomed themselves to inevitable perdition. But the inevitable doom of the Hitlerite invaders and their armies is determined not only by moral factors. There exist three more fundamental factors, the weight of which is growing from day to day and which must lead in the near future to the inevitable collapse of Hitlerite predatory imperialism:

First—there is the instability of the European war of imperialist Germany, the instability of the "New Order" in Europe.

The German invaders have enslaved the people of the European continent from France to the Soviet Baltic, from Norway, Denmark, Belgium, Holland and Soviet Byelorussia to the Balkans and the Soviet Ukraine. They have deprived them of elementary democratic liberties, deprived them of the right to decide their own fates, taken away their grain, meat and raw materials, transformed them into slaves. They have crucified the Poles, Czechs and Serbs. And, on achieving domination in Europe, they decided that they could now build on this foundation the domination of Germany over the whole world.

This is what they call the "new order in Europe." But what kind of "foundation" is this? What kind of "new order"? Only the Hitlerite self-enamored fools are unable to see that the "new order" in Europe and the notorious foundation of this order represent a volcano, ready to erupt at any moment and upset the German imperialist house of cards.

They refer to Napoleon, asserting that Hitler is acting like Napoleon and that he resembles Napoleon in every respect. In the first place, in asserting this, one should not forget Napoleon's fate. In the second place, Hitler no more resembles Napoleon than a kitten resembles a lion, for Napoleon fought against the forces of reaction, relying on the support of progressive forces, whereas Hitler on the contrary is relying on the support of reactionary forces and waging a struggle against the progressive forces.

Only the Hitlerite fools in Berlin are unable to understand that the enslaved peoples of Europe will struggle and will rise against Hitler's tyranny. Who can doubt that the U.S.S.R., Great Britain, and the United States will give full support to the peoples of Europe in their struggle for liberation against Hitler's tyranny?

Second—the instability of the German rear of the Hitlerite invaders.

While the Hitlerites were engaged in unifying Germany, which had been carved up by the Versailles Treaty, they could enjoy the support of the German people, inspired by the ideal of the restoration of Germany, but after this problem had been solved and the Hitlerites set out on the path of imperialism— on the path of seizures of foreign lands and conquests of other peoples, transforming the peoples of Europe and the U.S.S.R. into sworn enemies of present-day Germany—a profound change of attitude took place among the German people against the continuation of the war and for putting an end to the war.

Two odd years of sanguinary war, the end of which is not yet in sight; millions of human victims; starvation, impoverishment, epidemics; everywhere an atmosphere of hostility toward Germans; Hitler's stupid policy, which transformed the peoples of the U.S.S.R. into mortal enemies of the present-day Germany —all this could not but turn the German people against the unnecessary and ruinous war. Only the Hitlerite fools are unable to realize that not the European rear alone, but the German rear of the German troops as well represents a volcano ready to erupt and bury the Hitlerite adventurers.

GREAT BRITAIN—U.S.S.R.—U.S.A.

Finally, there is the coalition of the U.S.S.R., Great Britain, and the United States of America against the German Nazi imperialists.

It is a fact that Great Britain, the United States of America and the Soviet Union have united in a single camp, having set themselves the task of routing the Hitlerite imperialists and their invading armies.

Modern war is a war of motors. The war will be won by him who possesses an overwhelming superiority in the output of motors. If the production of motors in the U.S.A., Great Britain and the U.S.S.R. is combined, then we shall acquire at least a threefold superiority in motors as compared to Germany. This is one of the fundamental reasons for the inevitable doom of predatory Hitlerite imperialism.

The recent Three Power Conference in Moscow, with the participation of the representative of Great Britain, Lord Beaver-brook, and the representative of the United States, Mr. Harriman, decided to help our country systematically with tanks and aircraft. As is known, we have already begun to receive tanks and planes on the basis of this decision. Even earlier, Great Britain supplied our country with materials which we lacked, such as aluminum, lead, tin, nickel and rubber. If we add to this the fact that recently the United States of America decided to grant the Soviet Union a loan of $1,000,000,000, one may say with certainty that the coalition of the United States of America, Great Britain and the U.S.S.R. is very real, and that it is growing and will continue to grow for the benefit of our common cause of liberation. Such are the factors determining the inevitable doom of German Nazi imperialism.

SOVIET WAR AIMS

Lenin differentiated between two kinds of wars—wars of conquest, which are unjust wars, and wars for liberation, which are just wars.

The Germans are now waging a war of conquest—an unjust war, with the object of seizing foreign territory and conquering other peoples. Therefore, all honest people must rise against the German invaders as against enemies.

Unlike Hitlerite Germany, the Soviet Union and its allies are waging a war for liberation—a just war for the liberation of the enslaved peoples of Europe and the U.S.S.R. from Hitler's tyranny. Therefore all honest people must support the armies of the U.S.S.R., Great Britain and the other allies as armies of liberation.

We have not nor can we have such war aims as the seizure of foreign territories or the conquest of other peoples, irrespective of whether European peoples and territories or Asiatic peoples and territories, including Iran, are concerned. Our first aim is to liberate our territories and our peoples from the German Nazi yoke.

We have not nor can we have such war aims as the imposition of our will and our regime on the Slavic and other enslaved peoples of Europe who are waiting for our help. Our aim is to help these peoples in their struggle for liberation from Hitler's tyranny, and then to accord them the possibility of arranging their lives on their own land as they think fit, with absolute freedom. No interference of any kind with the domestic affairs of other nations!

But to realize these aims it is necessary to crush the military might of the German invaders. It is necessary to exterminate to the last man all the German invaders who have penetrated our native land to enslave it. To achieve this, it is necessary that our Army and our Navy enjoy the active and vigorous support of our entire country; that our workers—men and women —work in the factories without relaxing their efforts; that they give to the front more and still more tanks, anti-tank rifles and guns, airplanes, artillery, trench mortars, machine guns, rifles and ammunition.

CALLS NATION TO ARMS

It is necessary that our collective farmers—men and women —work tirelessly on their fields; that they give to the front and the country more and still more grain and meat and raw materials for our industries. It is necessary that our entire country and all the peoples of the U.S.S.R. organize themselves as one single fighting camp, waging, together with our Army and Navy, a great war for liberation, for the honor and liberty of our native land and for the destruction of the German armies.

This is our task. Now we can and must fulfill this task. Only by fulfilling this task and routing the German invaders can we achieve a lasting and just peace.

For the complete destruction of the German invaders!

For the liberation of all oppressed peoples groaning under the yoke of Hitlerite tyranny!

Long live the indestructible friendship of the peoples of the Soviet Union!

Long live our Red Army and our Red Navy!

Long live our glorious motherland!

Our cause is just!

Victory will be ours!

(At a military review held the next day, November 7, 1941, on Red Square in Moscow in honor of the Twenty-Fourth Anniversary of the October Revolution, Joseph Stalin delivered the following address.)

COMRADES, RED ARMY AND RED NAVY MEN, commanders and political instructors, men and women workers, men and women collective farmers, intellectuals, brothers and sisters in the enemy rear who have temporarily fallen under the yoke of the German brigands, our glorious men and women guerrillas who are disrupting the rear of the German invaders:

On behalf of the Soviet government and our Bolshevik Party I greet you and congratulate you on the twenty-fourth anniversary of the great October Socialist Revolution.

Comrades, today, in difficult conditions, we must celebrate the twenty-fourth anniversary of the October Revolution. The German brigands' treacherous attack and the war that they forced upon us have created a threat to our country. We have temporarily lost a number of regions, and the enemy is before the gates of Leningrad and Moscow.

The enemy calculated that our army would be dispersed at the very first blow and our country forced to its knees. But the enemy wholly miscalculated. Despite temporary reverses, our army and our navy are bravely beating off enemy attacks along the whole front, inflicting heavy losses, while our country—our whole country—has organized itself into a single fighting camp in order, jointly with our army and navy, to rout the German invaders.

There was a time when our country was in a still more difficult position. Recall the year 1918, when we celebrated the first anniversary of the October Revolution. At that time three quarters of our country was in the hands of foreign interventionists. We had temporarily lost the Ukraine, the Caucasus, Central Asia, the Urals, Siberia, and the Far East. We had no allies, we had no Red Army—we had only just begun to create it—and we experienced a shortage of bread, a shortage of arms, a shortage of clothing.

At that time fourteen states were arrayed against our country, but we did not become despondent or downhearted. In the midst of the conflagration of war we organized the Red Army and converted our country into a military camp. The spirit of the great Lenin inspired us at that time for the war against the interventionists.

And what happened? We defeated the interventionists, regained all our lost territories, and achieved victory.

SOVIET POSITION STRONG

Today our country is in a far better position than it was twenty-three years ago. Today it is many times richer in industry, food, and raw materials. Today we have allies who jointly with us form a united front against the German invaders. Today we enjoy the sympathy and support of all the peoples of Europe fallen under the yoke of Fascist tyranny. Today we have a splendid army and a splendid navy, defending the freedom and independence of our country with their lives. We experience no serious shortage either of food or of arms or clothing.

Our whole country, all the peoples of our country, are backing our army and our navy, helping them smash the Nazi hordes. Our reserves in man power are inexhaustible. The spirit of the great Lenin inspires us for our patriotic war today as it did twenty-three years ago.

NAZIS FACE DISASTER

Is it possible, then, to doubt that we can and must gain victory over the German invaders? The enemy is not so strong as some terror-stricken intellectuals picture him. The devil is not so terrible as he is painted. Who can deny that our Red Army has more than once put the much-lauded German troops to panicky flight?

If one judges by Germany's real position and not by the boastful assertions of German propagandists, it will not be difficult to see that the Nazi German invaders are facing disaster.

Hunger and poverty reign in Germany. In four and a half months of war Germany has lost four and a half million soldiers. Germany is bleeding white; her man power is giving out. A spirit of revolt is gaining possession not only of the nations of Europe under the German invaders' yoke, but of the Germans themselves, who see no end to the war.

The German invaders are straining their last forces. There is no doubt that Germany cannot keep up such an effort for any long time. Another few months, another half year, one year perhaps—and Hitlerite Germany must collapse under the weight of its own crimes.

"ONWARD TO VICTORY"

Comrades, Red Army and Red Navy men, commanders and political instructors, men and women guerrillas:

The whole world is looking to you as a force capable of destroying the brigand hordes of German invaders. The enslaved peoples of Europe under the yoke of the German invaders are looking to you as their liberators. A great mission of liberation has fallen to your lot.

Be worthy of this mission! The war you are waging is a war of liberation, a just war. Let the manly images of our great ancestors—Alexander Nevsky, Dmitri Donskoi, Kusma Minin, Dmitri Pozharsky, Alexander Suvoroff, Mikhail Kutuzoff—inspire you in this war!

Let the victorious banner of the great Lenin fly over your heads!

Utter destruction to the German invaders!

Death to the German armies of occupation!

Long live our glorious motherland, her freedom and her independence!

Under the banner of Lenin—onward to victory!